CHRONICLE OF THE OLD TESTAMENT KINGS

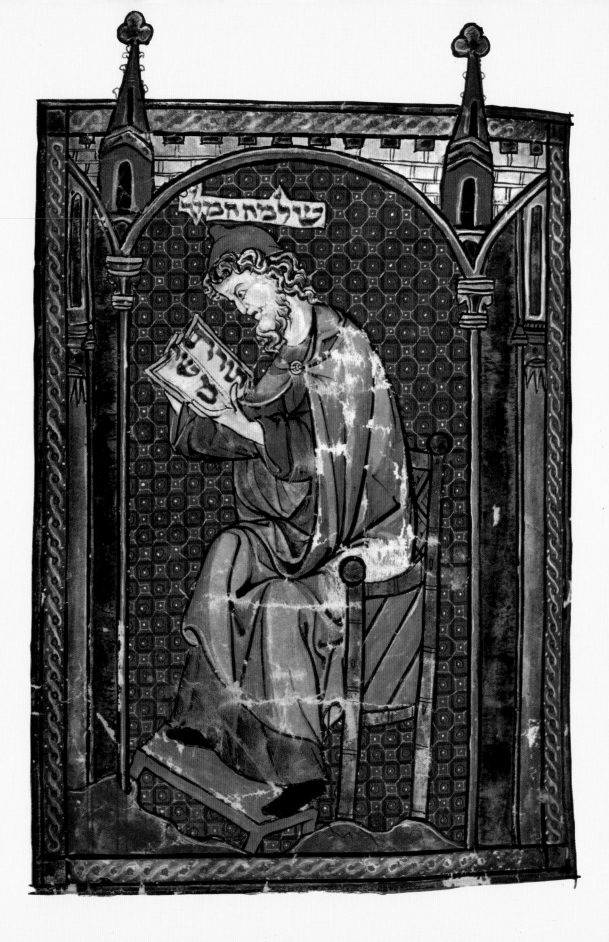

John Rogerson

CHRONICLE OF THE
OLD TESTAMENT
KINGS

THE REIGN-BY-REIGN RECORD OF THE
RULERS OF ANCIENT ISRAEL

WITH 260 ILLUSTRATIONS
100 IN COLOR

THAMES AND HUDSON

CONTENTS

(*Half-title*) A gilded glass dish from the Jewish catacombs in Rome. It shows various Jewish symbols, including the *menorah* (seven-branched candlestick) and the *shofar* (ram's-horn trumpet).

(*Frontispiece*) King Solomon reading the Torah, in a detail from a French 13th-century illuminated manuscript.

© 1999 Thames and Hudson Ltd, London

First published in hardcover in the United States of America in 1999 by Thames and Hudson Inc., 500 Fifth Avenue, New York, New York 10110

Library of Congress Catalog Card Number 98-61829
ISBN 0-500-05095-3

Printed and bound in Slovenia

Abraham

Moses

Saul

David

PREFACE: THE KINGS OF ANCIENT ISRAEL

Most readers will have heard of Old Testament characters such as Abraham, Moses, David and Solomon. They may even remember stories from childhood about some of them. Who can forget the story of David and Goliath, or of Moses in the bulrushes? But what do readers really know about these leaders? Do they realize, for example, that David was a deserter to Israel's enemies the Philistines? Are they aware that before he deserted he headed a desperate gang of men who went around the country operating a kind of protection racket? Do they recall that Moses had to flee from Egypt, otherwise he would have been executed for murdering an Egyptian, and that he spent some time in Midian before returning to lead the people out of slavery in Egypt?

The names mentioned above are well known; but how many readers have heard of king Josiah, or have any idea of his importance not only to ancient Israel but also to British history? Josiah, who came to the throne as a boy aged eight, was later responsible for one of the most far-reaching religious reforms ever carried out in Old Testament times, a reform that also affected the composition of the Old Testament itself. But his influence did not end there. When Henry VIII died in 1547 and was succeeded by the boy king Edward VI, religious reformers in England likened him to Josiah, and used the figure of the Old Testament king to justify the radical church reforms that were introduced during Edward's reign, and which helped to change the character of England as a nation.

All the above implies that we can read the Old Testament as a straight record of the lives of Israel's leaders. But is this possible? In the case of people such as Abraham or Moses many hundreds of years separate their lives from the times when the stories as we have them were written down. So, are they reliable accounts, or are they myths and legends?

Artists throughout the ages have found great inspiration in the tales of the heroic deeds of ancient Israel's leaders, and so these stories have become familiar as iconographic imagery as well as in their written form. This is *David with the Head of Goliath* (c. 1605/06) by Caravaggio.

The Exposition of Moses, by Nicolas Poussin (1654). In this painting of another familiar scene from the Bible, Moses is concealed in the bulrushes, later to be found by pharaoh's daughter. Here the biblical story is set in a European landscape, with Egyptianizing elements.

And does archaeology help us to know more about ancient Israel's leaders? In what follows here, the critical questions that arise when we seek to reconstruct the lives of Old Testament kings and other leaders will be faced fairly and squarely, and readers will get some insight into the complex but fascinating world of Old Testament criticism. But they will also get to know ancient Israel's leaders better. In some cases we shall only glimpse them through the mists of tradition – a tradition which, however, still tells us something about the people for whom it was important. In other cases – Herod the Great comes especially to mind – we shall glimpse only part of a complex figure about whom so much is known that an entire book would be needed to do him justice. The word 'him' is used advisedly. Are there any women in the record? The answer is yes, and an attempt will be made to do justice to them.

The complaint is sometimes made about the Old Testament that it is full of uninteresting history. This hardly does justice to the rich and varied content of the Old Testament, and it can also be strongly maintained that Israel's history is anything but dull. To approach it via a Chronicle of Old Testament kings and other leaders is a novel way of discovering just how interesting it is.

INTRODUCTION: CHRONOLOGY AND OLD TESTAMENT HISTORY

Recently there has been a revival of interest in the history of ancient Israel, but it has divided scholars sharply into two camps. In one camp are those who believe that a reasonably traditional but critical history of Israel can be reconstructed, at least from the time of the occupation of Canaan by proto-Israelites in the late 13th century BC. Although these scholars are aware of the problems of relating biblical texts to archaeological findings, they believe that archaeology does make a positive contribution to writing ancient Israel's history. The other group is sceptical about what can be known of Israel's history before the Babylonian Exile in 587 BC. It is a fact that the Old Testament historical records in the form that we have them date from during and after the Babylonian Exile. Further, some recent archaeological findings seem to indicate that Judah did not develop into a small state until the 8th century BC and that the neighbouring states of Israel, Moab, Ammon and Edom did not emerge before the 9th century BC. On this reading, it is possible to doubt the historical existence even of such figures as David and Solomon; and the bitter controversy that has been aroused by the publication in 1993 of an inscription from Dan that is claimed to contain a reference to the 'house of David' indicates how sharply the battle lines have been drawn.

In spite of, or indeed because of, these differences within Old Testament studies, it is important to have a volume about ancient Israel in a

THE 'HOUSE OF DAVID' INSCRIPTION

The publication, in 1993 and 1995, of fragments of an Aramaic inscription

A controversial inscription. The letters 'btdwd' are highlighted five lines from the bottom of the right-hand fragment; 'bt' is the word 'bet' meaning 'house' and the remaining letters are the name 'David'.

discovered at Tell Dan in northern Israel and apparently containing the name David sparked off a fierce controversy among scholars. Dated to the 9th century BC, the fragments were believed on the most positive interpretation to refer to a victory of the Syrian king Hazael around 845 BC over Jehoram king of Israel and Ahaziah king of Judah (see 2 Kings 8:28–29), the latter being referred to as 'Ahaziah son of Jehoram, king of the House of David'. It was suggested that Dan was later recaptured by Israelites, and that the inscription was smashed and its material used as part of a wall. On the negative side it has been questioned whether the fragments belong together (which the most positive interpretation depends on), and it has been pointed out that the names Jehoram and Ahaziah do not actually occur but are scholarly guesses.

Also, the words translated as 'House of David' do not have a word-divider between 'house' and 'David' while other words in the inscription are separated by word-dividers. It is indisputable that 'king of Israel' can be read in line 8 of fragment A. If the 'David' element does not refer to king David, it may be a divine name or may simply mean 'beloved'.

series that includes Egypt and Rome; for although Israel was tiny in comparison with those empires, its literature, in the form of the Old Testament, has had a greater impact upon western culture than theirs. But an important point should be noted. Old Testament historical traditions are unlike the records of the empires that surrounded ancient Israel. Israel's traditions were subjected to editing and re-editing, and they come from a context in which people wrestled with fundamental religious questions. The differing and occasionally contradictory answers that were given to these questions sometimes affected how past history was understood, as well as the uses to which it was put.

In view of this, it will come as no surprise that question marks or the sign 'c.' meaning 'circa' appear regularly before dates. For the period before the monarchy everything is guesswork, and in the case of figures such as Abraham, I am following convention and conforming to the format of this series in supposing that a rough date can be supplied at all. From the time of the monarchy, occasional cross-references to Egyptian or Assyrian historical sources make it possible to be more confident about dates. Within the books of Kings, reigns of kings of Judah are cross-referenced to those of kings of Israel and vice versa. A typical example would be 2 Kings 14:1–2, which reads, 'In the second year of Jehoash son of Jehoahaz king of Israel Amaziah son of Joash began to reign in Judah. He was 25 years old when he began to reign, and he reigned 29 years in Jerusalem.' Information such as this is valuable, but not without problems, as becomes evident when we look at the length of reigns given in 2 Kings for four kings of Judah who are usually placed in the 8th century BC:

Uzziah (Azariah)	52 years	(2 Kings 15:2)
Jotham	16 years	(2 Kings 15:33)
Ahaz	16 years	(2 Kings 16:2)
Hezekiah	29 years	(2 Kings 18:2)

The total of 113 years clearly does not fit into the century, and the figures are either wrong or it has to be supposed, not without reason, that Jotham reigned for some years as co-regent with his father. This is not the only difficulty. If the information in 2 Kings 16:2 that Ahaz was 20 when he began his 16-year reign is put with 2 Kings 18:2 that Hezekiah was 25 when he succeeded his father Ahaz as king, it means that Ahaz was aged around 11 when he fathered Hezekiah. Another problem is that Sennacherib's invasion of Judah in 701 BC (the date is secure from continuous Assyrian records) is said to have occurred in Hezekiah's 14th year in 2 Kings 18:13, which would mean that Hezekiah began to reign in 715. On the other hand, 2 Kings 18:9 states that Shalmaneser (V) began to lay siege to Samaria in Hezekiah's fourth year. We know from other sources that this siege began in 724 BC, which would mean that Hezekiah began to reign in 728/7 BC. Because no chronological scheme for the kings of Israel and Judah proposed so far has won universal acceptance, the dates adopted in the present work must be provisional.

N

0   40 km
0   30 miles

• Sidon

Damascus

MEDITERRANEAN SEA

• Tyre

• Dan   • Caesarea Philippi

Hazor •

Capernaum •

SEA OF
GALILEE

Tiberias •

Mt Carmel

Nazareth •   ▲
Mt Tabor   • Gadara

Megiddo •   • Shunem

Dor •

Taanach •   Jezreel •

Caesarea •   Beth-shean
(Scythopolis)   • Ramoth-gilead

Tirzah •

Samaria (Sebaste) •   • Gerasa

Mt Ebal ▲
• Shechem   Succoth •

Mt Gerizim ▲   • Penuel

Aphek •   Jabbok

Shiloh •   Jordan

Joppa •

Bethel •   Rabbat Ammon

Lydda •   Ai •   Jericho •

Gibeon •

Gezer •   Gibeah •

Aijalon •   Khirbet Qumran

Ashdod •   Ekron •   Jerusalem •

Medeba •

Azekah •   • Bethlehem

Gath •   Herodium •

Ashkelon •   Machaerus •

Lachish •

Gaza •   Hebron •   DEAD
SEA   Arnon

Beer-sheba •

Masada •

*Map of ancient Israel showing the principal
sites mentioned in the text and (opposite
above) the wider Mediterranean area.
(Opposite below) The northern end of the Sea
of Galilee, where the river Jordan enters.*

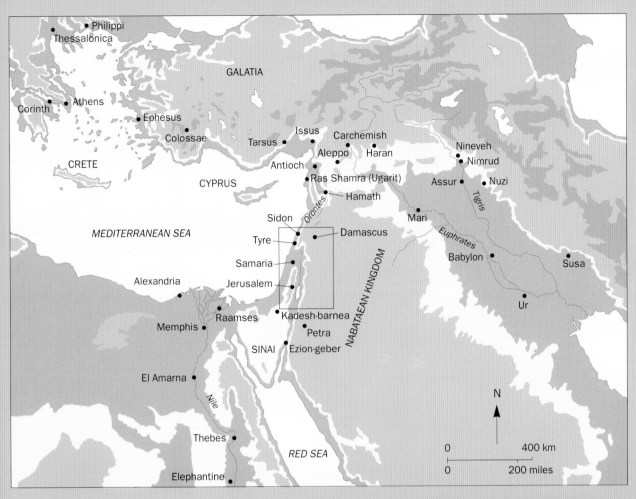

Philippi
Thessalonica
GALATIA
Corinth • Athens
Ephesus
Colossae
Tarsus • Issus Carchemish
Nineveh
Aleppo Haran Nimrud
Antioch Assur Nuzi
CRETE
CYPRUS Ras Shamra (Ugarit)
Hamath
Orontes
Mari
MEDITERRANEAN SEA Sidon
Tyre Damascus
Euphrates
Samaria Babylon Susa
Alexandria Jerusalem
Ur
Raamses Kadesh-barnea
Memphis Petra
SINAI Ezion-geber
NABATAEAN KINGDOM
El Amarna
Nile
Thebes
RED SEA
Elephantine
N
0 400 km
0 200 miles
Tigris

UNDERSTANDING OLD TESTAMENT HISTORY

Some 350 years ago scholars believed that the Old Testament could be used to date the creation of the universe precisely. Thus, in his book *The Annals of the World* (1650) Archbishop J. Usher (or Ussher) dated it to 'the entrance of the night preceding the twenty third day of October 4004'. This view of the value of the Old Testament as an historical source was, of course, undermined by the geological discoveries made at the beginning of the 19th century. Even so, until the discovery and decipherment of Egyptian, Babylonian and Assyrian records in the 19th century, the Old Testament remained a major source of information about those great empires, as well as about ancient Israel. Yet as early as 1806, scholars were warned that the value of the Old Testament for even ancient Israel's history could not be taken for granted.

The warning came from a 26-year-old German, Wilhelm Martin Leberecht de Wette, in a two-volume work which argued that the actual history of ancient Israelite religion had been different from the surface story given in the Old Testament itself. That surface story envisaged that, after their deliverance from slavery in Egypt, the Israelites gathered at Mt Sinai where, instructed by God, Moses instituted a complete system of priesthood and sacrifice, together with civil and moral laws for the guidance of the people. Against this picture, de Wette argued that Israel's actual system of priesthood and sacrifice had developed gradually over many centuries, and that in the period of the monarchy, from the time of Saul to Josiah, there was no centralized priesthood or sanctuary, but that families sacrificed at local shrines.

Much of de Wette's evidence for this interpretation came from the Old Testament itself and led him to conclude that books such as Deuteronomy were not accurate records of what had happened in the time of Moses but were later compositions which legitimated developments within Israelite religion by referring them back to the figure of Moses.

De Wette's researches were consolidated in the late 19th century into a critical scholarly consensus that divided Israelite religion into roughly three periods. The first, from the settlement of the Israelites in Canaan in the 13th century BC to the time of Josiah (640–609 BC), was one of religious diversity in which Israelites probably shared sanctuaries with Canaanites and even adopted some of their practices. The second was the time of Josiah when, under the influence of the teaching of prophets such as Hosea, Amos, Micah and Isaiah, and following a long period of Assyrian overlordship in the 7th century BC, Josiah undertook a reformation that abolished local

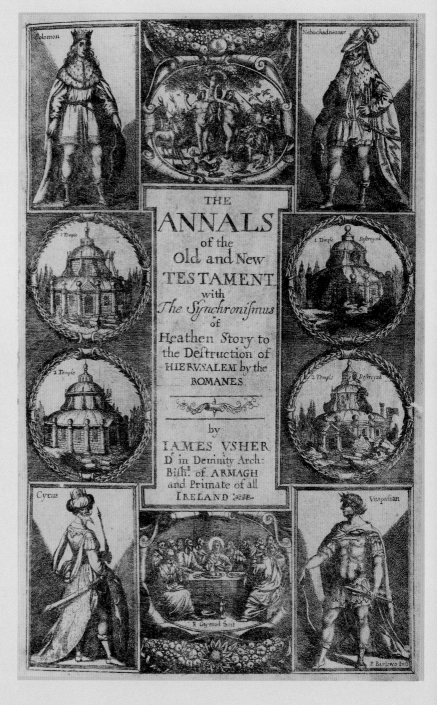

sanctuaries in an attempt to banish pagan influences from Israelite religion. The book of Deuteronomy was closely connected with this reform. The third period, from 539 BC, was that following the Exile when a small priestly community centred on Jerusalem established the detailed sacrificial system recorded in books such as Exodus and Leviticus, which they legitimated by projecting it back to the time of Moses.

The interesting thing about this critical consensus was that it assumed the general historical accuracy of books such as Judges, Samuel and Kings as witnesses for the first period. Indeed, the whole case rested on the contrast between religion as practised in that period according to these books, with many sanctuaries in use, and the type of sacrificial religion centred on a single sanctuary as commanded in Deuteronomy and implied in Exodus, Leviticus and Numbers.

It was accepted that, from the time of Solomon (c. 961 BC), conditions in ancient Israel were right for the task of collecting and writing down the traditions about the period before the monarchy. A quasi-historical work attributed to the Yahwist (so named because he used the divine name YHWH) and containing traditions about the Ancestors, the Exodus, the settlement in Canaan and the rise of the monarchy was held to have been compiled during Solomon's reign or in the century following it. There thus existed an early draft of parts of Genesis, Exodus, Numbers, Joshua, Judges, Samuel and the beginning of

1 Kings. The task of completing Israel's history was then a matter of continuing the story down to the destruction of the temple in 587 BC and of filling in periods such as the wilderness wanderings with the detailed sacrificial legislation.

This scholarly consensus has been gradually eroded in the past 30 years from several directions. First, it has been argued on internal literary grounds that the Yahwist more likely worked in the 6th century than the 10th or 9th centuries. This has opened up not simply an enormous gap between him and figures such as Abraham, but a gap of several hundred years between him and the time of David, and it has thus been questioned whether David and Solomon are any more than legendary figures. At the same time, archaeological research in Jordan as well as Israel seems to suggest that the peoples mentioned in the Old Testament as forming the empire of David and Solomon – Ammon, Moab, Edom – did not become small states until the 9th or 8th centuries, thus undermining the view that Solomon had presided over a small empire, the administration of which had put in place the conditions for the beginning of history writing in ancient Israel. A more plausible view, and one that can be sustained by archaeology, is that it was in the reign of Hezekiah, king of Judah (c. 728–698 BC) that Israel's history writing began in earnest, following the destruction of the northern kingdom, Israel, by the Assyrians.

The crucial question that has emerged from the contemporary discussion is

one that goes back, in a sense, to de Wette. He argued that the surface story of the Old Testament was incorrect in so far as it depicted the history of Israelite religion. However, the consensus that emerged from his initial researches depended upon the general accuracy of books such as Samuel and Kings. If this accuracy is now questioned, two issues arise. First, where, if anywhere, can we find an historical framework or skeleton on which to hang the historical traditions of the Old Testament? Second, if the books of Samuel and Kings are shown to be late compositions, what does this imply for the history of Israelite religion?

Two answers are currently being given to the first question. According to one, only archaeology can provide such a framework, in which case we know very little about Israel until the dynasty founded by Omri in the northern kingdom (c. 885–874 BC) and the time of Hezekiah (c. 728–698 BC) in the southern kingdom. In this interpretation, the traditions in the Old Testament about the period of the Judges and the times of Saul, David and Solomon have to be treated with great caution. A second, opposing view is prepared to accept the general outline presented in the Old Testament, with a period of existence of Israelite groups without centralized authority followed by the rise of 'kingship' at the time of a Philistine threat to the Israelites (c. 1020 BC), leading to the establishment of two small kingdoms of which one, Israel, was destroyed by the Assyrians in 722/1 BC and the other, Judah, was destroyed by the Babylonians in 587 BC.

As yet, the second main question, that of the history of Israelite religion, has not begun to be addressed, although the implications of the approach of the radical school of thought are that Israelite religion was far more pluralistic and even syncretistic than has been previously assumed.

The format of the series means that this book follows the line that the Old Testament provides a reliable historical framework for understanding ancient Israel's history. My own view is that the jury is still out, but that there is a need for a work that introduces some of the problems of handling the historical traditions of the Old Testament.

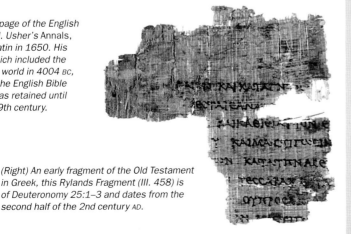

(Left) The title page of the English translation of J. Usher's Annals, published in Latin in 1650. His chronology, which included the creation of the world in 4004 BC, was added to the English Bible in 1701 and was retained until well into the 19th century.

(Right) An early fragment of the Old Testament in Greek, this Rylands Fragment (III. 458) is of Deuteronomy 25:1–3 and dates from the second half of the 2nd century AD.

THE ANCESTORS
(? 1450–1320 BC)

Abraham

Sarah

Hagar

Isaac

Rebekah

Jacob

Joseph

EXODUS AND SETTLEMENT
(? 1320–1230 BC)

Moses

Joshua

THE JUDGES
(c. 1230–1020 BC)

Othniel

Ehud

Deborah

Gideon

Abimelech

Tola

Jair

Ibzan

Elon

Abdon

Jephthah

Samson

Samuel

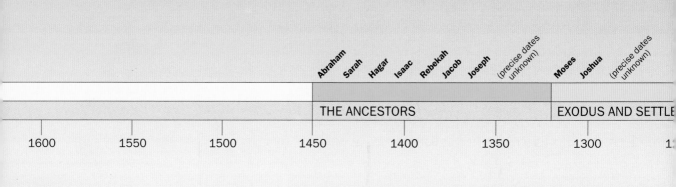

THE ANCESTORS

EXODUS AND SETTLE

1600   1550   1500   1450   1400   1350   1300

Abraham   Isaac   Jacob   Joseph

FROM THE ANCESTORS TO THE JUDGES
? 1450–*c.* 1020 BC

THE BIBLE BEGINS WITH THE CREATION OF THE WORLD and the history of the first humans. The writers of the Old Testament place these events in a 'beginning time' and seek to explain why the world existed and appeared as it did; this time was joined to theirs by a series of genealogies. The genealogies lead to Terah and to his son Abra(ha)m and to the stories of the Ancestors: Abraham, Isaac and Jacob. They are the heads of a family which journeys from Mesopotamia to Canaan, before settling in Egypt to escape famine. In Egypt the family becomes a nation large enough to be seen as a threat and so are oppressed as slaves. Their freedom comes when Moses leads them across the Red Sea and back to Canaan. Under Joshua twelve tribes, descended from the twelve sons of Jacob, occupy land allocated to them. After Joshua's death there is no institutionalized government, but God raises up leaders – these are the Judges.

The narratives of the Ancestors, the Exodus, the Wilderness Wanderings, the Occupation of Canaan and the period of the Judges, from Genesis 12 to the end of the book of Judges, are to the history of Israel what the first eleven chapters of Genesis are to the history of the world – foundation narratives that define the people and explain the origins of various institutions. Their purpose is not primarily historical; they have been shaped by centuries of liturgical practice and theological reflection, and they present great difficulties to anyone who tries to use them mainly for historical reconstruction.

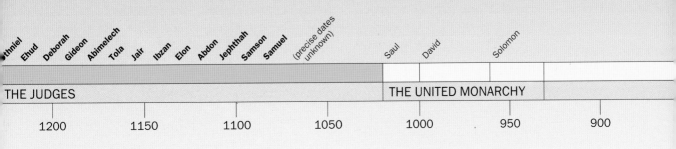

Othniel Ehud Deborah Gideon Abimelech Tola Jair Ibzan Elon Abdon Jephthah Samson Samuel (precise dates unknown) Saul David Solomon

THE JUDGES   THE UNITED MONARCHY

1200   1150   1100   1050   1000   950   900

אַבְרָהָם/אַבְרָם Abram/Abraham

שָׂרָה/שָׂרַי Sarai/Sarah

הָגָר Hagar

Portrait of Abraham from the 3rd-century AD synagogue of Dura-Europos in modern Syria.

ABRAM/ABRAHAM	

Born
  Ur of the Chaldees
Father
  Terah
Wives
  Sarai/Sarah
  Keturah
Sons
  Ishmael (born to
  Sarah's Egyptian
  maid Hagar)
	Isaac (born to
	Sarah)
	Zimran, Jokshan,
	Medan, Midian,
	Ishbak, Shuah (born
	to Keturah)
	Buried
	  Mamre (Hebron)
	Bible reference
	  Genesis
	  11:27–25:11

ABRAHAM

Now the LORD said to Abram, 'Go from your country and your kindred and your father's house to the land that I will show you. And I will make of you a great nation'.

Genesis 12:1-2

The biblical record

In the Old Testament story of the Hebrews Abram (his name is changed to Abraham when God makes a covenant with him in Genesis 17) is the founding father, without whose act of faith on a journey to an unknown destination there would be no Hebrew history at all. The biblical record tells of how Abram, his wife Sarai (later changed to Sarah) and their nephew Lot left Haran in northern Mesopotamia and travelled with their families, slaves and flocks the 400 miles (644 km) to Shechem in the northern hill country of Canaan, and on to the Negev desert, before famine forced them to go down to Egypt.

Whatever materials, oral or written, may have been utilized in forming the biblical story of Abraham, the following details emerge. Abraham is a foreigner, not a native-born Israelite, whose links with northern Mesopotamia later lead him to seek a wife for his son Isaac from among his kinsfolk who had remained in Haran. The religion of Abraham does not resemble that of Israel from the time of the monarchy onwards: there is no Israelite priesthood as he himself – rather than a priest – builds altars and offers sacrifice. His action in having a son by his wife's foreign maidservant Hagar is paralleled elsewhere in the Old Testament only by Jacob.

A map showing the travels of Abraham and his family, from his birthplace, Ur, to Egypt.

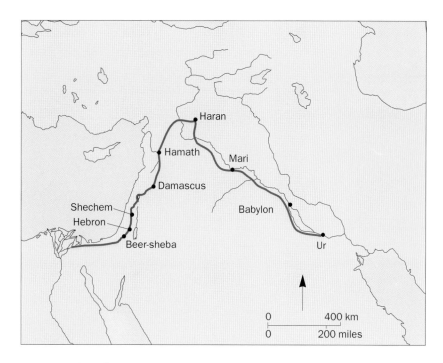

Interpreting the stories

Scholars are divided in their attitude to these differences between the religion of Abraham and that of later Israel, as presented in the Old Testament. For traditional critics, they are evidence that the stories contain genuine historical information about a person who lived in the period around 1500 BC. They point out that there are features in the Abraham story that resemble practices found elsewhere in the ancient Near East from the middle of the second millennium BC. Thus, Genesis 15:1-4 appears to say that the childless Abraham adopted Eliezer of Damascus

The visit of the three angels to Abraham is recounted in Genesis 18. They announce the birth of a son (Isaac) to Sarah. The illustration is from the Italian Hours of Alfonso of Aragon, dating to the 15th century.

The Haram el-Khalil (el-Khalil means 'the friend [of God] – the Muslim designation for Abraham) in Hebron is the traditional burial-place of the Ancestors. Built on foundations laid by Herod the Great and owing much to the Crusaders, the present building is used by both Muslims and Jews.

as his heir. The Old Testament itself contains no laws relating to adoption nor is there an account of an adoption anywhere else in the Old Testament. But such laws are known, for example, from Nuzi (near Kirkuk in Iraq) dating from the 15th century BC. Another parallel that has been drawn is between Hittite laws of the 16th–15th centuries BC and the account in Genesis 23 of Abraham buying a field from Hittites in which to bury Sarah. A common feature in the biblical and Hittite texts is the explicit reference to trees in the transaction details (Genesis 23:17).

The opposite opinion holds that the gap between 1500 BC and the time when the stories of Abraham reached their final form in the 6th–5th centuries BC is so enormous that it is quite impossible that genuine historical information can have been preserved over the intervening period. In this interpretation the differences between the religion and customs of Abraham and those of later Israel are explained as part of the literary artistry of the biblical writers.

A starting point for addressing these questions is the observation that, although the Old Testament is concerned primarily with an entity named Israel, the story begins not with the founding father of Israel, namely Jacob (p. 26), but with Jacob's putative grandfather Abraham.

THE SACRIFICE OF ISAAC

After these things God tested Abraham, and said to him, 'Abraham!' And he said, 'Here am I.' He said, 'Take your son, your only son Isaac, whom you love, and go to the land of Mori'ah, and offer him there as a burnt offering upon one of the mountains of which I shall tell you.' ... When they came to the place of which God had told him, Abraham built an altar there, and laid the wood in order, and bound Isaac his son, and laid him on the altar, upon the wood. Then Abraham put forth his hand, and took the knife to slay his son. But the angel of the LORD called to him from heaven, and said, 'Abraham, Abraham!' And he said, 'Here am I.' He said, 'Do not lay your hand on the lad ... for now I know that you fear God, seeing you have not withheld your son, your only son, from me.'

Genesis 22:1-2, 9-12

This 6th-century AD mosaic of the Sacrifice of Isaac comes from the floor of the synagogue at Beth Alpha in Galilee.

Further, many of the Abraham stories are set in the area of Hebron, which was the ancient chief city of the kingdom of Judah. In other words, the story of the Hebrews begins with a figure who was believed to be the founding father of Judah. Now Judah was much smaller than its northern neighbour Israel, was populated later than Israel, and was initially less significant in the development of Old Testament religion. Why, then, does the overall story begin with the ancestor of the initially smaller, less important country? The likely answer is that the story began to receive its final form at a time when Israel no longer existed as a political entity and Judah alone survived, representing itself as Israel. This could have been at any time after the destruction of the kingdom of Israel by the Assyrians in 722/1 BC. Three possible moments are the reign of either Hezekiah (c. 728–698 BC) or Josiah (640–609 BC), both kings of Judah, or the post-Exilic period (from 539 BC).

Any attempt to narrow the chronological possibilities further can only rest on plausible rather than probable theories. Hezekiah certainly had pressing needs for an overall story in which the founding father of Judah (i.e. Abraham) was also shown to be the founding father of Israel. He had seen the destruction of the northern kingdom, Israel, by the Assyrians in

722/1 BC and he was trying to preserve the independence of his own kingdom against Assyria by extending his influence into the former kingdom of Israel, as well as by forming alliances with other rulers of small kingdoms in the area. Josiah was in a similar position a century later. In favour of the post-Exilic period it can be said that Abraham's links with northern Mesopotamia in the biblical story may indicate that he was identified with the interests of those who returned from Exile in Babylon, and who argued that they, and not the people who had remained in Judah, constituted the true people of Israel.

The underlying religious theme

Abraham is one of those figures whose life has either been shrouded in the mists of time or remodelled in the image of those who put his story into writing. In fact, the importance of Abraham's story is not what it tells us about him, but what it tells us about the religious beliefs of those who wrote it.

The most important religious theme is that of divine promise and fulfilment, in the face of human distrust. Immediately after God has promised to Abraham that he will give him the land of Canaan and many descendants (in Genesis 12), Abraham leaves the land and goes to Egypt to escape from famine, in the process endangering his wife Sarah on whom the promise of descendants depends. Two attempts to get offspring – the apparent adoption of Eliezer in Genesis 15 and the fathering of Ishmael by his wife's maid Hagar in Genesis 16 – precede the birth of Isaac to Sarah in her old age (Genesis 21). There then follows the most important story in the cycle, the offering of Isaac (Genesis 22). God orders Abraham to sacrifice the natural son on whom the promise of descendants depends, and Abraham is only prevented from doing this by last-minute intervention from God.

What we have in the Abraham story are themes that express the deepest concerns of people of all ages: the desire for a homeland and for descendants, and for a way of understanding the perplexities of life. No doubt the placing of the story of the ancestor of Judah before that of the ancestor of Israel reflected the political realities of the time of the composition of the narratives, and enabled Judah to lay claim to the title of Israel. But the traditions also embodied a timelessness that enabled them to speak to various groups of Israelites at differing times.

SARAI/SARAH	
Born	*Buried*
Ur of the Chaldees	Mamre (Hebron)
Father	*Bible references*
Terah	Genesis
Husband	11:29–23:19
Abraham	
Son	
Isaac	

SARAH AND HAGAR

Sarah said to Abraham, 'Cast out this slave woman with her son'.

Genesis 21:10

Two women play a vital part in the story of Abraham: his wife Sarah and her Egyptian servant Hagar. While it is not possible to say anything about them as historical figures, the narrative is an illuminating description of

There are two versions in the Bible of the story in which Abraham pretends that Sarah is his sister rather than his wife. In Genesis 20 Abraham and his family are living in the territory of Abimelech, king of Gerar, who takes Sarah into his harem. This portrayal of the three characters is a 17th-century tapestry in the cathedral of Freiburg im Breisgau.

some of the dangers to which women were exposed in the ancient Near East, as well as male attitudes to them.

Sarah and Hagar were part of the retinue of a wealthy man without a permanent place of abode. Comparisons that have often been made between Abraham and modern bedouin sheikhs are highly misleading except in one aspect: that anyone travelling in unfamiliar country is dependent on the goodwill of those who control wherever the traveller happens to be. In one version of the Abraham story, the hero is forced to go to Egypt because of famine in Canaan and survives there only by allowing Sarah to become part of the pharaoh's harem, on the grounds that she is his (half) sister as well as his wife (Genesis 12:10-20). Although it is highly implausible that someone as powerful and remote as an Egyptian king would have been interested in the wife of a Semitic dis-placed person, the narrative no doubt hints at local deals that could be made, in which wives would be loaned or bartered in return for agree-ments between men.

In the second version of the story in Genesis 20 there are some signifi-cant differences. Here, Abraham is in the Negev and not in Egypt, and the king who takes Sarah into his harem is Abimelech of Gerar. In this account, God intervenes signally to save Sarah, by communicating the true state of affairs to Abimelech in a dream. Abimelech acts in an exem-plary way, restoring Sarah to Abraham and bestowing lavish gifts on Abraham in order to repay the wrong that had originated in Abraham's deceit! There is a powerful irony in the story as Abraham tries to excuse his behaviour by saying that he did not expect there to be any fear of God in the land and that Sarah had agreed to say in every place where they stopped that Abraham was her brother. Abimelech's behaviour proves

HAGAR	
Born	*Buried*
Egypt	Unknown
Father	*Bible references*
Unknown	Genesis 16:1-15,
Son	21:8-21
Ishmael	

The plight of Hagar and Ishmael, who have been driven out unprotected into the desert by Abraham, is vividly portrayed by Jean Charles Cazin (*c.* 1880).

Abraham's fears and assumptions to be quite false. Further, Abraham's behaviour towards Sarah shows that he does not trust God's ability to look after Sarah and to give him descendants as had been promised.

The theme of the non-Israelite (Abimelech) whose behaviour constitutes a judgment on Abraham is continued in the story of Hagar. It is on Sarah's insistence that Abraham agrees to have a child by the Egyptian maid-servant – an indication that women were not without influence. A child having been conceived, relations between Hagar and Sarah sour, and Abraham gives Sarah permission to do what she pleases to her servant. This is simply described as dealing harshly (Genesis 16:6); but it is sufficient to make the pregnant Hagar flee into the desert where, as a lone foreign woman, she would be at the mercy of anyone she met. Fortunately, the narrative tells how an angel of God met her and brought her back to Abraham, after which Ishmael was born. In this narrative it is God who has to act to protect a foreign slave whose treatment by Abraham and Sarah is implicitly censured.

A similar story (Genesis 21) relates how, after the birth of Isaac to Sarah, she grew angry when she saw Isaac playing with Ishmael. Sarah took the initiative in demanding that Hagar and her son should be cast out of the family. Abraham again complies, but this time it is because God tells him to, and so he supplies Hagar with provisions as he sends her away, confident that God will protect her. How Hagar and Ishmael survive in the wilderness of Beer-sheba is not related in detail, but the story ends happily with them both surviving and Ishmael marrying an Egyptian wife.

The significance of the narratives

The narratives about Sarah and Hagar detail the dangers that threatened women in the ancient Near East, especially if they were foreign slaves who could be cast out of the household on which their existence depended. They also express the narrators' conviction that if men, who had power, did not use it to protect their wives and their female slaves, God would do so instead. No doubt the belief in divine intervention in such cases expressed an ideal; but it was also a criticism of (male) human behaviour. Abraham's story is not complete without Sarah and Hagar; and their narratives contrast the sometimes questionable behaviour of the founding father of the Hebrews with that of God, who is represented as concerned to protect vulnerable women and foreigners.

יִצְחָק Isaac

רִבְקָה Rebekah

The aged and blind Isaac, in a detail from
Jacob Obtains by Fraud Isaac's Blessing
by Govaert Flinck (1615–1660).

ISAAC	
Born	*Buried*
Unknown	Mamre (Hebron)
Father	*Bible references*
Abraham	Genesis 21:1–28:5,
Wife	35:27-8, 49:31
Rebekah	
Sons	
Esau, Jacob	

REBEKAH	
Born	*Buried*
? Nahor	Mamre (Hebron)
Father	*Bible references*
Bethuel	Genesis 21:1–28:5,
Husband	35:27-8, 49:31
Isaac	
Sons	
Esau, Jacob	

ISAAC AND REBEKAH

Isaac went out to meditate in the field in the evening; and he lifted up his eyes and looked, and behold, there were camels coming. And Rebekah lifted up her eyes, and when she saw Isaac, she alighted from the camel, and said to the servant, 'Who is the man yonder, walking in the field to meet us?' The servant said, 'It is my master'.

Genesis 24:63-65

Compared with Abraham and Jacob, Isaac is a shadowy figure. As the son of Abraham and father of Jacob, Isaac naturally appears in both their stories. Thus, he is the son promised to Sarah, and the child almost killed by Abraham in obedience to God. As Jacob's father, he is the old man on whom Jacob plays the trick of pretending to be the elder brother Esau to steal the superior blessing due to the first-born. However, there is only one chapter (Genesis 26) in which Isaac figures as a person in his own right, and even then it provides us with a third version of the ancestor pretending that his wife is his sister, alongside the two versions of the story in the Abraham cycle already mentioned. Indeed, the Isaac version of the story is almost certainly dependent on the first of these.

In the earliest occurrence of this motif, Abraham goes down from Canaan to Egypt because of a famine. In the Isaac version, the famine in Abraham's time is explicitly mentioned, but God tells Isaac expressly *not* to go down to Egypt. He is promised that if he remains in the land, God will fulfil his vow to Abraham to grant him abundant posterity. The danger to Isaac and his wife Rebekah thus arises from the people among whom they dwell, named as Philistines in Genesis 26:8. The remainder of Genesis 26 also seems to be based on the Abraham cycle. It concerns a dispute between Isaac and Abimelech, king of Gerar, about wells, and looks back to a similar dispute between Abimelech and Abraham, even to the point of Abimelech's commander Phicol appearing in both.

While Isaac is apparently not an entirely invented figure, he is primarily a literary creation whose function is to link the traditions about Abraham, ancestor of Judah, with those of Jacob, ancestor of Israel. However, given the extent to which the Isaac stories both draw upon Abraham material and are also located in the Negev south of Judah, it is reasonable to look for the origins of the Isaac figure among Judahite circles. Isaac is located predominantly at Gerar, a site now usually identified as Tell Abu Hureira (modern Tel Haror), about 15 miles (25 km) north-west of Beer-sheba. The tell is near the wadi Esh-Shariah (modern Nahal Gerar) and was inhabited in the Bronze and Iron ages. According to

The blind Isaac is deceived by Rebekah and Jacob into giving his blessing meant for Esau, the first-born son, to Jacob. This engraving of the late 19th century is by Gustave Doré.

Now Rebekah was listening when Isaac spoke to his son Esau. So when Esau went to the field to hunt for game and bring it, Rebekah said to her son Jacob, 'I heard your father speak to your brother Esau, "Bring me game, and prepare for me savoury food, that I may eat it, and bless you before the LORD before I die." Now therefore, my son, obey my word as I command you. Go to the flock, and fetch me two good kids, that I may prepare from them savoury food for your father, such as he loves; and you shall bring it to your father to eat, so that he may bless you before he dies.' But Jacob said to Rebekah his mother, 'Behold, my brother Esau is a hairy man, and I am a smooth man. Perhaps my father will feel me, and I shall seem to be mocking him, and bring a curse upon myself and not a blessing.' His mother said to him, 'Upon me be your curse, my son; only obey my word, and go, fetch them to me.' So he went and took them and brought them to his mother; and his mother prepared savoury food, such as his father loved. Then Rebekah took the best garments of Esau her older son, which were with her in the house, and put them on Jacob her younger son; and the skins of the kids she put upon his hands and upon the smooth part of his neck; and she gave the savoury food and the bread, which she had prepared, into the hand of her son Jacob.

Genesis 27:1-30

Abraham sends his servant Eliezer to northern Mesopotamia to find a wife for his son Isaac. Eliezer's meeting with Rebekah is portrayed in the Vienna Genesis (Byzantine, 6th century).

PATRIARCHS AND MATRIARCHS

In Jewish and academic scholarly tradition the term Patriarchs describes the three founding fathers of the Israelites: Abraham, Isaac and Jacob. By the Matriarchs is meant Sarah, wife of Abraham, Rebekah, wife of Isaac, and Leah and Rachel, wives of Jacob. Recent usage has tended to prefer the term Ancestors to Patriarchs.

the Septuagint version of 1 Chronicles 4:24-43, the tribe of Simeon occupied Gerar (the Hebrew has the name Gedor) in the days of Hezekiah (c. 728–698 BC), and it could well be that it was at this time or after that traditions about Isaac, an ancestor in Gerar, were taken up and used to link the stories of Abraham and Jacob.

If Isaac is a shadowy figure in the tradition as we have it, his wife Rebekah is the opposite. Indeed, of the four matriarchs (Sarah, Rebekah, and Leah and Rachel, the two wives of Jacob) Rebekah is the strongest and most prominent. Brought from north-east Mesopotamia to be Isaac's bride so that he would not marry a local Canaanite woman (Genesis 24), Rebekah ensures that her favourite son Jacob gets the blessing due to Esau. She it is who organizes the ruse whereby Jacob impersonates Esau by wearing skins to make him feel hairy to his blind father, and thus deprives his older brother of his rightful blessing. It is also she who ensures that Jacob flees to her brother Laban in Haran, to escape Esau's anger. She is thus an instance of a woman in a male-dominated society who shapes events, even while lacking formal power. Although as a literary figure Rebekah stands out clearly, we know very little else about her. Unusually, we are not even told about her death, although that of her nurse Deborah who suckled her is mentioned at Genesis 35:8.

The account of the death of Isaac is part of the Jacob cycle (Genesis 35:28), as is the brief notice at 49:31 that Isaac and Rebekah were buried along with Abraham and Sarah in the cave in the field at Mach-pelah.

יַעֲקֹב Jacob

יוֹסֵף Joseph

Jacob: a detail from a mosaic in
the narthex of San Marco, Venice,
c. 1220–1300.

William Blake's vision of Jacob's dream,
in Genesis 28, of a ladder stretching to
heaven, with angels ascending and
descending (*c.* 1800). It is in this dream
that God promises to Jacob the land
where he is lying asleep.

*Then Jacob called his sons, and said, 'Gather yourselves together, that
I may tell you what shall befall you in days to come'.*

Genesis 49:1

In the Bible the Jacob cycle extends from Genesis 27 to 49, with the material devoted to the story of Joseph inserted from 37 to 49 in what is one of the greatest pieces of Hebrew narrative in the Bible. Indeed, no reader can fail to be struck by the skilful and dramatic way in which the Joseph narrative is constructed in comparison with the rather episodic Jacob story in which it is embedded, though the Jacob narrative does not lack an overall plot.

JACOB

Jacob's story begins with the machinations of Rebekah, his mother, his cheating his brother Esau out of their father's blessing and his subsequent flight to north-east Mesopotamia where he seeks refuge with his maternal uncle Laban. On the way north from Beer-sheba he stops at Bethel. It is here that he has a dream in which he sees a ladder stretching from earth to heaven. In this dream God promises to him and his descendants the land where he is lying asleep. Having reached Haran, Jacob falls in love with Laban's younger daughter Rachel, and serves Laban for 14 years to gain her hand in marriage, being tricked after seven years into first marrying the elder daughter Leah. Jacob thus has two wives who are sisters. Sons whose names are those of the (more than) Twelve Tribes of Israel begin to be born to the fertile Leah, to Bilhah the maid of the barren Rachel, and to Leah's maid Zilpah, until Rachel at last bears Joseph.

Jacob's meeting with Rachel at a well near Haran, painted by Palma il Vecchio (1515).

Jacob requests Laban's permission to return to Canaan. Both resort to stratagems over which sheep and goats can be taken by Jacob, and when he finally departs Rachel steals Laban's household gods and keeps them despite her father's pursuit. Jacob travels back with his family to Canaan along the eastern side of the Jordan valley. When he reaches the Jabbok gorge (modern wadi Zerqa) he faces the prospect of meeting Esau, from whom he had originally fled. Sending on elaborate gifts for Esau and ordering his entourage to go ahead, Jacob is left alone at Jabbok where he has a mysterious encounter. He wrestles with an unidentifiable angelic or divine assailant until daybreak, when Jacob emerges as both the winner in that he is blessed and his name is changed to Israel (which, according to Genesis 32:28 means 'he who strives with God') and a loser in that his thigh is disabled. Changed and chastened by this encounter, Jacob is rapturously received by Esau, after which he journeys to Bethel, the scene of his dream. On the way, Rachel dies after giving birth to Benjamin and is buried along the route to Ephrath which is not, as stated in 35:19, Bethlehem, but in the (later) territory of Benjamin (1 Samuel 10:2). This, in effect, concludes Jacob's story, except that Genesis 34 records the dealings of his sons Simeon and Levi with the city of Shechem, and their deceitful killing of its male inhabitants. When the Joseph story begins in Genesis 37, Jacob is no more than a background figure.

Jacob in history

Looking behind these traditions for scraps of historicity, scholars have noted that the stories have two locations – Haran in north-east Mesopotamia and Bethel in the northern hill country of Canaan. It has

JACOB	
Born	Bilhah); Gad, Asher
Gerar(?)	(born to Leah's
Father	maid Zilpah);
Isaac	Joseph, Benjamin
Wives	(born to Rachel)
Leah, Rachel	*Died*
Sons	Egypt
Reuben, Simeon,	*Buried*
Levi, Judah,	Mamre (Hebron)
Issachar, Zebulun	*Bible references*
(born to Leah); Dan,	Genesis
Naphtali (born to	25:1–50:26;
Rachel's maid	Joshua 24:32

Prior to crossing the river Jabbok Jacob wrestles until dawn with an unidentifiable angelic or divine assailant (Genesis 32:22-32). This is a key incident as it is at this point that Jacob's name becomes Israel. This painting, of 1856–61, is by Eugène Delacroix.

been suggested that the traditions therefore originate from two groups that occupied the territory of the northern kingdom, Israel, one of which had migrated from Haran. However, Haran is a feature of both the Jacob and the Abraham stories, with Rebekah being the link between the two. Although one cannot prove or disprove that the Haran theme originates from a Haran group, it is just as likely that it is a literary device to link the originally independent traditions of Jacob and Abraham. If this line is followed, the connection of Jacob with Bethel suggests that he was an ancestor whose traditions originated in the northern hill country.

Jacob's struggle with the unidentifiable manifestation of God at the river Jabbok in Transjordan in Genesis 32 is a key incident and it is here that his name becomes Israel. It will be pointed out (p. 43) that there is evidence that groups from northern Transjordan settled in Canaan in the 12th century BC, including elements that were to become Israel. It is therefore not impossible that this incident retains memories of a crossing from Transjordan into Canaan by an ancestor Jacob, which was later seen by his descendants as a defining moment. Other attempts to detect real events behind the traditions have noted the division of the tribes by their birth to the wives and maids of Jacob. Leah bears six sons who give their names to tribes: Reuben, Simeon, Levi, Judah, Issachar and Zebulun. To Leah's maid are born Gad and Asher, and to Rachel's maid are born Dan and Naphtali. Rachel is the mother of Joseph and Benjamin.

It is certainly not impossible that these associations do indeed represent different groups; and given that Reuben and Simeon disappear from Israelite history early on, and that Levi becomes, or always is, a priestly tribe with no territorial holdings, it could be supposed that the Leah tribes represent an earlier wave of occupation of Canaan. Another point is that Joseph (later the tribes of Ephraim and Manasseh) and Benjamin are the two Rachel tribes, and they occupy what will be the heartland of the northern kingdom. Their prominence, together with that of Rachel, suggests that the Jacob narrative comes from traditions preserved in the northern hill country, before the Jacob story was combined with Abraham's. Jacob was thus an ancestor of at least some of the northern tribes, and the group that he led possibly came from Transjordan.

Genesis 49 is devoted mainly to the so-called 'Blessing of Jacob' in which the dying patriarch utters a saying characterizing each of the tribes, either by describing its territory, or explaining its name, or alluding to its recent history. It is widely accepted that the sayings were probably originally independent. Jacob mentions the six Leah tribes first and the two Rachel tribes last, giving prominence to Judah and Joseph. This suggests that the 'Blessing' was compiled at a time when there were strong kingdoms in Judah and Israel, such as the reigns of Uzziah and Jeroboam II. The extensive saying about Joseph alludes to fighting with unnamed adversaries in which Joseph was victorious, and concludes by praising Joseph as one dedicated (Hebrew *nazir*) to deliver his brothers. Although the allusion cannot be identified for certain with any historical incident, it may well be the germ that gave rise to the story of Joseph.

JOSEPH

An underlying purpose of the narrative that runs from Genesis 37 to 50 is to link the patriarchs to the story of Moses by explaining how and why Jacob and his sons left Canaan and settled in Egypt. Its hero, Joseph, is his father's favourite because he is the son of Rachel, Jacob's beloved wife. As a sign of this favour Joseph wears a long-sleeved coat – the better-known translation 'coat of many colours' assumes that the Hebrew *passim* means strips, and that the phrase 'garment of strips' denotes a garment of multi-coloured strips. Joseph's dreams, which imply that his brothers and even his parents will one day be subservient to him, determine his brothers to sell him into slavery in Egypt, while pretending to Jacob that

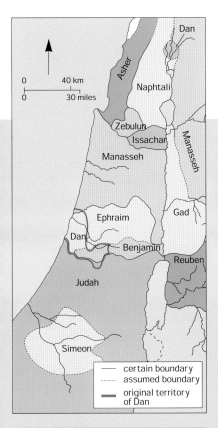

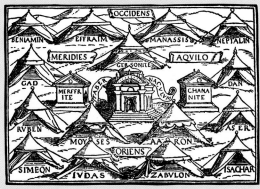

(Left) Map showing the distribution of territories of the Twelve Tribes. (Right) Hans Holbein's woodcut of the Israelite camp in the wilderness wonderings, with each of the Twelve Tribes occupying a tent arranged around the Tabernacle.

certain boundary
assumed boundary
original territory of Dan

THE TWELVE TRIBES OF ISRAEL

'All these are the twelve tribes of Israel; and this is what their father said to them as he blessed them, blessing each with the blessing suitable to him.'

Genesis 49:28

Behind the frequent references in the Bible to the Twelve Tribes of Israel lurk many problems. For instance, what was an Israelite tribe? Was it a descent group (i.e. extended families descended or believed to be descended from a named ancestor) or was it a geographical area? Did some of the tribes take their names from the area in which they lived (e.g. was the tribe of

Ephraim named after the hill country of Ephraim)? The fact that all these rhetorical questions can be answered affirmatively shows how complicated the subject is. The Old Testament contains indications that Israelite tribes were both descent groups and people defined by a geographical area and that several were named after their geographical locations.

We can further ask why are there twelve tribes and how far back in history does their association go? Answering these questions is complicated by the fact that the Old Testament contains more than twelve names of Israelite tribes, and that some groups (e.g. Reuben and Simeon) declined while others prospered; for example the tribe of Joseph divided into two tribes: Ephraim and Manasseh. And why twelve? A possible explanation is that this number corresponds to the months in a year and to religious or administrative arrangements which made each group responsible for

particular duties during a particular month. It is also possible, however, that the idea of twelve tribes is a theological construction, expressing the unity of the people of God. In the history of ancient Israel the southern tribe of Judah was mostly separated from the northern tribes, of which several (Gilead/Gad, Reuben, part of Manasseh) were located on the eastern side of the river Jordan.

There are two collections of sayings relating to the Twelve Tribes, in Genesis 49 (the so-called Blessing of Jacob) and Deuteronomy 33 (the so-called Blessing of Moses). The names in each vary: Simeon is absent from Deuteronomy 33 and Joseph has become two tribes. The saying about Reuben at Deuteronomy 33:6 'Let Reuben live, and not die, nor let his men be few' seems to imply the imminent demise of this tribe. The Twelve Tribes are best seen as an idealization whose precise history is difficult to reconstruct.

Jacob sends Joseph to look for his brothers, who sell him into slavery; in Egypt Joseph refuses to sleep with Potiphar's wife and is imprisoned.

JOSEPH AND HIS BROTHERS

The story of Joseph (Genesis 37, 39–48) is one of the high points of classical Hebrew narrative. Joseph, the eleventh and favourite son of Jacob, earns the displeasure of his brothers as his dreams imply that they will one day do obeisance to him, and due to his special coat of long sleeves

(or of different coloured strips of material), given to him by their father. His brothers rid themselves of him by selling him to merchants on their way to Egypt, but convince their father that Joseph has been killed by a wild animal when they show him the special coat stained with blood. In Egypt Joseph becomes the administrator of the estate of Potiphar, a high official, but is

imprisoned when Potiphar's wife falsely accuses Joseph of seducing her. In prison, Joseph correctly interprets the dreams of two of pharaoh's imprisoned officials, one of whom is released and who later remembers Joseph's skill in dream interpretation.

Pharaoh has a dream about seven well-fed cows emerging from the Nile only to be eaten by seven thin cows who

JOSEPH	
Born	*Buried*
Haran	Shechem
Father	*Bible references*
Jacob	Genesis 30:23-25,
Wife	37:2–50:26;
Asenath	Joshua 24:32
Sons	
Ephraim, Manasseh	

Then Jacob called his sons, and said, 'Gather yourselves together, that I may tell you what shall befall you in days to come. Assemble and hear, O sons of Jacob, and hearken to Israel your father.... Joseph is a fruitful bough, a fruitful bough by a spring; his branches run over the wall.... The blessings of your father are mighty beyond the blessings of the eternal mountains, the bounties of the everlasting hills; may they be on the head of Joseph, and on the brow of him who was separate from his brothers.'

The Blessing of Jacob,
Genesis 49:1-2, 22, 26

Joseph has been killed by a wild animal during a visit to his brothers as they graze the flocks in the northern hill country.

As a slave, Joseph soon gains the confidence of Potiphar his master and is put in charge of his estate. However, Potiphar's wife alleges that Joseph seduced her and he is imprisoned. He is released when the Egyptian pharaoh needs someone to interpret his dreams, and pharaoh's chief butler remembers that Joseph had accurately interpreted his dream when they were in prison together. Joseph now informs pharaoh what his dreams portend: Egypt will enjoy seven prosperous years followed by seven years of famine. To manage these events, Joseph is appointed by pharaoh to high office in Egypt and it is in this position that he encounters his brothers when they come to Egypt to buy grain during the famine. The story of the tricks that Joseph plays on his brothers and the account of the brothers' reconciliation with him are unsurpassed in the Old Testament for literary artistry. The cycle ends with Jacob and his family coming to join Joseph in Egypt: the stage is set for the next act of the drama – the oppression of the Israelites in Egypt and the Exodus.

The well-structured narrative of the Joseph stories is a far cry from what has preceded it in Genesis, and while such literary artistry is not necessarily a sign of late composition, few scholars now believe that the cycle originated in Egypt at an early date. Indeed, the material in the Old Testament that stands closest to the Joseph narrative is the cycle concerning Daniel and his companions, which in its present form is to be dated in the 2nd century BC. Both Joseph and Daniel are Israelites who

Joseph, governor of Egypt, meets his brothers who have come to buy grain. The story of Joseph, depicted by B. di Giovanni (1483–1511).

also emerge from the Nile. Joseph is called from prison to interpret pharaoh's dream. Its meaning is that seven years of plenty will be followed by seven years of famine; Joseph is empowered by pharaoh to ensure that the gains of the seven good years are preserved in order to provide food during the famine.

The famine affects Canaan as well as Egypt, and when Joseph's brothers arrive from Canaan to buy wheat, Joseph exacts his revenge. In particular, he manoeuvres his brothers (who do not recognize him) into bringing Joseph's younger brother Benjamin to him, and then charges Benjamin with stealing a special silver cup. The brothers are distraught because their father Jacob regards Benjamin as his most precious son following his loss of Joseph.

Joseph then breaks down with emotion and reveals his identity to the brothers. He is generous about their plot to be rid of him: 'it was not you who sent me here, but God' (Genesis 45:8). The reunion leads to Jacob and his whole family coming to sojourn in Egypt – the prelude to the narratives about the oppression in Egypt and the Exodus.

obtain prominence in the court of a great foreign ruler, who interpret dreams, and who are wrongly imprisoned. The date of the Joseph story will depend upon opinions about when Genesis and Exodus reached their final form; but a reasonable guess would place it either in the time of Hezekiah (*c.* 728–698 BC) or Josiah (640–609 BC) when the overall story of Israel was being forged, or in the post-Exilic period when the same process was being completed.

This mosaic from San Marco, Venice, depicts the moment when the aged Jacob is shown the blood-stained coat that he had given to his favourite son Joseph. Joseph's brothers intend thereby to persuade Jacob that Joseph has been killed by a wild animal, whereas they have sold him into slavery in Egypt.

מֹשֶׁה Moses

The head of Moses from the statue by Michelangelo in San Pietro in Vincoli, Rome, c. 1515. He is shown with horns because of a mistranslation of the Hebrew for 'rays of light'.

The words in Aramaic 'This is the bread of affliction which our fathers ate in the land of Egypt' are part of the liturgy used by Jews annually at the Passover, here illustrated in a 15th-century German Haggadah.

Moses said to God, 'Who am I that I should go to Pharaoh, and bring the sons of Israel out of Egypt?'

Exodus 3:11

If, in the Old Testament, Abraham, Isaac and Jacob are the physical ancestors of the Hebrews, Moses is the founder of their distinctive faith. According to Exodus 6:3 (see also Exodus 3:13-14) it was Moses to whom God revealed his special name YHWH, generally thought to have been pronounced Yahweh – a name not previously known to the Hebrews and one which occurs nearly 7,000 times in the Bible. Further, Moses was the leader who delivered the Hebrews from slavery in Egypt by bringing plagues upon the land, commanding the Hebrews to observe the Passover and leading them across the Red (or Reed) Sea. After the pursuing army of the Egyptian pharaoh had been engulfed by the returning waters of the sea, Moses led the people to Mt Sinai where God revealed to him the Ten Commandments, together with laws pertaining to the establishment of an Israelite priesthood, a sacrificial system and civil and judicial life. Moses then guided the Israelites on a long and difficult journey through the wilderness to the land of Canaan. The journey was characterized by lack of food, sickness, wars against enemies, and internal dissent and revolt. On the threshold of the Promised Land – which Moses was destined to see from afar but not enter – he delivered a final speech to the Israelites in the form of the book of Deuteronomy.

Looking beyond the biblical story

The Old Testament devotes more space to the life of Moses and the institutions he founded than to any other person; yet, paradoxically, we

The life of Moses as portrayed by Sandro Botticelli on the south wall of the Sistine Chapel in the Vatican. Of the various scenes, that at the top left depicts God's revelation to Moses in the burning bush, while in the foreground is the incident at the well in Midian where Moses meets his future wife and father-in-law (Exodus 2:15-22).

MOSES

Name	*Wives*
Probably Egyptian,	Zipporah; an
mes, mesu: 'child'	unnamed Cushite
and connected with	woman
the Hebrew verb 'to	*Sons*
draw [out of the	Gershom, Eliezer
rushes]'	*Buried*
Born	Plains of Moab
Egypt	*Bible references*
Father	Exodus 2:1 –
Amram	Deuteronomy 34:12

know almost nothing about him or his work. Indeed, any attempt to reconstruct the historical Moses involves a good deal of informed guesswork. To explain why this is so is to enter the heart of some of the most complicated problems of the critical study of the Old Testament, and to engage in a debate begun nearly 200 years ago by de Wette (p. 12).

Central to this debate is the view that the actual history of the development of Israelite religion, sacrifice and priesthood is quite different from the surface story presented in the Old Testament – as outlined in the opening paragraph of this section. There is now a broad consensus in Old Testament scholarship that Israelite religion in Canaan from the 12th century BC onwards was based on the main agricultural festivals of the barley and wheat harvests of spring, and the fruit harvest of autumn. Israelites worshipped at ancient local sanctuaries, and there was no centralized priesthood or system of sacrifice. It was only later, through the work of the prophets – especially those of the 8th century BC (Hosea, Amos, Isaiah, Micah) – and reforming kings of Judah such as Hezekiah and Josiah, that the organization of religion as presented in the stories about Moses actually began to emerge. A crucial point was the reform of Josiah in 622 BC, when local sanctuaries in Judah were closed and the hitherto royal temple in Jerusalem became the central, national sanctuary. The book of Deuteronomy, with its demand for worship at only one sanctuary, probably originates from this time. After the destruction of the temple in 587 BC and its rebuilding by the post-Exilic community in

Jerusalem in 515 BC, Judah became a small community centred around the temple. It was during this period that the priestly and sacrificial systems as described in books such as Exodus, Leviticus and Numbers were finally established but, in order to express a sense of authority and continuity with the past, the founding of these institutions was set in remote antiquity: the sojourn at Mt Sinai in the time of Moses.

To argue this in detail would require at least a large book, and aspects of it will be met with in other sections of the present work. All that can be done here is to outline a scholarly consensus based on painstaking study over the last 200 years, and to note how radically it differs from the Bible's own view of Moses and his works.

The Moses of history

What, then, can be surmised about the historical Moses? The name is probably Egyptian, from the verb *msy* meaning 'to be born', and therefore also *mes*, 'child'. In fact, it is only half a name, and would have been combined with the name of a god, as in the name of the pharaohs Thutmose(s). The fact that the Bible hebraizes the name by connecting it with the Hebrew verb *mashah*, 'to draw out' (Exodus 2:10) suggests that it is not an invented name. Tradition has clearly preserved a name that was not understood and which had to be accommodated into the language of the Bible. There was, therefore, someone called Moses, even if this may not have been his full name. The Bible further links him to Egypt in the story that he was taken from the bulrushes and brought up in the court of pharaoh (Exodus 2:1-10). There are, however, several internal difficulties in the story and its context. Thus, only two midwives service a growing Hebrew population that is threatening to overwhelm the Egyptians, while the Egyptians, needing the Hebrews to work as slaves on building projects, tell the midwives to kill the baby boys!

It is also remarkable that the tradition asserts that the founder of Israel's distinctive faith grew up, effectively, as a foreigner. Another intriguing 'foreign' element in Moses' background is his connection with Midian, in the Sinai wilderness. According to Exodus 2:11-22, Moses flees to Midian after he has killed an Egyptian who was mistreating a Hebrew, and indeed it is in Midian that Moses first encounters God as YHWH, and is commanded to lead the Israelites out of slavery. One approach, which combines the Egyptian and Midianite elements of the Moses tradition, sees him as a leader of a group of *shasu* nomads from southern Transjordan who had journeyed to Egypt and had been conscripted into labour gangs, probably during the reign of Ramesses II (1279–1212 BC). Led by Moses the group escaped, and later joined with proto-Israelite groups in northern Transjordan before they together crossed the Jordan into Canaan in the latter part of the 12th century BC. Moses' Egyptian name could have been given to him by an Egyptian overseer. Egyptian texts of the 14th century BC refer to 'Yhw in *shasu* land', which may mean that the name YHWH was originally associated with a mountain or region inhabited by the *shasu*. Thus, some ingredients of

SHASU AND HABIRU

Shasu is a term found in Egyptian texts in the period 1500 to 1100 BC. Whether it denotes both a land and a people is disputed, but the texts locate *shasu* in southern Syria, northern Palestine, the area between the Egyptian Delta and Gaza, and the area of Transjordan later occupied by the Edomites. They appear to have been organized into 'tribes' and to have been both sedentary and nomadic. Depictions of them show them to have been bearded and to have worn head-cloths and tasselled 'kilts'. Some scholars have tried to establish links between the *shasu* and proto-Israelites.

The *habiru* or *hapiru* are known from texts from Anatolia in the 19th century BC to Egyptian texts of the 12th century BC. The most dramatic references to them come in the Amarna letters of the mid-14th century BC, where they are described as groups who are attacking and destroying cities. Older scholarship linked these events with the Israelite invasion of Canaan. The general consensus is that the *habiru* were refugees or people on the margins of society who survived by becoming mercenaries or slaves or brigands. While a connection between the *habiru* and Hebrews cannot be ruled out, the available evidence does not enable such a connection to be described in any specific terms.

THE TEN COMMANDMENTS

And God spoke all these words, saying,

'I am the LORD your God, who brought you out of the land of Egypt, out of the house of bondage.

- 'You shall have no other gods before me.

- 'You shall not make for yourself a graven image, or any likeness of anything that is in heaven above, or that is in the earth beneath, or that is in the water under the earth; you shall not bow down to them or serve them. ...

- 'You shall not take the name of the LORD your God in vain; for the LORD will not hold him guiltless who takes his name in vain.

- 'Remember the sabbath day, to keep it holy. Six days you shall labour, and do all your work; but the seventh day is a sabbath to the LORD your God; in it you shall not do any work ....

- 'Honour your father and your mother, that your days may be long in the land which the LORD your God gives you.

- 'You shall not kill.

- 'You shall not commit adultery.

- 'You shall not steal.

- 'You shall not bear false witness against your neighbour.

- 'You shall not covet your neighbour's house; you shall not covet your neighbour's wife, or his manservant, or his maidservant, or his ox, or his ass, or anything that is your neighbour's.'

The Ten Commandments:
Exodus 20:1-5, 7-10, 12-17

Moses holding the two tablets on which the Ten Commandments are written, from the Alba Bible, Spanish, 1422. The tablets in the illustration contain only the essentials, not the full text.

the biblical tradition can be plausibly fleshed out historically, although the tradition as we now have it is based on much reflection and re-telling and, in its final form, displays considerable literary artistry.

Moses, Aaron and Miriam

Two figures closely associated with Moses are Aaron, his brother and later a priest, and Miriam, their sister. A consideration of these figures will take us into some of the detail of the Moses narratives and their problems. Moses often acts alone in stories about him, but there is a strand in which Aaron acts with Moses and where he seems to have been

Aaron pouring oil into a seven-branched lamp (*menorah*) from a Hebrew Bible dated 1278, from France.

inserted into the narrative. This is most obvious in the narrative of the plagues. In Exodus 9:22-26 the plague of hail occurs when Moses lifts up his rod at God's command, as do the plagues of locusts (10:12-15) and darkness (10:21-28). The plagues of blood and frogs (Exodus 7:19-24 and 8:1-7), on the other hand, occur when Aaron lifts up his rod on the instructions of God via Moses. The formula here is 'The Lord said to Moses, "Say to Aaron…".' It is noteworthy that God never speaks directly to Aaron who, indeed, is a completely passive figure. He says nothing and he initiates nothing. All his appearances are in the shadow of Moses, sometimes uneasily from a narrative point of view – if Aaron were to be deleted from Numbers 20:2-13 its flow would be improved.

There are, however, two exceptions to Aaron's silent and passive role, and both involve opposition to Moses. At Exodus 32:1-7, during Moses' absence from the Israelite camp while on Mt Sinai, Aaron directs the people to make and worship a Golden Calf. At Numbers 12:1-15 Aaron and Miriam criticize Moses for marrying a Cushite (Ethiopian) woman, and Aaron intercedes on Miriam's behalf when she is smitten with leprosy as a punishment for her remarks. To these narratives should be added Leviticus 10:1-3, where two of Aaron's sons, Nadab and Abihu, offer incense to God other than as prescribed, and are killed by divine fire.

How far these passages allow us to discover an historical Aaron is hard to say. The story of the Golden Calf is very similar to the incident in

A statue of Ramesses II in the temple of Luxor, Egypt. Ramesses is usually assumed to have been the pharaoh of the Exodus.

The triumphal dance of Miriam and the women after the destruction of pharaoh's army at the Red Sea (Exodus, 15:19-21), from the Golden Haggadah, Spain, 14th century.

1 Kings 12 where Jeroboam sets up bull images at Bethel and Dan and says to them, in words almost identical to those of Aaron in Exodus 32:4, 'Behold your gods, O Israel, who brought you up out of the land of Egypt'. Such similarity between the two stories has led to the theory that Aaron was the founder of a dynasty of priests at the ancient sanctuary of Bethel. According to this view, when Jerusalem became the sole legitimate sanctuary during Josiah's reform in 622 BC, the rival sanctuary at Bethel was discredited by the writing of a story in which its founding priest (Aaron) made a Golden Calf in opposition to Moses. However, this widely held theory assumes that readers will draw the far-from-obvious conclusion that Aaron was a priest of Bethel when they read Exodus 32; and in any case, if Aaron was the priest of a rival sanctuary to Jerusalem, why did he become the founding priest of a cultus that was ultimately located in Jerusalem? It is easier to suppose that Aaron was a priest in the Jerusalem cultus and that he owes his position in the Moses narratives to the incorporation of laws about priestly ritual into the tradition that Moses was the founder of the religion of Israel and its lawgiver in all matters.

Miriam is described in Exodus 15:20 as a prophetess who led the women in the singing of the 'Song of Moses' (Exodus 15:1-18) after Moses had sung it. Feminist writers have pointed out, with some justification, that the way in which the material is presented would allow the conclusion that Miriam was the person who composed the song of triumph, and that male bias in the formation of the tradition has ascribed the song to Moses and given Miriam simply an imitative role. If this is correct, it would account for the presence of Miriam in the stories. The date of Exodus 15:1-18 is much disputed. Depending on one's view of this, Miriam could have been present with Moses, or she could have been a prophetess at a much later date composing a song of victory in connection with a Passover celebration.

When the people saw that Moses delayed to come down from the mountain, the people gathered themselves together to Aaron, and said to him, 'Up, make us gods, who shall go before us; as for this Moses, the man who brought us up out of the land of Egypt, we do not know what has become of him.' And Aaron said to them, 'Take off the rings of gold which are in the ears of your wives, your sons, and your daughters, and bring them to me.' So all the people took off the rings of gold which were in their ears, and brought them to Aaron. And he received the gold at their hand, and fashioned it with a graving tool, and made a molten calf; and they said, 'These are your gods, O Israel, who brought you up out of the land of Egypt!'

The Story of Golden Calf,
Exodus 32:1-8

The 'Golden Calf' – a bronze bull statuette from the Samaria region, early 12th century BC.

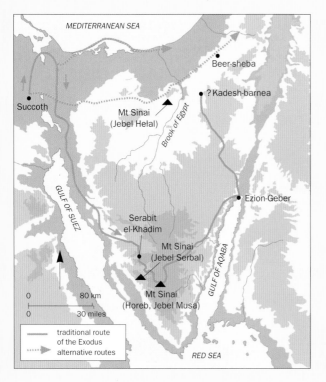

(Above) Jebel Musa, the traditional site of Mt Sinai, is part of a cluster of inhospitable mountains in the Sinai peninsula; it rises to a height of 7,455 ft (2,273 m). (Below) Map showing the possible routes of the Exodus, and the suggested locations of Mt Sinai.

(Right) The Israelites crossing the Red Sea on dry land between the parted waves, from the Ryland's Haggadah, 14th century.

(Opposite) The view from Mt Nebo in Jordan across the Jordan valley to the hills of Judah. The Dead Sea can be seen top left. According to Deuteronomy 34:1-3, this was Moses' view of the Promised Land, which he was destined never to enter, immediately prior to his death.

THE EXODUS

The word Exodus covers the whole complex of events of Israel's deliverance from Egypt, assisted by a series of miracles that included plagues upon the Egyptians and culminating in the crossing of the Red Sea, when the Israelites crossed on dry land and the pursuing Egyptians were engulfed by the returning waters. The location of the Red Sea implied in the biblical narratives is unknown. The term Red Sea (or, as some have argued on the basis of the Old Testament term *yam suph*, Sea of Reeds) referred in ancient times to the bitter lakes region to the north of Suez and to the Gulfs of Suez and Aqaba and possibly even further south; so there are many potential sites for the crossing. A widely accepted theory is that the Israelites crossed somewhere in this region (today crossed by the Suez canal) before making their way to the traditional location of Mt Sinai. The Exodus is usually dated in the reign of the pharaoh Ramesses II (1279–1212 BC).

Conclusion

In the tradition as we have it Moses is something of a tragic figure. A Hebrew growing up in a foreign court, he is initially rejected by his own people when he intervenes on their behalf (Exodus 2:11-14) and has to flee from Egypt when his intervention results in him killing an Egyptian. In exile in Midian he names his first son Gershom, the Hebrew name indicating that he is in exile in a foreign land (Exodus 2:22). His commission to deliver the Hebrews from slavery leads to renewed confrontation with his own people when his initial interview with the pharaoh merely increases their burdens (Exodus 5:21). After the deliverance Moses is faced with constant complaint from the people, opposition from Aaron, Aaron's sons and Miriam, and attempts from that quarter to usurp his leadership. Finally, along with the entire generation of those who left Egypt, he is not allowed to enter the Promised Land. He glimpses it only from Mt Nebo in Transjordan.

If historical research provides only a fleeting glimpse of the leader who proved to be such a powerful magnet for traditions to cluster round his person, the narrative itself makes it clear that to be the founder of a religion is no easy task. In the case of Moses it involves exile, rejection by those he comes to liberate, opposition to his leadership, ingratitude and, ultimately, failure to reach the goal of the Promised Land. How wise he was to be so reluctant to undertake his mission (Exodus 3:11–4:16)!

יְהוֹשֻׁעַ Joshua

Joshua, from the Arsenal Bible
(1250–54).

JOSHUA	
Born	*Bible references*
Egypt	Exodus 17: 9–13;
Father	32:17; 33:11;
Nun	Numbers 11:28;
Wives	13:16; 14:6-10,
None recorded	38; 27:18-22;
Sons	Deuteronomy 31:7-
None recorded	8, 14, 23; 34:9-12;
Buried	Joshua 1:1–24:31
Timnath-serah in	
the hill country	

So Joshua defeated the whole land, the hill country and the Negeb and the lowland and the slopes, and all their kings; he left none remaining, but utterly destroyed all that breathed.

Joshua 10:40

In the biblical tradition, Joshua's main role is as successor to Moses. He leads the people across the river Jordan and conquers the land of Canaan in a series of brilliant battles. At the end of the book of Joshua he summons the tribes to Shechem and there makes a covenant with the people, who pledge their undivided loyalty to God (24:25-7). However, Joshua also has a career prior to succeeding Moses; and his conquest of Canaan bristles with historical difficulties.

The biblical account

Joshua first appears in Exodus 17, when he leads the Israelite army to victory over the Amalekites. His introduction is so abrupt that it is taken for granted that readers know who he is. A special relationship between Joshua and Moses is assumed in Exodus 32:17, where it is implied that he was absent from the camp and with Moses when Aaron made the Golden Calf. A chapter later (33:11) he is described as 'his [Moses'] servant Joshua the son of Nun, a young man'. In Numbers 11:28 Joshua is called the 'minister of Moses' (Hebrew *mesharet*, one who serves or ministers to) but in chapter 13 he is simply one of the twelve spies, each of whom represents a tribe, sent by Moses from the Israelite camp at Kadesh-barnea to reconnoitre the lie of the land. At that point called Hoshea of the tribe of Ephraim, his name is changed by Moses to Joshua in Numbers 13:16. He and Caleb are the only two spies to bring a favourable

Scenes from the life of Joshua, including the campaign against Jericho, and Joshua's encounter with an angel dressed as a warrior holding a drawn sword; from the Joshua Roll, possibly 10th century, Byzantine.

report of their survey of Canaan and are thus the only ones who eventually enter the Promised Land. In Numbers 27:18, Joshua is officially designated as Moses' successor.

Historical questions

The historical problems raised by the book of Joshua's portrayal of Joshua as the conqueror of the whole of Canaan are two-fold – internal and external. Under the internal heading is the fact that, as opposed to the global claims of passages such as that quoted above, Joshua itself contains detailed accounts of only very limited operations. Thus, after the defeat of Jericho and Ai (Joshua 6–8), Joshua defeats a coalition of kings from cities in the hills and lowlands of Judah. The next and last action (Joshua 11) is in the far north, at Hazor, and although Joshua 12 gives a list of kings whom Joshua has defeated, it adds little to what has already been described. It is striking that there is no account of the conquest of the northern hill country which would later be the heartland of the northern

THE ISRAEL STELA

One piece of historical evidence of crucial importance for dating the presence of Israel in Canaan is the Stela of the Egyptian pharaoh Merneptah. In his 5th year (1207 BC) Merneptah campaigned throughout Canaan and in this stela he makes large claims about his successes. Among other victories, he asserts that he has wiped the people of Israel off the face of the earth.

This is the first mention of the nation of Israel and demonstrates that the Israelites were a distinct entity in Canaan by that time. Despite his claims, however, Merneptah obviously did not have such a devastating effect on the nation of Israel.

A word of caution is necessary: the stela implies that Israel as a nation is present in Canaan at a date around 1207 BC. This does not help in assessing when they first arrived. It may also refer to a group who already lived in the area, rather than a band newly settled there.

The Merneptah victory stela, now in the Egyptian Museum, Cairo, states that 'Israel is devastated, her seed is no more', as seen in the detail.

Shechem was the place where Joshua assembled the tribes after the conquest of Canaan. This is a sacred pillar at the site, cemented into place following the Drew-McCormick excavations in 1960 and 1962.

kingdom, Israel, and yet it is in this area, at Shechem, that Joshua assembles the tribes, in chapter 24. It has often been argued that he had no need to conquer Shechem because this had become Israelite several generations previously, when the two sons of Jacob, Simeon and Levi, took it by guile (see Genesis 34). But if this is accepted, it merely proves that the Israelite occupation took place in several stages spread out over a long period of time, rather than as a single operation led by Joshua.

The external questions are raised by archaeology and by theories based on archaeology and the biblical text. Twenty years ago there were three main competing views. The first, associated especially with the American archaeologist W.F. Albright and his students, was that archaeology confirmed that a violent campaign of destruction had been waged in the 12th century BC. Evidence was found that cities such as Lachish and Hazor had been destroyed at this time, as claimed by Joshua 10:31-2 and 11:10. Unfortunately, there was no evidence of destruction at other cities said to have been conquered by Joshua. Ai seems not to have been occupied at that period (and the name in Hebrew means 'ruin'). Perhaps even more telling, given its prominence in the biblical account, if Jericho was

The fall of Jericho, as depicted by Jean Fouquet (c. 1425–80). This version follows the biblical account which describes how the Israelites marched round the walls of the city carrying the Ark, with priests blowing on rams' horn trumpets. In fact, archaeologists have found no evidence that the city was occupied at this time.

CANAANITE RELIGION

'Canaanite' in the Old Testament is a term used to describe the inhabitants of ancient Israel prior to its occupation by the Israelites. It also denotes their descendants who lived alongside the Israelites. Their religion is known only from criticisms of it in the Old Testament, unless the questionable practice is followed of reconstructing it using texts from Ugarit, a maritime urban centre in northern Syria that was destroyed in the 12th century BC and which did not regard itself as belonging to 'Canaan'. The major accusation against Canaanite religion is that it involved child sacrifice (Psalm 106:34-9) and cult prostitution (Deuteronomy 23:17-18, Hosea 4:14). Among Canaanite deities mentioned are Baal and Asherah, although it is not clear whether Asherah was a goddess or the name of a sacred pole or tree. A popular view of Canaanite religion found in many textbooks is that it was an agricultural religion which used magico-religious practices to ensure the fertility of land and animals. There is, however, no direct evidence for this view, which also makes some questionable anthropological assumptions.

A cult mask found at Hazor, of the 14th century BC. Found in a potter's workshop, it was perhaps part of a temple sculpture.

inhabited at the time, no evidence of this has been found. In other words, archaeology both supported and embarrassed the conquest theory.

The second view, associated with the source-critical work of the German scholars A. Alt and M. Noth, and supported by their extensive researches on the geography and topography of ancient Canaan, was that the conquest had been a peaceful occupation over a long period of time in areas not controlled by the city states. In this view the book of Joshua at best contains genuine reminiscences of local skirmishes but not of a campaign of occupation by war. A third view, pioneered by the American George E. Mendenhall, saw the conquest not as an invasion by a group from outside the land at all, but as a revolt of peasants inside it against their overlords in the Canaanite city states.

More recent research based on field surveys carried out by German and Israeli archaeologists has provided yet a fourth picture, albeit one close to the views of Alt and Noth. These researches draw attention to an apparent depopulation of Canaan at the end of the Late Bronze Age (14th century BC), and suggest that the villagers withdrew to northern Transjordan where they lived largely in tented settlements. The reason for this movement of population can only be guessed at. It may have been because of prolonged periods of drought or due to a breakdown in authority in Canaan, resulting in anarchy. This depopulation was followed, in the 13th century, by a repopulation of Canaan, beginning with the more fertile eastern and central parts of the Bethel and Samaria hill country, and extending gradually to the more forested and less friendly western regions. The 'newcomers' were the descendants of those who had migrated to northern Transjordan, and they undoubtedly included people who, through traditions about common ancestors, identified themselves as Israelites, in contrast to other peoples who resettled in Canaan at the same time. These Israelites may have been joined in the meantime by groups who had come from Egypt, and who had begun to understand their identity in terms of the deliverance from Egypt.

Conclusion

In the light of present knowledge the account of the 'conquest' probably recalls a story of conflict between a consciously emerging people of Israel and their neighbours, all of whom had settled peacefully in the land but who began to fight for supremacy. It is noteworthy that Joshua's place of burial, Timnath-serah, was in the western section of the northern hill country, and that the tradition in which he asks the sun to stand still (Joshua 10:12) is in the context of a battle in the western valley of Aijalon. Joshua is therefore best thought of as a local Israelite leader who was remembered to have won victories for the Israelites in their struggle against local neighbours. Because tradition abhors a vacuum, and because Israelite tradition came to understand its history in terms of a succession of leaders, Joshua became the successor of Moses and his local victories were interpreted as the victory that possessed for Israel the whole of the land of Canaan.

עָתְנִיאֵל	Othniel	יָאִיר	Jair
אֵהוּד	Ehud	אִבְצָן	Ibzan
דְּבוֹרָה	Deborah	אֵילוֹן	Elon
גִּדְעוֹן	Gideon	עַבְדּוֹן	Abdon
אֲבִימֶלֶךְ	Abimelech	יִפְתָּח	Jephthah
תּוֹלָע	Tola		

According to the biblical narrative the interval between the death of Joshua and the anointing of Israel's first king, Saul, was the period of the Judges. Twelve such leaders are presented in the book of Judges, and they are described as having jurisdiction over the whole people. However, they do not constitute a 'succession'. The framework of the book of Judges portrays a recurring cycle of events in which the Israelites turn away from God to other gods; God then delivers them to the power of an enemy (the 'years of oppression'); the people repent and God saves them by raising up a judge; the judge defeats the enemy and the people enjoy a period of peace ('years of rest'), before the whole cycle begins again after the death of the judge. Thus the judges are *ad hoc* leaders, although the question of whether one or more of them might establish a dynastic succession is a recurring one.

On the Bible's own chronology the period of the judges lasted for over 400 years. Modern scholars allow around 200 years for a period of consolidation from the 'settlement' of the Israelites in Canaan to the beginning of the monarchy. The divergence is easily explained. First, the Bible uses round figures for periods of Judges' rule based on 40 years as a generation, when half that figure would be more realistic. Second, a close look at the stories indicates that a unified picture has been made up from disparate sources. Thus, some Judges, such as Gideon, Jephthah and Samson, feature in long stories, while other Judges are merely names in a list. Again, it is clear that, far from ruling all Israel, the Judges were in fact local leaders whose authority was limited territorially, and who could, theoretically, have ruled simultaneously in some cases.

Here we take the view that we are dealing with material that can plausibly be fitted within the historical context of 1230 to 1020 BC. However,

Foreign power	Years of oppression	Judge	Years of rule	Years of rest	Reference in Judges
THE BIBLICAL CHRONOLOGY FOR THE PERIOD OF THE JUDGES					
Cushan-rishathaim, king of Mesopotamia	8				3:8
		Othniel		40	3:11
Eglon, king of Moab	18				3:14
		Ehud		80	3:30
Jabin, king of Canaan	20				4:3
		Deborah		40	5:31
Midian	7				6:1
		Gideon		40	7:28
		Abimelech	3		9:22
		Tola	23		10:2
		Jair	22		10:3
Ammon	18	Jephthah	6		12:9
		Ibzan	7		12:9
		Elon	10		12:11
		Abdon	8		12:14
Philistines	40	Samson	20		16:31
Totals	111		99	200	

Grand Total: **410 years**

the material consists of popular stories and not historical reporting, although it may be possible to make some historical inferences.

OTHNIEL AND EHUD

The LORD raised up…a deliverer, Ehud…a left-handed man.

Judges 3:15

OTHNIEL AND EHUD	
OTHNIEL	EHUD
Father	*Father*
Kenaz	Gera
Bible reference	*Bible references*
Judges 3:7-11	Judges 3:15-30

The first Judge is Othniel (Judges 3:7-11), to whom a mere five verses are devoted, which contain the information that he delivered Israel from Cushan-rishathaim, king of Mesopotamia. Othniel is from Debir, a site not certainly identified, but probably in south-western Judah. How, or why, a leader from southern Judah should defeat an invader from northern Syria is not clear, and there is probably much truth in the view that, in the final and Judahite version of the book of Judges, Othniel is introduced simply in order to supply an otherwise lacking Judge from Judah.

Ehud, the first Judge about whom there is a story, delivers the people of Benjamin from Eglon, the king of Moab. Whether there was a state of Moab ruled by a king at this period is doubtful: this feature of the story probably reflects much later conditions. It is not impossible, however, that a chief from the country of Moab across the Jordan would have invaded and captured Jericho, given its agricultural riches (it is called at Judges 3:13 the 'city of palms'). Although the setting of the encounter between Ehud and Eglon is not explicitly stated, it is presumably Jericho, where Eglon could have had his winter quarters.

Ehud is described as being left-handed; the word in Hebrew takes the characteristic form of words for people with a physical handicap. Whether it was regarded as a handicap by the Benjaminites we do not know. In Judges 20:16 it is recorded that the Benjaminites could muster 700 picked men who were left-handed and who could sling a stone at a hair without missing. Viewed as a handicap or not, Ehud's left-handedness is crucial to the story because it enables him to conceal a sword on his right side under his clothing (swords are usually drawn diagonally across the body). Having tricked Eglon into granting him a private audience, Ehud is able to strike the oppressor down by using his left hand. It is some time before the Moabite king's servants discover their master's fate, during which interval Ehud makes good his escape, raises the men of the hill country of Ephraim (presumably from the tribes of Benjamin and Ephraim), seizes the fords of the river Jordan, and destroys the enemy.

The story of Ehud lacks two features often found in other accounts of the Judges. The spirit of the Lord does not come down upon him, and there is no mention of him judging Israel. What we have instead is a story about a popular local hero who turned what may have been considered to be a handicap to the advantage of his people.

DEBORAH	
Born	*Children*
Unknown	None recorded
Father	*Bible references*
Unknown	Judges 4–5
Husband	
Lappidoth	

Deborah, as depicted by Gustave Doré.

DEBORAH

Deborah, a prophetess...was judging Israel at that time.

Judges 4:4

Deborah is the only woman among the Judges, and she is the only Judge whom we actually see judging. She is described as a prophetess who sat beneath a palm tree somewhere between Bethel and Ramah (Judges 4:5). As a tree of the desert oases, plains and valleys of ancient Israel, Deborah's palm tree in the unusual habitat of the hill country must have been a well-known spot. Her ability to judge was no doubt based on her skill, insight and impartiality, while the people believed that she had supernatural powers as a prophetess.

The crisis that brought her to prominence was the threat posed to Israel by Sisera the commander of 'Jabin king of Canaan who reigned in Hazor' (Judges 4:2). This apparently simple statement presents us with some difficulties. A Jabin king of Hazor is defeated and killed by Joshua in Joshua 11:10 and Hazor is burned with fire. Further, Jabin plays no part in the story in Judges 4–5 apart from the initial and a concluding mention; the actual villain is Sisera. Again, Sisera's home city Haroshet-hagoiim (Harosh et of the gentiles) has not been identified.

A traditional scholarly view of Judges 4 and the magnificent 'Song of Deborah' that follows in chapter 5 is that it alludes to a final

confrontation between a coalition of Canaanite city states and the Israelite tribes in the pre-monarchic period, in which Israel won a decisive victory. The site of the confrontation was the valley of Jezreel where the attempt of the Canaanites to deploy their horses and chariots was frustrated by a cloudburst which swelled the river Kishon to a torrent, sweeping the Canaanites away (cf. Judges 5:20-21).

This is not an impossible or even an unlikely scenario but the details depend on difficult questions including the relationship between Judges 4 and Judges 5. In the latter poem six tribes – Ephraim, Benjamin, Machir (Manasseh), Zebulun, Issachar and Naphtali – are praised for joining in the fight while four tribes – Reuben, Gilead, Dan and Asher (there is no mention of Judah) – are blamed for their absence. In the prose account in chapter 4 only the tribes of Zebulun and Naphtali heed Deborah's call to assemble on Mt Tabor to take part in the battle. A case can be made for the superiority of either version, but certainty is impossible.

(*Above*) The valley of Jezreel, site of the battle between the Israelites and the forces of Sisera. (*Below*) Mt Tabor is the place where the Israelite forces assembled prior to engaging with Sisera, according to Judges 4:6-14.

Jael killing Sisera, while the battle rages around them, in a pen-and-ink drawing after the Master of Flemalle (c. 1430).

Awake, awake, Deborah!
  Awake, awake, utter a song!
Arise, Barak, lead away your captives,
  O son of Abinoam....
From Ephraim they set out thither into
  the valley,
  following you, Benjamin, with your
  kinsmen;
  from Machir marched down the
  commanders
  and from Zebulun those who bear the
  marshall's staff;
the princes of Issachar came with
  Deborah,
  and Issachar faithful to Barak;
  into the valley they rushed forth at his
  heels.
Among the clans of Reuben
  there were great searchings of heart.
Why did you tarry among the sheep-
  folds,
  to hear the piping for the flocks?
Among the clans of Reuben
  there were great searchings of heart.
Gilead stayed beyond the Jordan;
  and Dan, why did he abide with the
  ships?
Asher sat still at the coast of the sea,
  settling down by his landings.
Zebulun is a people that jeopardized
  their lives to the death;
  Naphtali too, on the heights of the
  field.
The kings came, they fought;
  then fought the kings of Canaan,
at Taanach, by the waters of Megiddo;
  they got no spoils of silver.
From heaven fought the stars,
  from their courses they fought against
  Sisera.
The torrent Kishon swept them away,
  the onrushing torrent, the torrent
  Kishon.
  March on, my soul, with might!

The Song of Deborah, Judges 5:12, 14-21

Although it is Deborah who is in charge of the Israelite resistance, in that it is she who summons the commander Barak and who accompanies him to the battle when he refuses to go without her (Judges 4:8), the real heroine of the story is Jael, the wife of Heber the Kenite, who lures Sisera into her tent and kills him while he is asleep. We are in the presence once more of popular stories about local heroes and heroines. Deborah, through her exceptional gifts, was able to function as an adjudicator in disputes and as a leader in war, although the actual fighting was carried out by the men. Jael used the intelligence and guile of any woman presented with the opportunity to rid her people of an oppressor. We need not doubt their deeds, even if the exact circumstances are less easily discerned.

GIDEON	
Born	Jotham and some
? Ophrah	70 others
Father	*Buried*
Joash	Ophrah
Sons	*Bible references*
Jether, Abimelech,	Judges 6–8

GIDEON

Gideon said … 'I will not rule over you'.

Judges 8:23

The story of Gideon (also called Jerubbaal) occupies chapters 6 to 8 of Judges, and is one of the longer accounts. Gideon's home is Ophrah, perhaps modern Afula in the valley of Jezreel (Judges 6:11), and he is a member of the tribe of Manasseh. His call to be a judge is occasioned by invasions of Midianites, by which is meant a nomadic people from the east. It is impossible to be more precise about whom the biblical narrator had in mind, except that the peoples concerned were not settled, and that drought forced them to invade and pillage parts of Israel. The information that they penetrated as far south as Gaza indicates that they came from the north-east, perhaps entering the valley of Jezreel near Beth-shean (note the mention of Harod and the hill of Moreh at Judges 7:1) before moving along the valley and down the coastal plain to Gaza. Gideon's location (if Ophrah was Afula) was thus a prime target for the invaders.

The biblical story

There are three clear sections to the story of Gideon: Gideon's call and his stand against the god Baal (Judges 6:1-32); the encounter with the Midianites in the valley of Jezreel (Judges 6:33–7:23); and the encounter with the Ephraimites leading to Gideon's expedition into Transjordan and the request to Gideon to become king (Judges 7:24–8:34).

The call of Gideon is unique among the Judges in that it comes from an angel of God who appears in the form of a human messenger. This messenger encourages Gideon to fight against the Midianites and assures

Gideon triumphant before the fleeing army of the Midianites. Following divine instructions, Gideon's men had concealed torches inside jars which they then smashed at the sound of trumpets to reveal the flames. From a French 16th-century Bible.

A gilded bronze statuette of Baal from Megiddo, dating to around 1200 BC.

The Jezreel valley is a triangular plain which connects the coastal plain north of Haifa with the Jordan rift valley. In biblical times it was liable to flooding, but it was the scene of various battles.

him of success, but Gideon is full of doubts, and requests a sign of reassurance. He sets a meal before his guest which is then consumed by fire at the touch of the angel's staff. The angel disappears and Gideon builds an altar to 'The Lord is peace'. As though to strengthen Gideon's resolve, God then commands him to destroy the altar to Baal and replace it with an altar to the God of Israel, using the wood of an Asherah pole to fuel the sacrifice. Fearful of the consequences, Gideon does this at night, and when the men of the town seek to kill him for his act, his father defends him on the grounds that if Baal is really a god he should be able to take care of his own interests. Clearly implicit in this first section is the contrast between the God of Israel, who can send his messenger and bring forth fire, and Baal, who is powerless to prevent the destruction of his altar. It is at this point that Gideon receives the name Jerubbaal.

The second section begins with an invasion of the Midianites and Amalekites across the river Jordan. They encamp in the valley of Jezreel by the hill of Moreh (Givat Hamoreh). Although the Spirit of God takes possession of Gideon and he summons the tribes of Asher, Zebulun and Naphtali in addition to his own tribe of Manasseh, Gideon still has doubts, and he demands a second sign as a proof of victory. A fleece left on the threshing floor should be wet when the ground is dry and dry when the ground is wet.

A theme now emerges that is well known from Joshua: in encounters with Israel's enemies, God gives the victory and Israel needs only to obey the divine instructions. In order to prove this, the Israelite army of 22,000 is reduced to 300, made up of those who drink at a stream by remaining standing and scooping up the water in their hands (a sign of alertness?).

Gideon receives a third sign when he and his servant Purah go at night to the Midianite camp and hear a man relating a dream which portends certain victory for Gideon and the Israelites. In the event the victory is easy. Following divine instructions, Gideon's 300 men surround the enemy camp with lighted torches concealed inside jars. At the signal of a trumpet the jars are smashed, the torches become visible, and the enemy flees in confusion.

The third section of the narrative is concerned with conflict of a different kind. Initially it is between Gideon and the Ephraimites who have joined in the battle and have killed two of the Midianite princes, but who are angry with Gideon because he did not call them to fight at the outset. Gideon's reply (Judges 8:1-3) makes it clear that the Ephraimites are stronger than him for he says 'God has given into your hand the princes of Midian, Oreb and Zeeb; what have I been able to do in comparison with you?' Gideon and his 300 men cross the Jordan to pursue the two kings of Midian and are refused help by the towns of Succoth and Penuel. Having captured the kings Gideon punishes the towns. There then follows an incident that has a bearing upon the matter of kingship in ancient Israel.

The Midianite kings Zebah and Zalmunna had evidently killed Gideon's brothers at Mt Tabor, either in the battle or before it (Judges 8: 19). It is hinted that they did this because 'as you are, so were they, every one of them; they resembled the sons of a king'; in other words they looked royal (in stature?). By implication Gideon, too, looked royal. Gideon decides to kill the Midianite kings in revenge and commands his first-born son Jether to carry out the execution. However, Jether is afraid to do so 'because he was still a youth' (Judges 8:20) and Gideon kills the kings himself.

At this point Gideon is asked by the men of Israel to rule over them and to establish a dynasty. Gideon refuses. He takes the golden earrings which his followers had plundered from the enemy, and makes an *ephod* (probably a religious image) and puts it in his home town of Ophrah. The birth of a son, Abimelech, to Gideon's concubine in Shechem prepares the way for the next episode in Judges, that of Abimelech's 'kingship'.

Interpreting the story of Gideon

The Gideon story can be read at many levels. Gideon has two names, Gideon and Jerubbaal, the latter being an explanation of, or justification for, Gideon's destruction of the altar of Baal, and his father said 'let Baal contend' (i.e. defend his own interests; one possible meaning of Jerubbaal). Because this incident is not germane to the story it is possible that Jerubbaal and Gideon were two different people whose separate traditions have been combined. The story of the sign of the fleeces is a piece of folklore, as is the stratagem of the torches concealed in jars. On the other hand the conflict between Gideon and his tribe of Manasseh, and the Ephraimites and the Transjordanian towns of Succoth and Penuel, no doubt reflects real tensions of an enduring or limited nature.

In the final form of the story the major theme is Gideon's unfittness to be a king, in spite of his achievements. Three times he needs a sign to be sure that God is with him and will grant victory. His son (who should succeed him) is afraid to execute the Midianite kings, and Gideon sets up an image which becomes a snare to Israel and to his family (Judges 8:27). Indeed, this theme of unfittness is so prominent that it is tempting to suggest that Gideon was indeed a powerful chief who established a rule in his region that transcended his tribe and was on the way to becoming something like a king. This would explain why the narrative is so keen to stress his faults and those of his son. It would also explain the 'kingship' of his son Abimelech, as well as the meaning of Abimelech's name – 'my father is king'!

ABIMELECH

ABIMELECH	
Born	*Children*
? Ophrah	None recorded
Father	*Buried*
Gideon	? Thebez
Wife	*Bible reference*
Unknown	Judges 9

They made Abimelech king, by the oak of the pillar at Shechem.

Judges 9:6

Abimelech is the son of Gideon by a concubine from Shechem. His story contains a number of obscurities and is a strange incident in itself. He first goes to his mother's kin in Shechem, encourages them to rebel against the 70 sons of his father and hires a band of brigands with money taken from the temple of Baal-berith. He then murders Gideon's sons in Ophrah, save one, the youngest. It is ironic that the money for this

Mts Ebal (on the right) and Gerizim flanked the ancient city of Shechem (Tell Balata). Mt Gerizim and Shechem are the setting for Jotham's fable. Today the area is occupied by the modern city of Nablus.

When it was told to Jotham, he went and stood on the top of Mt Gerizim, and cried aloud and said to them, 'Listen to me, you men of Shechem, that God may listen to you. The trees once went forth to anoint a king over them; and they said to the olive tree, "Reign over us". But the olive tree said to them, "Shall I leave my fatness, by which gods and men are honoured, and go to sway over the trees?" And the trees said to the fig tree, "Come you, and reign over us". But the fig tree said to them, "Shall I leave my sweetness and my good fruit, and go to sway over the trees?" And the trees said to the vine, "Come you, and reign over us". But the vine said to them, "Shall I leave my wine which cheers gods and men, and go to sway over the trees?" Then all the trees said to the bramble, "Come you, and reign over us". And the bramble said to the trees, "If in good faith you are anointing me king over you, then come and take refuge in my shade; but if not, let fire come out of the bramble and devour the cedars of Lebanon."'

Jotham's Fable, Judges 9:7-15

is taken from a temple of Baal, whereas Abimelech is specifically called the son of Jerubbaal, with its implication that Baal was powerless (see p. 50).

Abimelech is then proclaimed king by the men of Shechem. Gideon's one surviving son, Jotham, ascends Mt Gerizim which overlooks the town, and tells the people the fable that when the trees wanted a king, the only 'tree' prepared to reign was the bramble – a tree that offers nothing except its propensity to catch fire and destroy other trees. The implication that Abimelech's rule will end in disaster is borne out by events. In language which must deliberately anticipate what is said about Saul in 1 Samuel 16:14, God sends an evil spirit to put Abimelech and the men of Shechem at loggerheads. From the narrative it can be guessed that Abimelech was residing in Ophrah and that Zebul was his appointed governor in Shechem. However, the men of Shechem begin to act lawlessly, ambushing and robbing passers-by (Judges 9:25), and revolt against Abimelech is fermented by an otherwise unknown Gaal and his kinsmen. Shechem was clearly a divided city (between Canaanites and Israelites?), for Zebul informs Abimelech of the revolt in Shechem and advises him how to defeat the rebels by surrounding the town at night. The stratagem succeeds, and Abimelech takes the city, razes it to the ground and sows it with salt (Judges 9:45), though its destruction is not attested archaeologically. Even the people sheltering in the tower of Shechem are burnt out. Abimelech now proceeds against Thebez (probably modern Tubas, north-east of Shechem). Here he is killed when a woman in the besieged tower throws a millstone down, breaking his skull. Abimelech's armour-bearer kills him at his request. Thus ends the reign of the first 'king'.

Although the narrative speaks of Abimelech ruling over Israel (Judges 9:22), it is clear that his authority was restricted to the northern central hill country and the valley of Jezreel. None the less, the narrative presents an alarming picture of this early attempt to be king. Abimelech's rule begins with fratricide, destroys the city that was his original base and ends in ignominious death. Abimelech, as predicted in the parable of the trees, brings only harm to his subjects. The whole story, whatever its origins, fits plausibly into a period when Israel was a collection of small chiefdoms with no central authority and experienced a good deal of conflict between towns and groups.

TOLA TO ABDON: THE 'MINOR JUDGES'

In the book of Judges there are twelve 'judges' who succeed each other. As has been pointed out, the 'judges' were probably localized leaders whose activities overlapped. Further, it is the biblical writers who created the scheme whereby the period from the death of Joshua to the kingship of Saul is bridged by twelve 'all Israelite' leaders. The number is clearly symbolic, and is made up only by the inclusion in the narrative of two lists of 'minor judges'.

THE 'MINOR' JUDGES	
TOLA	Daughters
Born	30
Issachar	
Buried	ELON
Shamir	Born
	Zebulun
JAIR	Buried
Born	Aijalon
Gilead	
Sons	ABDON
30	Born
Buried	Pirathon (Ferata)
Kamon (Qunem?)	Sons
	40
IBZAN	Buried
Born	Pirathon
Bethlehem	
(Zebulun)	Bible references
Sons	Judges 10:1-5,
30	12:8-15

Tola from the tribe of Issachar who resided at Shamir (an unidentified site) in the hill country of Ephraim. He 'judged' for 23 years and was buried in Shamir (10:1-2).

Jair from Gilead 'judged' for 22 years; he had 30 sons who ruled 30 cities, and was buried in Kamon, a site not identified for certain but possibly Qunem on the road from the Jordan valley to Irbid (10:3-5).

Ibzan of Bethlehem (probably the site in Zebulun; Joshua 19:15), who had 30 sons and 30 daughters, and 'judged' for seven years (12:8-10).

Elon of Zebulun 'judged' for ten years and was buried in Aijalon in Zebulun (not identified for certain; 12:11-12).

Abdon the Pirathonite (i.e. from the town of Pirathon, modern Ferata, 5 miles (8 km) west-south-west of Shechem) in Ephraim; he had 40 sons and 'judged' for eight years (12:13-15).

They are called 'minor judges' simply because nothing is known about them other than the details given above. With the exception of Jair from Gilead in Transjordan, they are identified with the northern tribes of Ephraim, Zebulun and Issachar, although Tola, the representative of Issachar, lived in Ephraim. The details about their families – Jair and Ibzan have 30 sons and Abdon 40 sons – suggests that they were heads of leading families, or possibly local chiefs, whose rule was exercised through the numerous sons born to the many wives they received in return for the leadership and protection they offered their subjects.

It is quite possible that these men were, in fact, judges in the sense of arbitrators to whom disputes that arose within the chiefdom were brought. Men whose fairness and wisdom in judging won renown would be greatly mourned on their death, and their places of burial would be marked by a small building. Disputants would then meet at their tombs, hoping that the influence of the deceased judge would still assist them to resolve their differences. The passages in Judges mention the burial places of each judge – not in itself unusual, but significant if they had become special sites in the life of the local people.

Whatever the origin of the traditions about the 'minor judges', they provide five names to add to the six about whom there are stories (Ehud, Deborah, Gideon, Abimelech, Jephthah and Samson) and the solitary representative of Judah, Othniel, to make up the total of twelve.

JEPHTHAH	
Born	Buried
Unknown	Mizpah(?) in Gilead
Father	Bible references
Gilead	Judges 11–12
Daughters	
1	

JEPHTHAH

Jephthah ... was a mighty warrior, but he was the son of a harlot.

Judges 11:1

Sandwiched between the two lists of 'minor judges' is the story of Jephthah in Judges 11:1–12:7. Its tragic element is famous. On the eve of a decisive battle Jephthah vows that if God gives him victory he will offer as a burnt sacrifice 'whoever comes forth from the doors of my house to meet me' (Judges 11:31). Jephthah is victorious but, tragically, it is his only child, his daughter, who comes to meet him,

Jephthah's daughter, with tragic results for her and her father, comes to greet him as his returns victorious from battle, as portrayed by Matthäus d. Ä. Merian (1593–1630).

and who therefore has to be sacrificed. If this story has seized the imagination of artists such as Blake, Degas and Millais and poets such as Byron and Tennyson, its tragic element was softened in Handel's oratorio of 1751. An angel appears and announces the reprieve of Jephthah's daughter, who will in future serve God as a priestess. This tradition is also found in a Jesuit drama of 1686, 'Jephthes Tragoedia'.

The biblical tradition

In the biblical tradition the details of the story are rather more earthy, and not always clear. Jephthah is introduced as the son of a harlot who is driven out by his brothers to prevent him from inheriting any part of his father's wealth. He withdraws from his unnamed city in Gilead in Transjordan to the land of Tob in the north (possibly Taiyibe in southern Syria), where, anticipating David (see 1 Samuel 22:2), he becomes the leader of a group of bandits who spend their time raiding the area. When the Ammonites, Gilead's foreign neighbours in Transjordan, make war on Israel, Jephthah is sought out and asked to lead the resistance against the enemy. This he agrees to do on condition that he becomes the head of the inhabitants of Gilead.

A limestone statue probably of an Ammonite king, from Amman, Jordan.

A long passage in Judges 11:12-28 records negotiations between Jephthah, who has been accepted as head of Gilead, and the king of Ammon. This is clearly a reference to claims in Numbers that the Israelites as they journeyed through Transjordan to the land of Canaan did not take any land from the Ammonites but merely possessed what God gave to them, just as the Ammonites possessed what their god Chemosh gave them. There is therefore no legitimate ground for the Ammonites to wage war against Israel. The passage in Judges thus presupposes the existence of the book of Numbers in something like its present form, which cannot be before the 6th–5th centuries BC.

Jephthah's overtures are rejected and battle ensues, with the victorious and tragic consequences already mentioned. Judges 11 completes the story of the sacrifice of Jephthah's daughter, two months after the victory. In Judges 12:1-6 an obscure incident is described that presumably occurred immediately after Jephthah's defeat of the Ammonites. As in the case of Gideon, the men of Ephraim are angry that a battle has taken place to which they were not called. They cross the Jordan (Ephraim is on the west side), confront Jephthah in Zaphon (not identified for certain) and threaten to burn down his house. Jephthah counters by saying that the Ephraimites were indeed called upon to help but did not do so.

A fight now begins between the men of Ephraim and Jephthah's Gileadites, inflamed by an insult – 'you are fugitives of Ephraim, you Gileadites, in the midst of Ephraim and Manasseh' – the meaning of which is unclear. Jephthah is victorious, and presses home his advantage by securing the fords across the Jordan. Ephraimites who then try to cross back over the river to return to their own side are made to say 'Shibboleth' (Hebrew for an ear of grain). However, the unfortunate Ephraimites can apparently only say 'Sibboleth', and this pronunciation proves to be a death warrant for them.

This peculiar incident raises several questions. If Ephraimites and Gileadites were separate 'tribes' living on opposite sides of the river Jordan, why was it necessary to ascertain whether those who wanted to cross the river from east to west were Ephraimites by their pronunciation of 'Shibboleth'? Surely Gileadites would not want to cross! The answer may well be that Ephraimites and Gileadites were not as separate and distinct as might be supposed. In 2 Samuel 18:6 a battle takes place in the 'forest of Ephraim', which scholars usually locate in Transjordan. This suggests that some Ephraimites may have lived on the eastern side of the Jordan, while the insult directed by the Ephraimites against the Gileadites implies that some Gileadites lived on the western side. This could explain why the Ephraimites were angry not to be asked to help fight the Ammonites (the Ephraimites on the eastern side were also threatened but would their cry for help be unheeded?), but it still does not explain the 'Shibboleth' incident. If Ephraimites and Gileadites lived together, is it likely that there would be such a large difference of pronunciation between them?

The tradition leaves much unexplained, although Jephthah was clearly a local brigand-turned-hero whose deeds were recounted among Gileadite groups who lived in Ephraim. In the context of the book of Judges Jephthah is important as he illustrates a theme that becomes more prominent as the book progresses – the inability of any 'judge' to establish a dynasty. All the 'judges' seem to have disadvantages. Ehud is left-handed (regarded as a physical defect), Deborah is a woman, Gideon refuses to begin a dynasty and, in any case, leads Israel into idolatry. Abimelech tries to become a dynastic king but fails spectacularly, while Jephthah, born illegitimate, has to sacrifice his only child in fulfilment of his vow. As it progresses, Judges reads less like an account of the period it claims to describe, and more like an introduction to the books of Samuel, in which God's truly chosen leader, David, is presented.

The river Jordan takes a tortuous path between the Sea of Galilee and the Dead Sea, covering three times the shortest distance (105 km or just over 62 miles) between the two points. It often formed a natural and important boundary in ancient Israel's history, as shown by the story of the 'Shibboleth' incident.

שִׁמְשׁוֹן Samson

Samson blinded, a detail from Rudolf
von Ems' *World Chronicle*.

SAMSON	
Born	*Children*
Zorah	None recorded
Father	*Buried*
Manoah	Between Zorah and
Wives	Eshtaol
unnamed Philistine,	*Bible references*
Delilah (if married)	Judges 13–16

And Samson said, 'With the jawbone of an ass, heaps upon heaps, with the jawbone of an ass, have I slain a thousand men'.

Judges 15:16

While many readers will be familiar with the story of Samson and Delilah, this incident is only one of a series of events that make up the whole. The figure of Samson has succeeded in attracting a cluster of traditions, and his story is the longest of the cycles found in the book of Judges.

The biblical account

The cycle is set in the territory of Dan as it was before that tribe migrated to the north, as related in Judges 18. This was a wedge of land bordered on one side by the sea and on the south by the territory of the Philistines and the area of Judah. It is thus a plausible geographical setting for the initial encounters – presumably often antagonistic – that must have taken place in the second half of the 11th century BC between the Philistines and their Israelite neighbours.

The opening chapter of the cycle gives no indication of what is to follow. Samson's parents are a pious, childless couple who are visited by an angel, and promised a son who will be a Nazirite (a Hebrew word derived from a verb meaning 'to dedicate'). The son's special relationship to God as a person 'dedicated' to him requires that he abstain from wine and strong drink and that the hair of his head should not be cut. As the story of Samson unfolds, it soon appears that being 'dedicated' to God does not in fact exempt him from a good deal of morally questionable behaviour.

One of Samson's first extraordinary feats was killing a lion with his bare hands (Judges 14:6); from a 13th-century French manuscript.

The first main recorded incident in Samson's life, in 14:1–15:8, introduces themes that recur throughout the cycle: Samson's great physical strength; his love of riddles; and his inability to resist female entreaties. He is betrothed to a Philistine woman and before his wedding kills a lion with his bare hands. Samson then composes a riddle based on the fact that bees make a hive in the lion's carcass and challenges the guests at his wedding feast to explain his riddle: 'Out of the eater came something to eat. Out of the strong came something sweet'. Unfortunately, he loses the challenge when his wife, who has been threatened with death by the guests if she fails to do so, prevails upon him to reveal the answer.

In his anger Samson kills 30 men from the town of Ashkelon in order to procure the 30 sets of festal garments that he has to provide as loser of the challenge. His wife is now given to Samson's best man, and in order to avenge his humiliation, Samson catches 300 foxes (some modern translations prefer 'jackals') ties a torch to each pair of tails and, having set them alight, sends the animals into the Philistine grain fields and

THE PHILISTINES

The Philistines were part of a larger migration of peoples from Asia Minor around 1200 BC. It seems to have been a period of great unrest, though the exact causes of these movements of peoples are unknown. They came by sea and land and tried, unsuccessfully, to settle in Egypt, being defeated by Ramesses III (1182–1151 BC). In Egyptian sources they are called the Sea Peoples. Some, however, succeeded in settling in the coastal area of southern Palestine. Biblical sources inform us that they occupied the five cities of Gaza, Gath, Ekron, Ashdod and Ashkelon (1 Samuel 6:17), that they worshipped the god Dagon and that they were uncircumcised. Their possession of horses and chariots gave them a military advantage over the Israelites. In the latter part of the period of the Judges they expanded northwards and

A relief showing the battle of Ramesses III and the Sea Peoples, carved on the outer north wall of Medinet Habu, the pharaoh's mortuary temple at Thebes, Egypt.

A detail of a Philistine prisoner from the reliefs at Medinet Habu. He is identifiable by the distinctive headdress.

eastwards, to the disadvantage of the tribes of Dan and Judah. Their attempt to take over the whole of ancient Palestine (the name itself derives from 'Philistine') was one of the factors that precipitated the rise of dynastic kingship in Israel at the end of the 11th century BC, beginning with Saul.

olive orchards. The Philistines respond by burning Samson's erstwhile wife and her father; Samson then kills a further unspecified number of Philistines.

The next incident, in Judges 15:9-20, brings us closest to what must have been the historical realities of the period. Geographically, the Philistines were not only in closer proximity to Judah than any tribe other than Dan, they also had easy means of expansion into Judah's territory via the hills of the Shephelah. That the Philistines should have exerted their influence on Judah is entirely to be expected, and it is perhaps only surprising that this is the single incident recorded in the Bible that indicates such Philistine pressure.

The Philistines demand that the men of Judah deliver Samson to them; Samson agrees, provided that the Judahites do not harm him and that he is bound with two new ropes. On being handed over he immediately snaps the ropes and kills 1,000 Philistines using an ass's jawbone as a weapon. His subsequent thirst is slaked when God opens the ground and water comes from it. Both the place of the slaughter of the Philistines and the well are given special names in Hebrew: 'the hill of the jawbone' and 'the spring of him who called'.

It is only now that the story of Samson and Delilah occurs (chapter 16). Delilah is described simply as 'a woman in the valley of Sorek' whom Samson loved. The story revolves around Delilah's repeated but vain attempts to learn the secret of Samson's great strength, until he can hold out against her entreaties and wiles no longer. His subsequent capture, enslavement and blinding provide a sad and tragic conclusion to his story, which is alleviated by the return of his strength as his hair grows, and his pulling down of the temple of Dagon 'so that the dead whom he slew at his death were more than those whom he had slain during his life' (Judges 16:30).

Samson's story must have been very popular in ancient Israel, as it has been ever since, embodying as it does the timeless themes of revenge on enemies, the great physical strength of the hero and the vulnerability of that strength to female entreaties. It has provided inspiration for artists and poets through the ages, most notably for Milton's great poem *Samson Agonistes*. This cycle also contains the largest number of legendary feats by a single man in Judges: among other things Samson kills a lion, catches 300 foxes (jackals would be easier!), slaughters 1,000 of his enemies simply using the jawbone of an ass as a weapon and then prevails upon God to create a well. What history, if any, lies behind these extraordinary events?

The history behind the legends

Probably the closest we can get to the 'historical Samson' is as a hero of the tribe of Dan who possessed great strength and courage and who was eventually captured by the Philistines after inflicting considerable damage on their lives and property. Places associated in popular memory with his exploits were specially named, and provided the opportunity for

SAMSON AND DELILAH

When Delilah saw that he had told her all his mind, she sent and called the lords of the Philistines, saying, 'Come up this once, for he has told me all his mind'. Then the lords of the Philistines came up to her, and brought the money in their hands. She made him sleep upon her knees; and she called a man, and had him shave off the seven locks of his head. Then she began to torment him, and his strength left him.

Judges 16:18-19

The story of Samson and Delilah in Judges 16 has inspired dramas (for instance, Milton's *Samson Agonistes*), oratorios (such as Handel's *Samson*) paintings, opera and films. This is because it is, depending on one's point of view, the story of the fall of a hero, the unfaithfulness of a wife, the seductive powers of a harlot, failure to keep religious vows, or the revenge of a physically strong woman. The similarity of the Hebrew names Samson and Delilah with the Hebrew words for sun and moon has led some interpreters to look for the origins of the story in solar mythology. Parallels have long been drawn between Samson and Hercules.

In the biblical story Samson falls in love with Delilah, a woman in the valley of Sorek. Whether she is Israelite,

Philistine or Canaanite is not made clear, neither does the account tell us whether Samson married her, or whether her co-operation with the Philistines was willing or forced. The Philistines offer her a large sum of money to discover the source of Samson's strength and how he can be overcome. The reader knows from the story of Samson's birth that, for religious reasons, he has been brought up not to cut his hair, and this becomes the focus of the story. Three times he gives Delilah false information about the secret of his strength, but the fourth time he tells her the truth: if his hair is shaved off, he will lose his great strength. Delilah calls a man to shave off Samson's hair while he sleeps, his strength departs, and he is taken prisoner by the Philistines. Blinded and humiliated, he grinds at the mill in prison; but he has his revenge on the Philistines when, his hair having grown again, he has sufficient strength to pull down the pillars of a building in which 3,000 men and women are feasting. He perishes along with them when the roof collapses. No fate of Delilah is recorded.

Two episodes from the tragic fate of Samson, depicted in a coloured engraving by Matthäus d. Ä. Merian (1625/27): Delilah cutting off Samson's hair while he sleeps; and Samson pulling down the temple of Dagon, killing 3,000 people as well as himself. According to the biblical account, it was a man who shaved off Samson's hair.

Samson is blinded by the Philistines, by Rembrandt (1636).

the tradition to grow and embellish what had happened. Whether Samson really did kill a lion with his bare hands, or became weak once his head had been shaved, is improbable. His story may well have absorbed mythological themes from traditions about Hercules – a process that some suggest may have been helped by the similarity between the name Samson and the word for 'sun' in Hebrew. On the other hand, the involvement of the tribe of Judah in the story does have the mark of authenticity, and perhaps the hero Samson was eventually betrayed to the Philistines by the men of Judah, an incident mirrored in Judges 15:9-13.

Within the context of Judges, as we can detect the shadow of David beginning to be cast back upon this period, Samson is another instance of a leader who is unable to establish a dynasty. His first wife was a Philistine; we are not told whether Delilah was Philistine or Israelite. It seems in neither case, however, were children born. A story that begins with such great expectations – a divine visitation announces the birth of a special child, dedicated to God – ends surprisingly, spectacularly and tragically. But Israel is still far from having a leader 'after God's own heart'.

שְׁמוּאֵל Samuel

Samuel from the wall-paintings in the mid-3rd-century AD synagogue at Dura-Europos, Syria.

SAMUEL	
Born	*Sons*
Ramathaim-zophim	Joel, Abijah
Father	*Buried*
Elkanah	Ramah
Mother	*Bible references*
Hannah	1 Samuel
Wife	1:1–28:20
Unknown	

The dedication of Samuel by Eli, from the painting by F.W.W. Topham, exhibited in 1889.

The word of Samuel came to all Israel.

1 Samuel 4:1

As presented in the biblical sources, Samuel is not so much an individual as a set of individuals, each fulfilling a different role. These include judge, priest, soothsayer, prophet and king-maker. Even after his death Samuel is consulted by occult means by the distraught Saul on the eve of the latter's final battle. The first task in dealing with Samuel is to disentangle his various personae.

Samuel as judge

It is possible to read 1 Samuel 1 and 7:3-17 as a continuation of the book of Judges. Chapter 1 is reminiscent of the story of the birth of Samson, although the actual details are different. A childless woman, Hannah, prays that she might have a son. She promises that if God answers her prayer she will give the child to God 'all the days of his life, and no razor shall touch his head' (1 Samuel 1:11). The prayer is answered, a son is born, and Hannah lends him to God by entrusting him to the sanctuary at Shiloh, where the priest Eli had assured her that God would grant her petition. It is also possible to compare the story of Gideon, in which a divine messenger commissions Gideon to his task of delivering the Israelites from the Midianites.

In 1 Samuel 7:3-17 Samuel delivers the Israelites from the Philistines at Mizpah (either Tell en-Nasbeh or Nebi Samwil in the territory of Benjamin). The method of the deliverance resembles Gideon's victory in that God is the prime worker and the Israelites merely have to pursue an enemy that has already been thrown into confusion by God thundering at

The exact appearance of Ark of the Covenant is unknown, and it has been represented in many different ways by artists. This is a mosaic in the Oratory of Theodulf, Germigny des Prés, France.

The Ark of the Covenant as visualized in a fresco in the synagogue at Dura-Europos, mid-3rd century AD, now in the National Museum, Damascus. The scene shows the Ark being returned to the Israelites after the destruction of the temple of Dagon at Ashdod.

THE ARK OF THE COVENANT

Perhaps the most famous – and mysterious – symbol of ancient Israel, the Ark of the Covenant was a portable shrine which symbolized the warlike presence of God among his people. It was closely associated with the divine title 'Lord of Hosts' – hosts meaning the earthly and heavenly armies commanded by God. In 1 Samuel 4:4 its full title is given as 'the ark of the covenant of the LORD of hosts'. Its origins are unknown. According to traditions in the books of Exodus and Numbers it was made in the wilderness to store the tablets of the Ten Commandments; but modern scholarship believes that the description of the Ark and the tent in which it was housed, in Exodus 36–7, are based on the furnishings in Solomon's temple. Whatever its origins, it was an important cult object which was probably carried by the Israelites into war, and which was later kept in the temple in Jerusalem. It was probably destroyed by the Babylonians in 587 BC and never replaced.

them with a mighty voice (1 Samuel 7:10). The passage concludes with the information that Samuel judged Israel 'all the days of his life' and that he went on circuit from Ramah to Bethel, Gilgal (east of Jericho, possibly Khirbet el-Mefjir) and Mizpah. He is thus identified as a Benjaminite who administered justice in the eastern half of that tribe's territory.

Samuel as priest

The fact that Samuel's role as a judge is not treated as fully as such accounts in the book of Judges is because his other roles have probably displaced material about this aspect of his activity. The story of Samuel as a priest is complicated – the fact that he offered sacrifices does not necessarily mean that he was a priest. In the book of Judges, sacrifices are offered by Gideon, Jephthah and Manoah (Samson's father), none of whom were priests. However, Samuel is associated with the temple at Shiloh and this enables the biblical tradition to incorporate the narrative about the loss of the Ark of the Covenant (temporarily housed at Shiloh) to the Philistines, and its recovery after it had brought misfortune upon them (1 Samuel 4:1b–7:2). It is noteworthy that Samuel appears nowhere in the story about the loss and recovery of the Ark, although the famous incident about the boy Samuel hearing the voice of God in the temple and mistaking it for that of Eli the priest (1 Samuel 3:1-18) prepares the reader for the introduction of the Ark story.

An interesting 'loose end' occurs in 2:35 when an unnamed prophet informs Eli that his sons will be killed and that God will raise up a 'faithful priest'. In the context of the opening chapters of 1 Samuel we might expect this to be Samuel, but Samuel's priestly role disappears after 3:18, and the 'faithful priest' refers forwards to Zadok, who replaced Eli's descendant Abiathar in the reign of Solomon (1 Kings 2:27, which explicitly refers to the judgment on the house of Eli). Thus Samuel as a priest is largely a literary device to enable stories about the fate of the Ark and the future of the priesthood to be inserted into the narrative. These stories in their present form probably presuppose the destruction of Jerusalem in 587 BC, and express hopes for its restoration.

Samuel as soothsayer and prophet

A persistent feature of the Samuel narratives is the presentation of him as a 'prophet', and the head of groups of ecstatic prophets whose 'prophesying' included stripping off their clothes and lying naked (1 Samuel 19:24). 'Soothsayer' has been added to the heading above to indicate that Samuel and his prophets should not be thought of as identical with later prophets in the Old Testament such as Isaiah, Amos or Hosea. There are, of course, some similarities. Later prophets (a good example is Ezekiel) had strange, ecstatic experiences. Again, prophets such as Isaiah, Amos, Micah and Jeremiah involved themselves actively in political matters, as did Samuel in his role as as king-maker. One difference, however, is that Samuel and his groups were probably believed to have access to hidden knowledge, such as how to find lost animals (1 Samuel 9:6), as well as the ability to work miracles. Through music (1 Samuel 10:5) and ecstatic utterance, such prophets believed that they could be possessed by the deity, and they probably represented a fanatical and nationalistic force utterly opposed to foreign political and religious domination. The origin of such prophetic groups in Israel is unknown, and their appearance in the books of Samuel is the first in the Old Testament, though the phenomenon that they represent is known from elsewhere in the ancient world. For present purposes the important thing is that these prophetic groups offer a plausible setting for the historical Samuel and his influence in the history of ancient Israel.

Samuel as king-maker, anointing Saul, by Julius Schnorr von Carolsfeld (1794–1874).

Samuel as king-maker

If in reality Samuel was the leader of a group of ecstatic prophets whose religious and national fervour led them to support and then undermine Saul's leadership against the Philistines, then Samuel as king-maker is presented in the tradition as a much more 'sanitized' and 'comfortable' figure. Even so, there are several portrayals of Samuel in this role. In 1 Samuel 10:1-13 the ecstatic Samuel anoints Saul and introduces him to, or perhaps into, a group of ecstatics; in 1 Samuel 8:1-22 the spurned 'judge' Samuel warns the people of the dangers of having a 'king ... like all the nations'. Again, the Samuel who is the king-destroyer, who declares that God has rejected Saul and who anoints David and protects him against Saul (17:18-24), is portrayed differently in the accounts in chapters 13:8-15 and 15:1-35.

Conclusion

Samuel is a composite figure who literally embodies differing concerns and enables varying types of tradition to be harmonized. We are probably closest to the historical figure in the traditions about Samuel as a leader of ecstatic prophets. The material that turns him into a 'judge' subordinates him to typical themes that occur elsewhere in the book of Judges, while his overt political actions present a 'sanitized' Samuel, no doubt reflecting times when ecstatic prophets were either non-existent or totally marginalized. Samuel as priest is a purely literary device. Few figures in the Old Testament offer such interesting resources for seeing how Israelite tradition transformed and combined material about historical personages.

THE UNITED MONARCHY

Saul
c. 1020–1000 BC

David
c. 1000–961 BC

Solomon
c. 961–931 BC

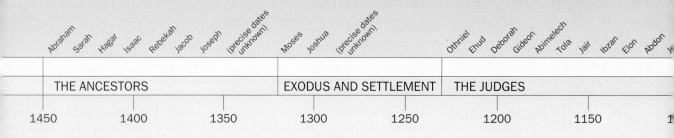

Abraham Sarah Hagar Isaac Rebekah Jacob Joseph (precise dates unknown)	Moses Joshua (precise dates unknown)	Othniel Ehud Deborah Gideon Abimelech Tola Jair Ibzan Elon Abdon Je	
THE ANCESTORS	EXODUS AND SETTLEMENT	THE JUDGES	

| 1450 | 1400 | 1350 | 1300 | 1250 | 1200 | 1150 | 1 |

Saul

David

Solomon

THE UNITED MONARCHY
c. 1020–931 BC

THE TERM 'UNITED MONARCHY' is used to denote the period in ancient Israel's history between the Judges, when Israel was not ruled by a king, and the Divided Monarchy, when the two rival kingdoms, Israel and Judah, were each ruled by a king. By traditional critical reckoning the United Monarchy spans nearly 100 years, from the appointment of Saul as king in around 1020 BC to Solomon's death in *c.* 931 BC.

The term United Monarchy is, in fact, unfortunate. If we accept the picture given in 1 and 2 Samuel and 1 Kings 1–11 the period saw more disunity than unity. Saul was appointed as king over the northern tribes only, and Judah either opted in or was forced into a coalition with him. Following David's banishment from Saul's court there was virtual civil war, and after Saul's death, David became king of Judah while one of Saul's sons, Eshbaal, was nominally king of the northern tribes. Even after the murder of Eshbaal and the establishment of David's rule over the whole kingdom, David was faced by two revolts.

The reign of Solomon gives the impression of having been a tranquil period, but a closer look at the biblical text reveals hints of opposition. Jeroboam, an Ephraimite in charge of forced labour, is encouraged by a prophet to rebel against Solomon. Jeroboam flees to Egypt and remains there until Solomon's death, but his return is one of the factors that leads to the break-up of the united monarchy. For later biblical writers this period of 'unity' among the tribes became an ideal whose restoration was earnestly desired. Thus do hopes often fly in the face of reality.

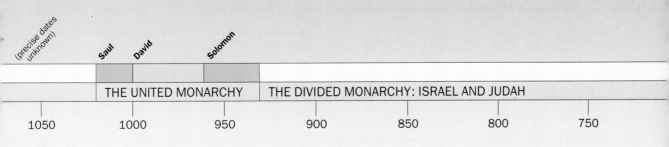

(precise dates unknown)

Saul   David   Solomon

THE UNITED MONARCHY | THE DIVIDED MONARCHY: ISRAEL AND JUDAH

1050   1000   950   900   850   800   750

שָׁאוּל Saul
c. 1020–1000 BC

Saul, by Rembrandt.

SAUL	
Born	Abinadab, Eshbaal
Unnamed town in	*Buried*
Benjamin	Jabesh-gilead
Father	*Bible references*
Kish	1 Samuel 9–11,
Sons	13–29, 31
Jonathan, Malchish,	

Ye daughters of Israel, weep over Saul.

2 Samuel 1:24

Saul, like Samuel, is a composite figure in the biblical tradition. We get glimpses of him as an ecstatic prophet, 'judge' and king. Unlike Samuel, however, one role predominates. Saul is first and foremost a king in his own right, and subsequently a foil to David whom Samuel anoints while Saul is still the effective ruler.

The idea of kingship

Recent scholarship has questioned whether 'king' is the correct designation for Saul, and whether it would not be more correct to call him a chief. This is a key question, if only because it is a reminder that when a Hebrew word such as *melekh* is translated into English as 'king', there is the danger that readers will impose notions of kingship that would have been unknown to ancient Israelites. The point at issue is whether 'king' is a general classificatory term, to deserve which a number of institutions need to be in place, such as an administration that can organize public life from regional centres. If one wishes to study the development of ancient Israel in the context of the general development of societies,

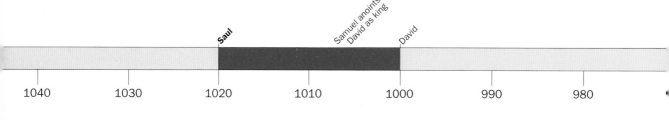

Saul

Samuel anoints
David as king

David

1040   1030   1020   1010   1000   990   980

Saul and his master, from a French 15th-century manuscript.

classificatory terms are necessary, and minimal conditions for their use need to be agreed. In such a context it may well be more accurate to call Saul a chief rather than a king.

Within the Old Testament's own view of its cultural development, however, Saul was regarded as a *melekh*, which, for the sake of convenience, will be translated as 'king'. He is also called a *nagidh* at 1 Samuel 10:1 (usually rendered as 'prince' or 'leader'), but whether this is significant is doubtful. If, in sociological terms, kings need to fulfil certain conditions to qualify for the title, the Old Testament also has a view of what constitutes an acceptable king, and it is a theological one. No doubt this was worked out over many centuries within Israel and was also affected by ideas of kingship widely current in the ancient Near East. We should recognize that even if these ideas of kingship were worked out centuries later than the period of Saul, it was in terms of such theories that Saul was viewed in the biblical tradition. Any attempt to penetrate back to the 'historical Saul' must take account of this.

Among many statements in the Old Testament about what makes an ideal king, two can be considered here: Deuteronomy 17:14-20 and Psalm 72. Deuteronomy specifies that a king should not be a foreigner, should not 'cause the people to return to Egypt in order to multiply horses', should not multiply wives for himself, and should not greatly multiply for himself silver and gold. The obscure reference to Egypt and horses may be a prohibition against sending an Israelite army to help a foreign king. Positively, a king must copy out, study and observe God's law and statutes. Psalm 72, while exuding a rather different spirit – the ideal king is to be successful in battle, to preside over a huge empire and to be internationally famous – emphasizes the king's duty to support the weak:

> *For he delivers the needy when he calls,*
> *the poor and him who has no helper.*
> *He has pity on the weak and the needy, and saves the lives of the needy.*
> *From oppression and violence he redeems their life;*
> *and precious is their blood in his sight.*

In contrast to these ideals, at 1 Samuel 8:10-17 we get an extremely negative view of kingship. It comes at the point where the people ask Samuel to appoint a king for them and he lists the likely disadvantages that will accrue. A king will conscript young men to serve in the army and young women to serve as perfumers, cooks and bakers. He will take land away from the legitimate owners to give to his officers and servants; he will tax grain and cattle. He will enslave the people. This list no doubt reflects the realities of kingship over a long period in Israel: the account of Saul's kingship is therefore written against the background of developed views in Israel about ideal kings and actual personalities.

Looking behind the biblical tradition

Although later views about kingship have affected the narratives about Saul, he is not necessarily judged in terms of them. His chief failures as a king, according to the biblical narrative, were that he offered a sacrifice at Gilgal when Samuel, who was supposed to offer the sacrifice, did not appear on time (1 Samuel 13:8-14) and that he failed to kill the Amalekite king Agag when Samuel had ordered him to spare no

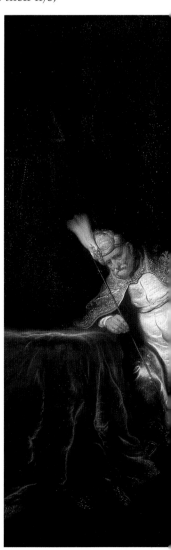

one. These seemingly trivial offences look rather like rationalizations, and if we can begin to penetrate behind the traditions, Saul's failure may have been no more than that he fell in battle against the Philistines while defending his country whereas David eventually defeated them.

A close look at the biblical tradition reveals Saul as a 'judge' in 1 Samuel 11. The Ammonites besiege the Transjordanian town of Jabesh-gilead, whose elders send for help to the western Israelites. When Saul hears the news, God's spirit comes down mightily upon him, he musters the Israelites, and defeats the Ammonites. He is reminiscent here of 'judges' such as Gideon and Jephthah. Saul as ecstatic prophet is hinted at in two incidents that end with the proverb 'Is Saul also among the prophets?' (1 Samuel 10:12, 19:24) and which describe two different circumstances in which he behaved ecstatically. In the remainder of the traditions Saul is presented as a somewhat desperate man, fighting localized battles against Philistines. He is estranged from Samuel and

(*Below left*) David's harp-playing soothes the troubled Saul (1 Samuel 16:23); a painting by Salomon Koninck (1609–1656). (*Below right*) In this vivid depiction by Salvator Rosa (1615–73) Saul cowers before Samuel, whom the Witch of Endor has conjured from the realm of the dead.

The suicide of Saul (left) in his final battle against the Philistines, portrayed by Pieter Bruegel the Elder (1562).

feels deep suspicion of the motives of David as well as jealousy of his achievements in battle and popularity. Shortly before his final battle, unhappy and fearful, Saul seeks by occult means to consult the dead Samuel.

However, it is also clear that the tradition has lost or suppressed material about Saul. In the incident of consulting the dead Samuel we are told that Saul had put the mediums and wizards out of the land (1 Samuel 28:3), and in 2 Samuel 21:1-14 David is told by God that a three-year famine in the land is the result of Saul's action against the Gibeonites when he slew them because they were not Israelites. While the famine and the need to avenge Saul's deed give David a convenient excuse for executing seven sons from Saul's family, thus protecting his own dynasty, Saul's action may well have been an attempt to purge his land of foreigners and their religion. This religious and nationalist zeal would fit well with sometime membership of a group of ecstatic prophets.

Conclusion

Saul remains something of an elusive figure. We do not even know how long he reigned. The Hebrew text of 1 Samuel 13:1, according to which he was one year old when he began to reign and he reigned two years, is corrupt. Thus, it is not known whether he gained a few local victories over Ammonites and Philistines during a brief two-year reign, or whether

THE BATTLE OF MICHMASH

The battle of Michmash was a brilliant individual assault on the Philistine garrison at Michmash by Saul's son Jonathan (see 1 Samuel 14:1-15). Although the biblical account minimizes the part played by Jonathan and his armour-bearer in order to attribute the victory entirely to God, it is clear that Jonathan surprised the Philistines by approaching them unseen along a narrow valley before engaging them in hand-to-hand fighting. The account claims that 20 Philistines were killed.

he achieved a more comprehensive set of victories that gave his people a period of freedom from their enemies during a reign of twenty years, before his eventual defeat. Tradition asserts that he was very tall (1 Samuel 9:2) and there is no doubt that he was a brave man, able to inspire bravery in others. After he had been badly wounded in battle he killed himself when his armour-bearer refused to do the deed for him. When his body and those of his sons were displayed on the walls of Beth-shean, the men of Jabesh-gilead undertook a dangerous sortie to rescue and bury them. But the last word on Saul was spoken, literally and metaphorically, in the lament ascribed to David on hearing of Saul's death (2 Samuel 1:19-26):

> *Ye daughters of Israel, weep over Saul,*
> *who clothed you daintily in scarlet,*
> *who put ornaments of gold upon your apparel.*
> *How are the mighty fallen in the midst of the battle!*

One thing at least is clear. After Saul, things were never the same again in ancient Israel. The people had accepted a type of leadership that implied establishing a dynasty, and which put power on an unprecedented scale into the hands of one man or, rarely, one woman. And the implications were not simply political, but theological, in that the figure of an anointed royal servant of God provided the focus for later hopes of the coming of a Messiah (the Hebrew means 'anointed one').

An aerial view of the mound on which Beth-shean was situated, and where the bodies and armour of Saul and his sons were displayed by the Philistines. In the background, at the foot of the mound, are the remains of the city of Scythopolis, dating from the Roman to Byzantine periods.

דָּוִד David

c. 1000–961 BC

David as an aged and experienced king; a sculpture by Claus Sluter (*c.* 1396).

DAVID	
Born	Ithream, Shimea,
? Bethlehem	Shodab, Nathan,
Father	Solomon, Ibhar,
Jesse	Elishama, Eliphelet,
Wives	Nogah, Nepheg,
Michal, Ahinoam,	Japhia, Eliada
Abigail, Maacah,	*Buried*
Haggith, Abital,	Jerusalem
Eglah, Bathsheba	*Bible references*
Sons	1 Samuel 16–31;
Amnon, Daniel,	2 Samuel; 1 Kings
Absalom, Adonijah,	1–2:11
Shephatiah,	

The LORD has sought out a man after his own heart.

1 Samuel 13:14

With the reign of David the biblical tradition reaches a peak that from our perspective we can see has already cast its shadow back over the narrative since the death of Joshua. Who is to lead God's people in the Promised Land? The books of Judges and 1 Samuel tell of various leaders who, in spite of great achievements in some cases, were unable to establish permanent leadership in the form of a dynasty. In David, the biblical tradition sees a 'man after God's own heart' whom Samuel anoints as the chosen one among the sons of Jesse and with whom God makes a covenant that promises that David's dynasty will endure for ever (2 Samuel 7:16).

David's reign not only casts its shadow backwards, however. David becomes the ideal by which subsequent kings are judged; and the hope, in difficult times, that a second David will arise to shepherd his people is a recurring theme in prophecy (cf. Ezekiel 34:23-4). Yet, paradoxically, the account of David is by no means all flattering. A key feature is the narrative of David's adultery with Bathsheba, beginning at 2 Samuel 11:2, his attempts to avoid responsibility for the resulting

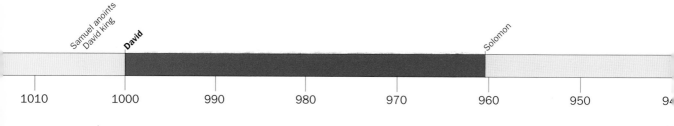

Samuel anoints David king

David

Solomon

1010   1000   990   980   970   960   950   94

Samuel anoints David, in an illuminated manuscript of 1480.

Bathsheba at her Toilet, by Rembrandt (1654). David's adultery with Bathsheba brought censure from the prophet Nathan and was the cause of many misfortunes.

pregnancy by recalling Bathsheba's husband, Uriah, from the heat of battle in the expectation that he will have intercourse with Bathsheba; and his cynical 'murder' of Uriah by getting the army commander Joab to expose him to acute danger in battle, when Uriah observes the custom of soldiers on active duty of abstaining from sex with their wives. David's actions call forth the rebuke of Nathan the prophet, and bring retribution upon his family in the form of rape and fratricide among his children, a rebellion against him by his son Absalom and a revolt of the northern tribes led by a kinsman of Saul. This remarkable cycle, from 2 Samuel 11 to 20, concerns the same David who has defeated Israel's enemies and established a great kingdom, ruling over Israel and Judah. What does the tradition say about earlier events?

Here the narrative is confusing and, at one point (1 Samuel 16 and 17), even contradictory, and it is clear that at least two strands of tradition have been woven together. In 1 Samuel 16, David is introduced to the court of Saul as an already accomplished fighter who by his musical skills can soothe Saul when the latter is tormented by an evil spirit from God and who becomes Saul's armour bearer. In chapter 17 the famous story of David and Goliath occurs. David is a shepherd lad taking food to his older brothers who are fighting for Saul against the Philistines. He hears the challenge of the Philistine giant, and offers to meet it, declining armour which he has never worn, and relying instead on his skills with sling and stone. Following David's defeat of Goliath, Saul enquires of his commander, Abner, who David is – an extremely odd question given that David is already Saul's bodyguard!

The historical David

If it is assumed that we can use the material in 1 and 2 Samuel to penetrate back to the historical David (and not all agree that this is possible), the following plausible outline can be reconstructed. David (if this was his original name: it has been suggested that it was a name taken when he became king or that it meant 'commander') grew up in Judah in a family that possibly had links with the Ammonite royal family (cf. 2 Samuel 10:1-2, 17:25-7). When, as undoubtedly was the case, the Philistines exerted pressure on Judah, David distinguished himself in fighting against them. It is in this period that David's encounter with Goliath can plausibly be set, in which case Saul was not present (there is also the problem that in 2 Samuel 21:19 Goliath is said to have been killed by Elhanan). Thus, by the time he joined Saul's inner circle David had already acquired a formidable reputation as an accomplished fighter. His entry into Saul's service denoted the uniting of the resources of Judah and Israel against the Philistines, and David became not only Saul's son-in-law by marrying his daughter Michal, but also the close companion of Saul's son Jonathan.

Saul became jealous of David's achievements and evident popularity ('Saul has slain his thousands, and David his ten thousands', 1 Samuel 18:7) and, following several attempts by Saul on his life, David fled from court and formed a private army of distressed and discontented people (1 Samuel 22:1-2). Among them may have been David's group of 30 heroes and its inner group of three (2 Samuel 23:8-9) – incidents such as the challenge of David to the three to get water from the well at Bethlehem under the noses of a Philistine garrison (2 Samuel 23:13-17) may also belong to this period. David appears to have run a kind of protection racket to provide food for his band, and he was pursued by Saul and his army.

The narrative goes out of its way to emphasize David's loyalty to Saul at this time. Twice David has the opportunity to kill Saul but spares him (1 Samuel 24:1-22; 26:6-25). When David finally deserts to the

David the musician, whose skill at playing the harp soothed Saul's torments, pictured in a mosaic from a 4th-century AD synagogue in Gaza.

NATHAN

No details are given of Nathan's ancestry or place of birth. In 1 Samuel 7 Nathan acts as the intermediary between David and God. In reply to David's request about building a temple Nathan conveys the divine answer that it is David's son who will build it; God will build a house (dynasty) for David that will last for ever. Nathan's second appearance follows David's adultery with Bathsheba. Nathan prophesies that the child conceived by them will die and that David's family will be the scene of continual strife (2 Samuel 12:10-11). At the end of David's life, Nathan sides with the priest Zadok and the commander of the royal bodyguard Benaiah in supporting Solomon, Bathsheba's son, against David's eldest surviving son, Adonijah, for the succession (1 Kings 1). The narratives in which Nathan appears are part of the 'Succession Narrative', the date of which is hotly contested.

Nathan's narrative function is to emphasize that even God's most favoured servants are human and their misdemeanours stand under divine judgment and need divine pardon.

The prophet Nathan admonishing king David, in a detail from a Byzantine psalter of c. 950.

Philistines out of desperation (1 Samuel 27) he avoids any attacks on his own people. He is also spared from having to take part in the final battle between Saul and the Philistines (1 Samuel 29:1-11), and he executes the Amalekite who brings him the news of Saul's death and who claims to have slain him (2 Samuel 1:5-16; cf. 1 Samuel 31:4-6).

Following Saul's death, the situation in Israel was confused. Although the Philistines were nominally in charge of the whole country, Saul's commander, Abner, had set up Saul's son Eshbaal as king in Mahanaim in Transjordan. In the south, David had been made king of Judah with his capital in Hebron. Presumably the Philistines approved of this situation and used David as a vassal ruler to help enforce their authority. Certainly, the incident in 2 Samuel 3 in which the forces of David led by Joab confront the forces of Saul's dynasty led by Abner at Gibeon looks like a case of the Philistines employing David to keep Saul's forces at bay. In the encounter Joab's brother Asahel is killed by Abner and Joab

DAVID AND GOLIATH

And there came out from the camp of the Philistines a champion named Goliath, of Gath, whose height was six cubits and a span. He had a helmet of bronze on his head, and he was armed with a coat of mail, and the weight of the coat was five thousand shekels of bronze. And he had greaves of bronze upon his legs, and a javelin of bronze slung between his shoulders. ... He stood and shouted to the ranks of Israel, 'Why have you come out to draw up for battle? Am I not a Philistine, and are you not servants of Saul? Choose a man for yourselves, and let him come down to me. If he is able to fight with me and kill me, then we will be your servants; but if I prevail against him and kill him, then you shall be our servants and serve us.' When Saul and all Israel heard these words of the Philistine, they were dismayed ....

And David said to Saul, 'Let no man's heart fail because of him; your servant will go and fight with this Philistine.' ... Then he took his staff in his hand, and chose five smooth stones from the brook, and put them in his shepherd's bag or wallet; his sling was in his hand, and he drew near to the Philistine. ... When the Philistine arose and came and drew near to meet David, David ran quickly towards the battle line to meet the Philistine. And David put his hand in his bag and took out a stone, and slung it, and struck the Philistine on the forehead; the stone sank into his forehead, and he fell on his face to the ground.

1 Samuel 17:4-6, 8-9, 48-49

David the warrior, by Andrea del Verrocchio (c. 1472/75). Here David is portrayed as the young, boyish slayer of the champion of the Philistines.

uses trickery to kill Abner in revenge. Abner's death hastens the collapse of Saul's dynasty: Eshbaal is murdered by two of Saul's former captains who are then themselves executed by David when they bring him what they suppose to be the good news. David is invited to be king over Israel and the Philistines are suddenly faced by a united Israel led by an outstanding warrior.

According to 2 Samuel 5, David captured the Jebusite city of Jerusalem and made it his capital before confronting and defeating the Philistines.

When David first became king, his capital was at Hebron (*right*), the burial place of the Ancestors Abraham and Sarah – a mosque, visible in the centre, now marks their tombs. However, the city was situated too far south to be able to control the whole country effectively.

In a brilliant decision, David chose the Jebusite site of Jerusalem as his new capital (*below*). This view shows the Haram al-Sharif, the sacred Muslim enclosure on which stands the Dome of the Rock (centre) and the El-Aqsa mosque. The area of David's city was to the left of the enclosure.

Excavations carried out in the 'City of David' in the 1970s and 1980s discovered this 'stepped stone structure', which some scholars date to the time of David.

Some scholars reverse these events. Whatever the truth, the choice of Jerusalem as capital was a brilliant move. Hebron was too far south to serve as a capital of all Israel, while to have chosen an ancient northern town such as Bethel or Shechem would have taken David away from his natural power base in Judah. Jerusalem straddled excellent routes to all four points of the compass and was a neutral city for Judah and Israel alike. Having consolidated his power, David brought into Jerusalem the Ark of the Covenant, a sacred object that symbolized God's warlike presence among his people, and which, according to the biblical tradition, had accompanied Israel through its journeying in the wilderness. Jerusalem thus became both the political and religious capital of Israel.

David: an assessment

It is no surprise that David should be one of the most important figures in the Bible. As presented in the tradition his achievements were outstanding. Before his reign, Israel was a defeated, vassal people. Within a few years David had made Israel free, and even extended his control over some small neighbouring peoples. Before his reign there was no one dominant political or religious centre in Israel. Within a few years Jerusalem had attained a centrality that it never subsequently lost. Prior to David, no leader had established a dynasty. David established a dynasty that was so enduring that after its physical extinction around 400 years after his death, it supplied the hopes for the coming of a future ideal king. In addition to all this, the entrance of Jerusalem into Israelite religion enriched the symbolism, worship and psalmody of that religion.

'As presented in the tradition...'. It needs to be noted that recent research indicates that the extent of Jerusalem's power as portrayed in the biblical account of David was not, in fact, realized until at least 200 years later, probably in the reign of either Uzziah or Hezekiah. But it is also noteworthy that, if the Bible has exaggerated David's achievements, it has not presented him as a superman. David is also one of the most human figures in the Bible. He is glimpsed as an extremely brave and shrewd soldier, who could command the absolute loyalty of outstandingly strong and brave men, yet whose actual performance as king and father was characterized by self-indulgence, self-delusion and vacillation. He is unable to inspire in his close family and his people the devotion that he won from his soldier colleagues. He is, perhaps, a man's man, happier with comrades in arms such as Jonathan, and his group of heroes; less at home in the intrigues of a royal family and the demands of presiding over peace.

Map showing the extent of the kingdom of Israel during the United Monarchy, under Saul, David and Solomon, according to the biblical material. Recent research, however, casts doubts on these claims.

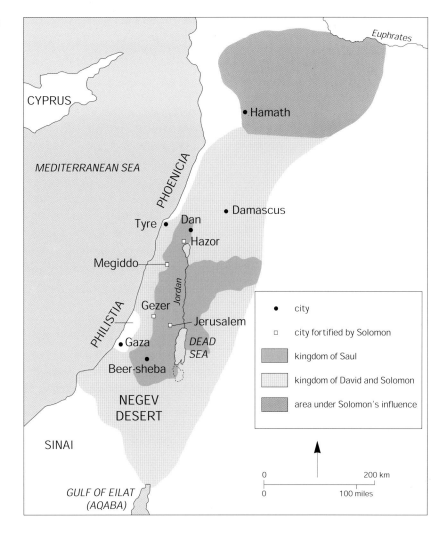

שְׁלמֹה Solomon

c. 961–931 BC

Detail from the Judgment of Solomon
from a French medieval manuscript.

SOLOMON	
Born	*Son*
Jerusalem	Rehoboam
Father	*Buried*
David	Jerusalem
Mother	*Bible references*
Bathsheba	1 Kings 1–11;
Wives	2 Chronicles 1–9
700, and 300	
concubines	

… even Solomon in all his glory was not arrayed like one of these.

Matthew 6:29

Glory and magnificence are words that come readily to mind when the name Solomon is mentioned. After all, was he not the first great builder among the kings of Israel, with the temple in Jerusalem as his crowning achievement? And was he not also a cultivated man of letters whose wisdom was as famed as his material wealth?

Such was the impact of the reputation of Solomon that later tradition credited him with the authorship of several books. Proverbs, Ecclesiastes and the Song of Songs (called in some Bibles the Song of Solomon) are traditionally ascribed to him, as well as Psalm 72. Further, the 'Wisdom of Solomon' in the Apocrypha bears his name in the title. So what do the biblical record and modern historical and archaeological studies have to say about him?

The biblical record

Although Solomon's reputation rests entirely upon the biblical material in 1 Kings 1–11, a close reading shows that the account is not simply uncritical hagiography. Even the beginning of Solomon's reign is inauspi-

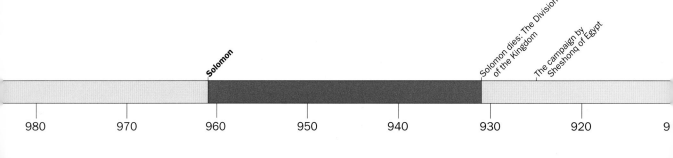

Solomon

Solomon dies: The Division
of the Kingdom

The campaign by
Sheshonq of Egypt

980   970   960   950   940   930   920   9

This depiction of the anointing of Solomon from a fresco by Raphael (1483–1520), Vatican Loggia, captures the biblical account of a hastily improvised ceremony outside the city.

cious. Handel's coronation anthem 'Zadok the priest, and Nathan the prophet anointed Solomon King', which has been sung in Westminster Abbey at the coronation of every British monarch since George II in 1727, gives the impression that Solomon's coronation was a formal occasion in dignified surroundings. The biblical narrative indicates otherwise.

The account in 1 Kings begins by portraying a king David who is old and infirm and who has lost his sexual potency. Once this latter point is established, David's oldest surviving son Adonijah makes a bid for the succession. He is supported by the army commander Joab and one of the two principal priests, Abiathar. Adonijah arranges an elaborate sacrifice and feast at En-rogel, a water source with cultic associations just outside Jerusalem (the site known today as *Bir-eyyub*, 'Job's well'). Although no coronation is described, a report of the proceedings is brought to David by Nathan the prophet, who claims that the guests are proclaiming 'Long live King Adonijah!' (1 Kings 1:25). This enables a group inspired by Bathsheba, David's wife and Solomon's mother, and headed by Nathan, the other principal priest Zadok, and Benaiah the commander of David's guard, to get David's permission for the coronation of Solomon. At a hastily improvised ceremony at Gihon, the other main source of water just outside Jerusalem, Zadok anoints Solomon king (1 Kings 1:39). Thus Solomon's reign begins in rivalry. Solomon's main rival Adonijah and his main supporter Joab are later executed and the priest Abiathar expelled from Jerusalem, as described in 1 Kings 2.

An account of Solomon's achievements is given in 1 Kings, chapters 3 to 10. These include his prayer for wisdom and the demonstration of it in his adjudication between two women who claim the same child, his fiscal reorganization of the kingdom, the building of the temple and

Solomon demonstrates his wisdom in judging between two women who both claim to be the mother of the same child. This version of the famous scene is on a silver reliquary casket from San Nazaro Maggiore, Milan, end of the 4th century.

The Queen of Sheba's visit to Solomon, graphically depicted in an Ethiopian manuscript.

the royal palace, and the visit of the Queen of Sheba from south-western Arabia, who wishes to see for herself Solomon's wealth and wisdom. However, even this account contains implicit criticisms of Solomon. The adjacent verses in 1 Kings 6:38 and 7:1 laconically mention that Solomon took 7 years to build the temple but 13 years to build his palace. Then, in chapter 9 God appears to Solomon in a dream and gives him a

Now when the queen of Sheba heard of the fame of Solomon concerning the name of the LORD, she came to test him with hard questions. She came to Jerusalem with a very great retinue, with camels bearing spices, and very much gold, and precious stones; and when she came to Solomon, she told him all that was on her mind. And Solomon answered all her questions; there was nothing hidden from the king which he could not explain to her....

The Visit of the Queen of Sheba,
1 Kings 10:1-3, 6-7, 10

stern warning that the temple will become a heap of ruins if he or his descendants turn aside from God. This is followed immediately by the statement that Solomon gave 20 cities in Galilee to Hiram king of Tyre, Solomon's chief supplier of materials and craftsmen for the temple and palace. This was no doubt payment in kind, but it involved giving away part of the land of Israel and its inhabitants.

The chief criticisms of Solomon are reserved for 1 Kings 11, which forms the transition to the account in the following chapter of the division of Solomon's kingdom into Judah and Israel under his successor. For the biblical narrative Solomon's main wrongdoing is religious. He marries foreign women and they lead him astray to worship foreign deities and even to build holy places for them. God punishes Solomon by raising up adversaries in the form of Hadad the Edomite and Rezon of Damascus. The successful revolts of these leaders indicate the breaking-up of Solomon's empire. Most seriously, there is an attempted revolt by Jeroboam, of the tribe of Ephraim, an able man who is in charge of the forced labour from his tribal area. He is encouraged in his revolt by a prophet, Ahijah, and seeks refuge in Egypt when Solomon tries to kill him. Thus, even from a superficial reading of the biblical material, the epithet 'glory' as applied to Solomon is not untarnished.

Historical criticism and archaeology

In addition to using forced labour to build the temple and palace in Jerusalem, we are told in 1 Kings 9:15 that Solomon built Hazor, Megiddo and Gezer. Verse 17 also attributes to Solomon the rebuilding of Lower Beth-horon, Baalath and Tamar in the wilderness and (unspecified) store cities. In 2 Chronicles 8:4-6 Tadmor is added to this list (which can hardly

A reconstruction of the city gate at Gezer. Whether or not this was actually built in Solomon's reign is a matter of debate.

The site of Hazor, in northern Galilee, with a detail (inset) of what has been identified as the Solomonic gate, with the characteristic plan also found at other sites attributed to Solomon's reign.

be the great oasis city of Palmyra in the Syrian desert and is most likely a textual mistake for Tamar in 1 Kings 9:17), as well as store cities in Hamath, Upper Beth-horon and (unspecified) fortified cities and store cities, including sites in Lebanon.

Here archaeology does provide some possible corroboration. Excavations at Hazor, Megiddo and Gezer have uncovered city gates with similar plans, casemate walls (double city walls wide enough to contain dwellings) and, in the case of Megiddo, two palaces and other public buildings, which have been dated to the time of Solomon. Although scholars are not unanimous on all the details, one archaeologist, A. Mazar, can write of 'the emergence of Israelite royal, monumental architecture characterized by ashlar masonry, stone moulding and specific plans'. No Solomonic remains have been identified in Jerusalem, but archaeologists have reconstructed both the temple and the palace on the basis of the biblical account and actual examples of such buildings found elsewhere in the ancient Near East. According to Mazar the temple was a rectangular building about 82 ft (25 m) by 164 ft (50 m), with an exceptional height of 49 ft (15 m). It had three divisions: a porch; the sanctuary; and the Holy of Holies. There were also three storeys of chambers on either side of the main building. Mazar plausibly suggests that the palaces at Megiddo contained architectural features that were also employed in the Jerusalem palace.

If the attribution of these gates, walls and palaces to Solomon is correct – and several leading younger Israeli archaeologists have recently

Excavated remains of the city gates at Megiddo and Gezer, usually dated to the reign of Solomon.

questioned this – then his kingdom must have been organized in something like the manner described in the Bible. Israel would have been a small but major power in the region, taking advantage of Egyptian weakness and of Israelite control over neighbouring peoples, such as those of Edom and Damascus. The claim that Solomon built a fleet of ships to operate from Ezion-geber on the Red Sea (1 Kings 9:26) and that he exacted tribute from small kingdoms (1 Kings 4:21) would also accord with this picture, as would his fiscal organization of the land into twelve districts (1 Kings 4:7-19) and his use of forced labour both of Israelites and of non-Israelites living within the kingdom (1 Kings 9:20-1). Israel would indeed have passed overnight from being a loose association of chiefdoms to a centralized small state, the ambitious projects of whose ruler would have weighed heavily on the people.

There is today growing scepticism in some scholarly circles about the claims made in the Bible about the extent, or even existence, of an empire of David and Solomon. Evidence from several directions suggests that Judah (the southern kingdom of which Jerusalem remained the capital after the division of the kingdom) did not become a state capable of controlling a small empire until 200 years after Solomon. It would be wrong in the current state of our knowledge to disagree with the opinions of expert archaeologists and to dismiss their findings and the support that these give to the biblical account. However, the most recent research is beginning to re-draw the archaeological map and require a reconsideration of the evidence for Solomon's reign.

The biblical account of Solomon was written many hundreds of years later than the times it describes. Here, as always, it is necessary to distinguish between the final form of the narrative and much older material, perhaps taken from archives, which the narrative might contain, such as material about the construction of the temple. There can be no doubt, however, that when the account of Solomon's reign reached its final form his temple lay in ruins following its destruction by the Babylonians in 587 BC. Not only is this indicated by the warning about the possibility of the temple's destruction in 1 Kings 9:6-9, but Solomon's prayer of dedication of the temple (8:22-53) implies that the temple is no longer standing. In this prayer he envisages a number of situations in which, disaster having overtaken the Israelites, they will pray towards the temple in penitence; and Solomon requests God to hear and to act when such prayers are made. The situations include the defeat of Israel in battle, the occurrence of drought, or famine caused by pestilence, sickness caused by plague or, most significantly, that the Israelites are defeated and taken into captivity by their enemies. What is astonishing is that no mention of sacrifice, or any other activity of praise or worship in the temple, is made in the prayer. The temple is not a place *in* which worshippers offer sacrifice and worship; it is primarily a place *towards* which worshippers *pray*. This would be most appropriate for a people in exile praying in hope towards a ruined temple. Thus even the 'temple' material in 1 Kings 1–11 contains the paradox that the built temple is also the ruined one.

SOLOMON'S TEMPLE

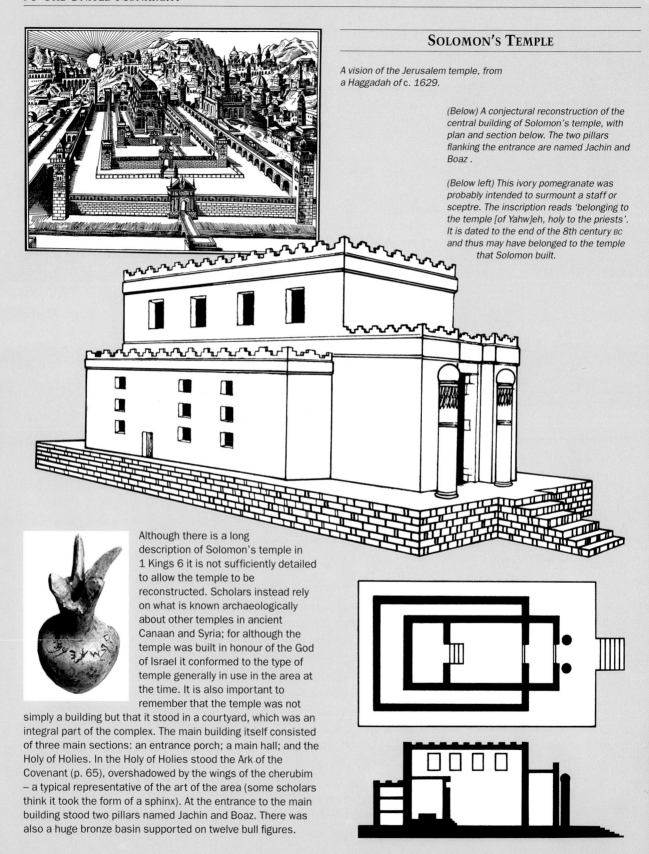

A vision of the Jerusalem temple, from a Haggadah of c. 1629.

(Below) A conjectural reconstruction of the central building of Solomon's temple, with plan and section below. The two pillars flanking the entrance are named Jachin and Boaz.

(Below left) This ivory pomegranate was probably intended to surmount a staff or sceptre. The inscription reads 'belonging to the temple [of Yahw]eh, holy to the priests'. It is dated to the end of the 8th century BC and thus may have belonged to the temple that Solomon built.

Although there is a long description of Solomon's temple in 1 Kings 6 it is not sufficiently detailed to allow the temple to be reconstructed. Scholars instead rely on what is known archaeologically about other temples in ancient Canaan and Syria; for although the temple was built in honour of the God of Israel it conformed to the type of temple generally in use in the area at the time. It is also important to remember that the temple was not simply a building but that it stood in a courtyard, which was an integral part of the complex. The main building itself consisted of three main sections: an entrance porch; a main hall; and the Holy of Holies. In the Holy of Holies stood the Ark of the Covenant (p. 65), overshadowed by the wings of the cherubim – a typical representative of the art of the area (some scholars think it took the form of a sphinx). At the entrance to the main building stood two pillars named Jachin and Boaz. There was also a huge bronze basin supported on twelve bull figures.

COMPARISON BETWEEN THE BOOK OF PROVERBS AND AN EGYPTIAN TEXT	The Wisdom of Amenemope	Proverbs
	First Chapter *Give thine ears, hear what is said,* *Give thy mind to interpret them.*	Chapter 22:17-18a *Incline your ear, and hear the words* *of the wise,* *and apply your mind to my knowledge;* *for it will be pleasant if you keep them* *within you*
	Second chapter *Guard thyself against robbing the* *wretched* *And against being puissant over the* *man of broken arm*	Chapter 22:22 *Do not rob the poor, because he is* *poor,* *or crush the afflicted at the gate*
	Thirtieth chapter *See for thyself these thirty chapters* *They give pleasure; they instruct;* *They are the foremost of all books;* *They instruct the ignorant.*	Chapter 22: 20-21 *Have I not written for you thirty sayings* *of admonition and knowledge;* *to show you what is right and true,* *that you may give a true answer to* *those who sent you?*
Some of the similarities between the biblical book of Proverbs and the Egyptian 'Wisdom of Amenemope' (c. 1300): they probably indicate the widespread nature of such teachings, rather than literary dependence.	*As for the scribe who is experienced in* *his office,* *He shall find himself worthy to be a* *courtier.*	Chapter 22:29 *Do you see a man skilful in his work?* *he will stand before kings;* *he will not stand before obscure* *men.*

Modern study of the reign of Solomon has been sharply critical of the effect of his policies on the ordinary people of his kingdom; and the biblical narrative itself tells how the Israelites asked Solomon's successor to make their burdens lighter (1 Kings 12:4). Some writers have even seen implicit criticisms of Solomon in Genesis 3, linking the tradition of Solomon's wisdom with the desire of Adam and Eve to eat the fruit of the tree of knowledge. On the basis of this link, the expulsion of Adam and Eve from the garden of Eden is seen as an adverse verdict upon Solomon.

What of Solomon's 'wisdom'? The claim in 1 Kings 4:32 that he uttered 3,000 proverbs and that his songs were a thousand and three (a claim responsible for the traditional attribution to Solomon of the book of Proverbs, for example) is variously regarded. Collections of proverbs in ancient Near Eastern literature pre-date Solomon, and he could certainly have uttered proverbs. Indeed, scholars have long noticed similarities between Proverbs 22:17 to 24:22 and the Egyptian text the 'Wisdom of Amenemope', dated around 1300 BC. Whether Solomon actually did utter proverbs and compose songs will depend on views about the nature and extent of his reign.

Solomon remains a somewhat enigmatic figure. His architectural achievements were carried out at the expense of alienating his people; and if he was extremely wise, he did not have the ability to see the contradiction between his own luxury and the hardship of his people on which his luxury depended, and the consequences this would have.

THE DIVIDED MONARCHY:
ISRAEL

Jeroboam I
c. 931–910 BC

Nadab
c. 909 BC

Baasha
c. 909–886 BC

Elah
c. 885 BC

Zimri
c. 885 BC

Omri
c. 885–874 BC

Ahab
c. 873–853 BC

Ahaziah
853–852 BC

Jehoram
852–841 BC

Jehu
841–813 BC

Jehoahaz
813–797 BC

Jehoash
797–782 BC

Jeroboam II
782–747 BC

Zechariah
747 BC

Shallum
747 BC

Menahem
747–742 BC

Pekahiah
742–740 BC

Pekah
740–731 BC

Hoshea
731–722/1 BC

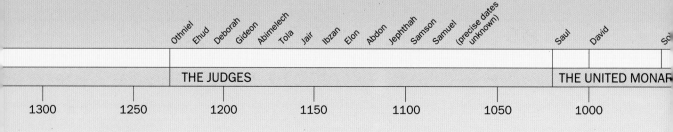

Othniel Ehud Deborah Gideon Abimelech Tola Jair Ibzan Elon Abdon Jephthah Samson Samuel (precise dates unknown) Saul David So

THE JUDGES

THE UNITED MONAR

1300   1250   1200   1150   1100   1050   1000

Jeroboam I

Ahaziah

Jehu

THE DIVIDED MONARCHY: ISRAEL
931–722/1 BC

AFTER THE DEATH OF SOLOMON the so-called United Monarchy finally and irrevocably broke apart. For nearly 200 years, from 931 to 747, four dynasties ruled the northern kingdom, Israel, of which two, those of Omri and Jehu, held power for nearly 140 years. The beginning and especially the end of the northern kingdom were marked by instability, coup and counter-coup. The last 25 years saw no fewer than five kings, until the Assyrians put an end to the northern kingdom of Israel in 722/1.

This instability was caused by several factors. Israel was not only composed of ten tribes, but stretched as far north as Dan, and included Transjordanian territory. There was no one centre of authority in the north, and Israel did not enjoy stable government until Omri established Samaria as the northern capital. The northern kingdom was also more fertile than Judah and it was closer, and more accessible, to enemies such as its neighbour Damascus, and its ultimate destroyer, Assyria.

During the 9th century Israel dominated Judah as well as other local small kingdoms, and it was also during this century that prophetic opposition to the paganizing policies of northern kings, led by the prophets Elijah and Elisha, brought about the overthrow of the powerful dynasty of Omri and its replacement by a dynasty initially committed to prophetic ideals. The fate of Israel was finally sealed by the expansionist policies of the Assyrians under Tiglath-pileser III and his successors. After its fall, the northern kingdom would not come under sustained Jewish control again for over 600 years.

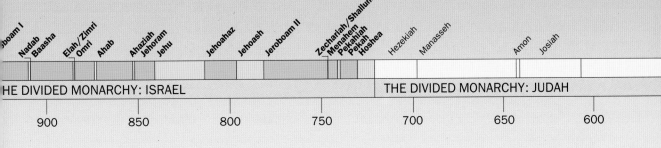

Jeroboam I · Nadab · Baasha · Elah/Zimri · Omri · Ahab · Ahaziah/Jehoram · Jehu · Jehoahaz · Jehoash · Jeroboam II · Zechariah/Shallum · Menahem · Pekahiah · Pekah · Hoshea · Hezekiah · Manasseh · Amon · Josiah

THE DIVIDED MONARCHY: ISRAEL   THE DIVIDED MONARCHY: JUDAH

900   850   800   750   700   650   600

יָרָבְעָם **Jeroboam I**
c. 931–910 BC

נָדָב **Nadab**
c. 909 BC

בַּעְשָׁא **Baasha**
c. 909–886 BC

Jeroboam I, a detail from the painting
Jeroboam's Idolatry, by J.H. Fragonard
(1752).

JEROBOAM I	
Born	Nadab
Zeredah	*Bible references*
Father	1 Kings
Nebat	12:20–14:19
Sons	
Abijah	

JEROBOAM I

When all Israel heard that Jeroboam had returned, they sent and called him to the assembly and made him king over all Israel.

1 Kings 12:20

The biblical narrative concerning Jeroboam is unique in the Old Testament in that it appears in two distinct versions. This is not apparent to readers of the Bible in English or standard translations in other languages, which follow the traditional Hebrew text. The other version is contained in the ancient Greek translation of the Old Testament, the Septuagint. The main differences between the two accounts can be summarized as follows.

In the Hebrew version Jeroboam rises to prominence during Solomon's reign as an organizer of forced labour in Ephraim and Manasseh. He is designated as a future king by Ahijah, a prophet from Shiloh, and has to flee from Solomon and take refuge in Egypt. When he hears that Rehoboam has succeeded Solomon, Jeroboam returns to Israel and takes part in the meeting between Rehoboam and 'all Israel' at Shechem which ends in the revolt of the ten tribes (p. 124). Jeroboam is made king.

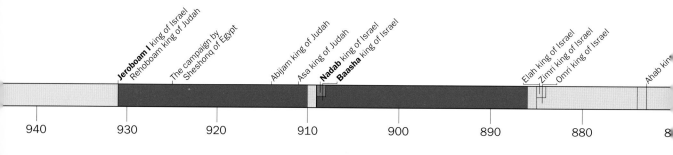

Jeroboam I king of Israel
Rehoboam king of Judah
The campaign by Sheshonq of Egypt
Abijam king of Judah
Asa king of Judah
Nadab king of Israel
Baasha king of Israel
Elah king of Israel
Zimri king of Israel
Omri king of Israel
Ahab king

940   930   920   910   900   890   880   8

THE CAMPAIGN OF SHESHONQ

According to 1 Kings 14:25-6 Judah was invaded in King Rehoboam's fifth year by Shishak (i.e. Sheshonq I), king of Egypt (cf. also 2 Chronicles 12 : 1-16). The biblical account records that Shishak took away the treasures from the temple and the royal palace. While Sheshonq did not record the details of his campaign, he did set up a relief in the temple of Amun at Karnak which listed captive cities. From this list it is difficult to reconstruct the exact sequence of the campaign, and an older view has recently been re-stated, according to which the list contains at least an element of propaganda. Two points do

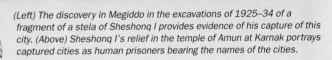

(Left) The discovery in Megiddo in the excavations of 1925–34 of a fragment of a stela of Sheshonq I provides evidence of his capture of this city. (Above) Sheshonq I's relief in the temple of Amun at Karnak portrays captured cities as human prisoners bearing the names of the cities.

emerge, however. First, if Sheshonq's list really does represent cities which he captured, then the northern kingdom, Israel, suffered more than Judah, although the Bible says nothing about an Egyptian invasion of Israel by Shishak. Second, the list does not mention Jerusalem, which has led to the view that Rehoboam sent tribute to Sheshonq to persuade him not to come up against the city. The claim of 2 Chronicles 12:2-4 that he did come up against Jerusalem is therefore discounted.

An invasion of Israel by Rehoboam is prevented by the prophet Shemaiah. Jeroboam builds Shechem and Penuel and sets up calf images at Bethel and Dan. When his son falls sick, Jeroboam sends his wife disguised to Ahijah for help, but Ahijah sees through the deception, denounces Jeroboam's apostasy and prophesies the death of the child and the destruction of Jeroboam's dynasty.

The Greek version is not entirely self-consistent, perhaps because it was revised to try to make it conform to the Hebrew account in some particulars. It has Jeroboam returning to Israel *before* Rehoboam

Jeroboam's Idolatry, by J.H. Fragonard (1752) illustrates Jeroboam's setting up of sacrilegious calf images at Bethel and Dan, and the prophetic disapproval of this act.

becomes king and places the incident of the sick child *before* the assembly of the tribes at Shechem to meet Rehoboam. Also, the prophet who declares that Jeroboam will be a future king is Shemaiah not Ahijah.

The variations can be explained in at least two ways. The Greek version may be a 'midrash' (interpretation) of the Hebrew version, although it then needs to be asked why some important details have been altered, such as the name of the prophet who designated Jeroboam as a future king. Another view is that the Greek represents an independent composition, originally in Hebrew, from a time when the tradition was somewhat fluid. A similar phenomenon is found in the differences between the Hebrew and Greek versions of Jeremiah. This latter view would imply that the books of Kings reached their final form, in, say, the 4th century BC, rather later than is usually thought.

The importance of Jeroboam

Whatever the exact sequence of events, Jeroboam's significance lies in the fact that he became the focus of northern opposition to the southern dynasty of David, such that he was appointed the first northern king. The account in 1 Kings 12:28, in which Jeroboam sets up golden calves in Bethel and Dan and says of them 'Behold your gods, O Israel, who brought you up out of the land of Egypt', represents Jeroboam as an idolater. However, it is possible to interpret Jeroboam's revolt as an attempt to restore to Israel the 'old' faith in God as the redeemer from Egyptian slavery, as opposed to the 'new' faith of David and Solomon centred in a city (Jerusalem) that was not connected with Israel's ancient traditions and which contained a temple designed and built by the non-Israelite, Hiram, king of Tyre. Moreover, the fiscal and labour demands of Solomon's kingdom upon his northern subjects made them long for independence. If Jeroboam was a conservative reformer rather than an idolater, the golden calves must be understood as the

The 'high place' of the sacred precinct of Dan and the reconstructed four-cornered altar (centre). These remains represent several phases of construction, from the 10th to the 8th centuries.

The city walls and towers of Dan, parts of which probably date from the time of Jeroboam I (late 10th century).

throne of the invisible God of Israel, and as a recognizable part of the traditional cult.

Soon after Jeroboam's rebellion, in around 925 BC, both Israel and Judah were invaded by Sheshonq I (945–924 BC) of Egypt. The incident is recorded in 1 Kings 14:25-27 (where the pharaoh's name is given as Shishak), but it only mentions it in regard to Jerusalem. From what can be reconstructed of Sheshonq's campaign from his own inscription, he wreaked more destruction upon Israel (ruled by Jeroboam I, whom he had once protected) than upon Judah. It is possible that the reference to Jeroboam building Penuel in Transjordan (1 Kings 12:25) indicates that he took refuge in Transjordan; however, Sheshonq claimed to have captured Mahanaim, also in Transjordan. Following this setback, Jeroboam reigned for another 14 years. Perhaps the Egyptian invasion weakened the kingdom and fuelled opposition – at any rate, Jeroboam's dynasty lasted for just one generation. His son Nadab was killed by Baasha after two years on the throne. Baasha then killed Jeroboam's entire family.

NADAB	
Born	*Bible references*
Unknown	1 Kings 15:25–26,
Father	31
Jeroboam	
Son	
Unnamed	

A Syrian archer, depicted in a relief from Tell Halaf in northern Syria.

NADAB

Nadab, Jeroboam's son, receives only three verses in the Bible: 1 Kings 15:25-6 and 31. According to the meagre information given, he reigned for just two years and did what was evil in God's sight. Modern dating systems reduce this to only one year because of the way in which years were counted in ancient Israel. To put it in modern terms, a king who reigned for six months, from 1 October to 31 March, would be credited with a reign of two years, since it occupied part of two separate years.

BAASHA

As soon as he was king, Baasha killed all the house of Jeroboam.

1 Kings 15:29

The information about Baasha is also sparse and contained in twelve verses (1 Kings 15:27-31 and 1 Kings 15:16-22; though the latter are concerned primarily with Asa, king of Judah). We learn that Baasha, of the tribe of Issachar, killed Nadab, while the Israelites were besieging the Philistine town of Gibbethon. He then exterminated Jeroboam's entire family and besieged the Judahite town of Ramah. He was forced to break off the siege, however, when Ben-hadad king of Damascus raided northern Israel, having been persuaded to do so by gold and silver sent from the Jerusalem treasury by king Asa of Judah. As a result of his invasion Ben-hadad occupied several towns in the extreme north and 'all Chineroth, with all the land of Naphtali'. Given that the territory of Naphtali was a strip to the west of the Sea of Galilee, this indicates that the Syrians advanced down the west side of the Jordan valley as

BAASHA	
Born	*Buried*
Unnamed town in	Tirzah
Issachar	*Bible references*
Father	1 Kings 15:27-31,
Ahijah	16-22
Son	
Elah	

The northern end of the Sea of Galilee, showing (bottom right) the Greek Orthodox monastery on the site of Capernaum.

far south as the Sea of Galilee, without occupying the mountainous and forested Upper Galilee or very much of the more hospitable Lower Galilee.

The accounts raise many unanswerable questions. For instance, why was Nadab besieging a Philistine city in the coastal plain, probably not far from Gezer and of far more interest to the southern kingdom, Judah? Why did Baasha besiege Ramah? What was the reason for the coup d'état, and what were Baasha's origins? Issachar, Baasha's tribe, was to the immediate north of Ephraim and Manasseh, occupying the northernmost Samaria hills and across the valley of Jezreel to the southern hills of Lower Galilee. His coup may have sprung from tribal rivalries. If the saying of the prophet Jehu ben Hanani against Baasha – 'I exalted you out of the dust' (1 Kings 16:2) – can be relied on, we might deduce that Baasha was a commoner who had risen to a position in the army that allowed him to get sufficiently close to the king to be able to assassinate him during a siege. The sieges against Gibbethon and Ramah would be attempts to encircle and harass Judah.

It has been suggested that Baasha was killed resisting Ben-hadad's invasion. There is no evidence for this; but the foreign occupation of an area of Israel could well have been the prelude to the instability and civil war from which emerged the dynasty of Omri.

אֵלָה Elah
c. 885 BC

זִמְרִי Zimri
c. 885 BC

עָמְרִי Omri
c. 885–874 BC

ELAH AND ZIMRI

ELAH	ZIMRI
Born	*Bible references*
? Tirzah	1 Kings 16:9-13,
Father	15-20
Baasha	
Buried	
? Tirzah	
Bible references	
1 Kings 16:8-10, 14	

[Omri] bought the hill of Samaria from Shemer for two talents of silver; and he fortified the hill, and called the name of the city which he built, Samaria, after the name of Shemer, the owner of the hill.

1 Kings 16:24

ELAH AND ZIMRI

Between the death of Baasha (*c.* 886 BC) and the accession of Omri (*c.* 885 BC) Israel saw two kings and much violence. Baasha was succeeded by his son Elah, who is credited with having reigned for two years (1 Kings 16:8). However, the actual period could have been only a matter of months given the way that the reigns of kings were calculated. All we know of Elah is that he was assassinated while drunk in his capital of Tirzah, and that the assassin, Zimri, commander of half the royal chariots, took the throne. Zimri's reign, in turn, lasted a mere seven days (1 Kings 16:15). When the army heard of Zimri's coup it lifted the siege of Gibbethon, proclaimed its commander Omri as king, marched to the capital Tirzah, and besieged it until Zimri took his own life as he destroyed the king's house with fire. Omri's rule was not undisputed, however, even with the death of Zimri. In 1 Kings 16:21-22 is a description of a civil war between

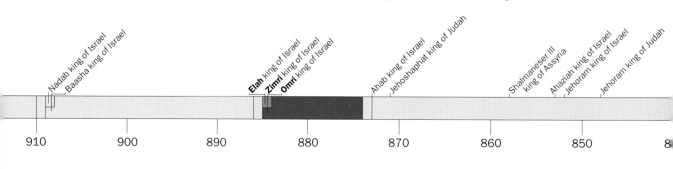

supporters of Omri and a certain Tibni, son of Ginath. The duration of the troubles is not given, only its outcome, which saw Omri triumph.

We do not know why the reign of Baasha was followed by a period of such turmoil; but a reasonable guess is that Ben-hadad's invasion of Israel and the occupation of the strip of Upper Galilee bordering on the Jordan valley (1 Kings 15:20), even if only temporary, led to a demand for strong leadership which would guarantee the security of the country. In such circumstances, it would be likely that the initiative would come from the army, especially if the information that Elah was drunk in Tirzah while the army was many miles to the south implies that Elah was not a military man.

OMRI

OMRI	
Born	*Buried*
Unknown	Samaria
Father	*Bible references*
Unknown	1 Kings 16:16-28
Son	
Ahab	

Because the uncertainties surrounding Omri outweigh the certainties, we will consider the latter first. Omri took over a kingdom that had suffered military defeat at the hands of Damascus, and which had recently experienced coup, counter-coup and civil war. By the end of his brief reign of some twelve years he had stabilized the country, had built (or begun to build) a new capital city at Samaria, had forged alliances with Judah and Tyre, and had extended his rule in Transjordan to the point where the inscription of the Moabite king Mesha conceded: 'Omri humbled Moab for many years'. Omri thus has the honour of being the first king of the northern kingdom to be mentioned in extra-biblical sources – and not only in the Mesha Inscription; he is also mentioned in Assyrian inscriptions, the most flattering mention being in the annals of the later ruler Tiglath-pileser III (745–727 BC) where Israel is called *Bit Hu-um-ri-a* – 'the house of Omri'! Omri clearly made a considerable impression on his own and succeeding generations, even beyond the boundaries of his kingdom.

Relief from Dhiban in Jordan (ancient Dibon), possibly showing a Moabite.

Samaria was chosen by Omri as the site of the capital of the northern kingdom, Israel, in the first half of the 9th century BC, and it remained so until the Assyrians destroyed it in 722/1 BC.

If we do not get such a picture of Omri from the Bible, it is because the biblical writers regarded him as an evil king religiously, and therefore chose to record only the bare minimum of information about him. The first of many uncertainties concerns his name and origins. His father's name and his tribal affiliation are not given in the biblical record. Does this mean that he was a foreign mercenary soldier? Is his name to be connected with an Arabic verb meaning 'to live', with the implication that he came from 'foreign' stock within Israel? Or can he be connected with the tribe of Issachar on the basis of 1 Chronicles 27:18? All three possibilities have been argued. Again, it is disputed whether Omri is short for Omriyah, which ends in an abbreviated form of the divine name YHWH and possibly therefore means 'Yah gives life'.

Another uncertainty arises from within the biblical material. In 1 Kings 20:34 the king of Damascus says to Omri's son Ahab: 'I will restore the towns that my father took from your father; and you may establish bazaars for yourself in Damascus, as my father did in Samaria'. If this is accepted at face value, then Omri suffered defeats at the hands of Damascus and had to accept humiliating terms. This hardly fits with a king who was able to 'humble Moab for many years'. Further, Samaria, once completed, was such an impregnable fortress that it withstood a three-year Assyrian siege before it capitulated in 722/1 BC. As we shall see when we come to Omri's son Ahab, the problems of reconstructing this period are formidable.

A final uncertainty is whether it was Omri or his son Ahab who fortified towns such as Hazor and Megiddo and constructed their magnificent water systems. If it was Ahab, he could not have done it without the conditions created by his father. And by moving Israel's capital to the impregnable and strategically-placed Samaria, Omri changed the face of Israel's history. It is no accident that, in spite of the Bible's overwhelming theological interests, the main theatre of action for its narratives immediately following Omri, from 1 Kings 17 to 2 Kings 11, is Israel rather than Judah.

The inscription of Mesha, which contains a mention of Omri.

THE MESHA INSCRIPTION

The Mesha Inscription, also known as the Moabite Stone, was discovered in 1868 in the town of Dhiban (ancient Dibon) in southern Transjordan just to the north of the spectacular wadi el-Mujib, the ancient Arnon gorge. It contains 34 lines of text written in a language very similar to Hebrew, and is one of the most important non-biblical inscriptions ever discovered. The original monument is now in the Louvre in Paris.

Dating from around 850 BC it was set up by Mesha, king of Moab, in honour of the Moabite god Chemosh. Its value for biblical studies is immense because it mentions Omri, and the fact that Omri had afflicted Moab for many years in the days of Mesha's father or grandfather. It also mentions that Israelites belonging to the tribe of Gad had dwelt 'in the land of Ataroth from of old' and how Mesha had fought against and captured the city at the command of Chemosh, killing all 7,000 inhabitants. This latter claim, which may be more rhetoric than reality, is to be compared with those parts of the book of Joshua in which God commands Joshua to kill all the inhabitants of cities captured by him (cf. Joshua 6:21). In 2 Kings 3:4-27 there is an account of an expedition against Mesha led by Omri's grandson, Jehoram. The coalition of the kings of Israel, Judah and Edom inflicts heavy casualties on Mesha, until Mesha sacrifices his eldest son to Chemosh, bringing him victory and great wrath upon Israel.

אַחְאָב Ahab

c. 873–853 BC

Ahab, a detail from the painting
Jezebel and Ahab with Elijah, by
Frederic Leighton (1836–96).

AHAB	
Born	*Buried*
Samaria	Samaria
Father	*Bible references*
Omri	1 Kings
Son	16:29–22:40
Ahaziah	

Ahab the son of Omri did evil in the sight of the LORD more than all that were before him.

1 Kings 16:30

In contrast to the meagre information offered by the Bible on the reign of Omri (1 Kings 16:15-28), a full six chapters (1 Kings 16:29–22:40) are devoted to his son Ahab. Ahab also appears in Assyrian records, but while the Mesha Inscription does mention Omri's son (unnamed), this is more likely to be a reference to Omri's grandson Jehoram. One reason for the comparatively large amount of space devoted by the Bible to Ahab is that his reign coincides with the time when the prophet Elijah was active. Thus, some of the material in 1 Kings 17–22 concerns Elijah rather than Ahab.

A bronze ring inscribed 'Ahab King of Israel'. Unfortunately it was not found in an excavation and so its exact date and context are unknown.

Frustratingly, whereas it might be expected that the greater availability of evidence both in the Bible and in Assyrian records might ease the task of reconstructing Ahab's reign, the opposite is the case. The biblical and extra-biblical material disagree, and it is likely that events from a slightly later period in Israel's history were mistakenly transferred to the time of Ahab.

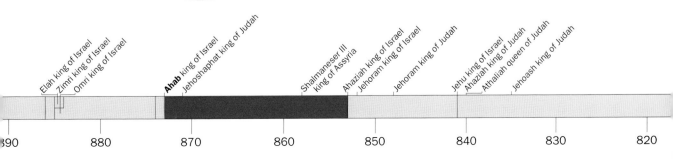

Elah king of Israel
Zimri king of Israel
Omri king of Israel
Ahab king of Israel
Jehoshaphat king of Judah
Shalmaneser III king of Assyria
Ahaziah king of Israel
Jehoram king of Israel
Jehoram king of Judah
Jehu king of Israel
Ahaziah king of Judah
Athaliah queen of Judah
Jehoash king of Judah

890   880   870   860   850   840   830   820

The letters on this grey stone seal are the Phoenician form of the name Jezebel, and the seal possibly therefore belonged to the queen. It dates to the 9th–8th century BC, but it is not known exactly where it was found.

A dejected Ahab and a defiant Jezebel face the wrath of the prophet Elijah over the judicial murder of Naboth. Elijah foretells a violent death for them both. *Jezebel and Ahab with Elijah*, by Frederic Leighton (1836–96).

In the thirty-eighth year of Asa king of Judah, Ahab the son of Omri began to reign over Israel, and Ahab the son of Omri reigned over Israel in Samaria twenty-two years. And Ahab the son of Omri did evil in the sight of the LORD more than all that were before him. And as if it had been a light thing for him to walk in the sins of Jeroboam the son of Nebat, he took for wife Jezebel the daughter of Ethbaal king of the Sidonians, and went and served Baal, and worshipped him.

1 Kings 16:29-31

The biblical account

Pulling no punches, the biblical account of Ahab begins by describing him as the most evil Israelite king so far. Two features are singled out for criticism: not only does Ahab marry Jezebel, a princess of the maritime city of Sidon, but he even builds a temple to Baal in Samaria. Having thus aroused the anger of God, Ahab is confronted by the prophet Elijah. As punishment, Elijah proclaims a prolonged drought lasting for two to three years (1 Kings 17:1). Towards the end of this period he presents himself once more before Ahab and enters into a contest on Mt Carmel with the prophets of Baal, whom Jezebel has favoured. Elijah is victorious and the prophets of Baal are killed. To escape Jezebel's anger Elijah flees to Mt Horeb (usually taken to be Mt Sinai) where he is instructed by God to anoint Hazael as king over Damascus and Jehu as king over Israel (1 Kings 19:15-16). This last detail creates problems for us. Jehu became king of Israel in 841 BC, and Hazael usurped the throne of Damascus at around the same time, that is, some twelve years after the death of Ahab. However, the impression is given in 1 Kings 19:15 that Elijah is to anoint Hazael immediately.

There then follow three wars between Ahab and the king of Damascus who is named Ben-hadad. In the first, Ben-hadad besieges Samaria, and it

ELIJAH

The prophet Elijah and the ravens (1 Kings 17:6) in an Ethiopic manuscript.

Elijah is introduced abruptly into the biblical narrative at 1 Kings 17:1 and remains a dominant figure until he is taken up into heaven in 2 Kings 2. His town of origin is Tishbe in Transjordanian Gilead, and he is presented as the leader of prophetic groups that live on the margins of society. Elijah himself is involved in the politics of the nation, challenging the actions of Ahab and queen Jezebel and upholding the religion of the God of Israel against that of the Canaanite god Baal. In one famous passage he challenges the prophets of Baal to bring down fire upon a sacrifice on Mt Carmel, and in another, having fled to Mt Horeb, he witnesses the divine presence not in a strong wind, an earthquake or fire, but in a 'still small voice'.

is only by acting on the instructions of an unnamed prophet that Ahab brings off a surprise counter-attack, lifts the siege and routs the Syrians. The second encounter is at Aphek (possibly at En-gev on the south-east shore of the Sea of Galilee) when Ahab again defeats the Syrians, and captures and spares Ben-hadad. It is on this occasion that the Syrian king promises to restore to Israel the cities which his father took from Omri (see p. 102). The third battle is at Ramoth-gilead (possibly Tel Ramith in Jordan) at which Ahab is killed. Interspersed with these battles is the story of Naboth's vineyard (1 Kings 21). Naboth, having refused to sell his vineyard to Ahab, is found guilty on a false charge of blasphemy contrived by Jezebel, and stoned to death. Elijah confronts Ahab and foretells a violent death for him and Jezebel (1 Kings 21:19).

The Assyrian account

In the records of the Assyrian king Shalmaneser III (858–824 BC), there is a description of an expedition in 853 in which Shalmaneser marched down through northern Syria, capturing Aleppo and Hamath on the way, until, at Karkara, he defeated a coalition of twelve kings including Adad-'idri (i.e. Hadadezer) of Damascus who had contributed 1,200 chariots and 20,000 foot soldiers, and Ahab the Israelite, who had contributed 2,000 chariots and 10,000 foot soldiers.

Several questions are raised by this information. First, why is the king of Syria (Damascus), who was Ahab's contemporary, called Ben-hadad in the Bible but Hadadezer in the Assyrian records? Three answers are possible: that Adad-'idri is an alternative form of Ben-hadad; that Ben-hadad is a title and not a name (and thus there is no discrepancy); or that one source (probably the Assyrian) is correct and the other (probably the Bible) is incorrect. A second question is why, given that Shalmaneser's expedition was in the year that the king of Damascus is supposed to have killed the king of Israel in battle, the two kings were on the same side in opposing Shalmaneser. This is not an insoluble problem – it is not unknown for allies to fall out with each other. A third point is that Ahab's large number of chariots (2,000) sits uneasily with that part of the narrative of the second war between Ahab and Ben-hadad (1 Kings 20:23-25) in which it is stated that the Israelites excel in fighting in the hills whereas the Syrians are stronger on the plains. This can only mean that the Syrians are superior in chariotry; yet Ahab fielded more chariots against the Assyrians than did his Syrian ally.

It is certainly possible to reconstruct the reign of Ahab to harmonize the biblical and extra-biblical materials. The view taken here, however, is that 1 Kings 17–22 gives a largely misleading account, and that material from a later reign – that of Jehoram – has been mistakenly attributed to Ahab. This interpretation can probably also be extended to the account of the death of Ahab in 1 Kings 22. At 2 Kings 8:28-9 Jehoram, Ahab's grandson, is badly wounded when fighting the king of Damascus at Ramoth-gilead, and this is most likely the basis also for 1 Kings 22.

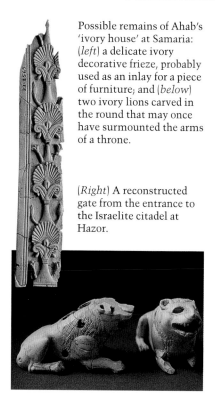

Possible remains of Ahab's 'ivory house' at Samaria: (*left*) a delicate ivory decorative frieze, probably used as an inlay for a piece of furniture; and (*below*) two ivory lions carved in the round that may once have surmounted the arms of a throne.

(*Right*) A reconstructed gate from the entrance to the Israelite citadel at Hazor.

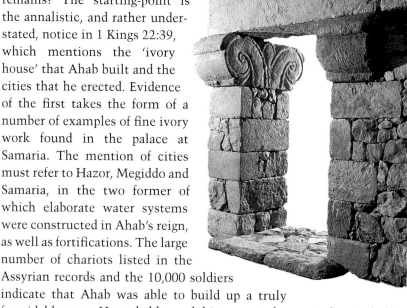

This staircase forms part of the massive water system at Hazor, which was probably constructed in the reign of Ahab. Five flights of steps lead to a tunnel 82 ft (25 m) in length which reaches to the level of the water.

Overview

If the general picture provided by 1 Kings 17–22 is abandoned, what remains? The starting-point is the annalistic, and rather under-stated, notice in 1 Kings 22:39, which mentions the 'ivory house' that Ahab built and the cities that he erected. Evidence of the first takes the form of a number of examples of fine ivory work found in the palace at Samaria. The mention of cities must refer to Hazor, Megiddo and Samaria, in the two former of which elaborate water systems were constructed in Ahab's reign, as well as fortifications. The large number of chariots listed in the Assyrian records and the 10,000 soldiers indicate that Ahab was able to build up a truly formidable army. He probably used this to control Transjordan, including Moab, and it is likely that Judah was also under his control. He continued his father's policy of alliances with other small states where necessary, for example through his marriage – with its disastrous consequences – to Jezebel, daughter of the king of Sidon.

On the religious side, Ahab was a pragmatist rather than a devout man. There is no reason to doubt that he encouraged his wife's religion, and that he built a temple to Baal in Samaria. The confiscation of Naboth's property on a trumped-up charge and the prophetic opposition which this (and probably other unrecorded incidents) provoked is conso-nant with an autocratic style of strong leadership backed by economic prosperity and a power-ful army. If Ahab had a need for a religion at all, it would have been one that sanctioned his actions rather than the prophetic Yahwism that condemned him for his abuse of power. It is understandable that the biblical tradition should want to blacken him and to ascribe to him a violent death. He probably died peacefully, leaving to his descendants a world troubled by the growing ambitions of the Assyrian king Shalmaneser III.

אֲחַזְיָה **Ahaziah**
853–852 BC

יְהוֹרָם **Jehoram**
852–841 BC

Ahaziah; a detail from a Bible illumination of the first half of the 12th century AD.

AHAZIAH	
Born	*Buried*
? Samaria	Samaria
Father	*Bible references*
Ahab	1 Kings 22:51-3;
Son	2 Kings 1:1-18
None	

AHAZIAH

Ahab was succeeded by his son Ahaziah, whose reign lasted for only two years, according to 1 Kings 22:51. However, this figure is not without difficulties as will be seen when Jehoram's reign is discussed. The biblical record implies (1 Kings 22:52) that Ahaziah's mother was the foreign princess Jezebel. However, his name could be taken to mean 'Yah has grasped'; that is, it is compounded with a form of Yahweh although he is described as a servant of Baal.

Virtually all we are told about his reign is that he was seriously injured in a fall in his palace in Samaria and that he later died of his injuries (2 Kings 1:2-17). His injury serves as the context for the reappearance of Elijah, who intercepts a group of messengers sent by Ahaziah to the god Baal-zebub of Ekron, to enquire whether he would recover. On hearing of the whereabouts of Elijah, Ahaziah sends a captain with 50 men to conduct the prophet to his presence. It is only after two such groups have been destroyed by fire from heaven that a third group brings Elijah to Ahaziah, where the prophet tells the king that he will not recover. While the legendary and folkloristic features of the story are obvious, the kernel is probably true – that Ahaziah died from a serious accident in his palace.

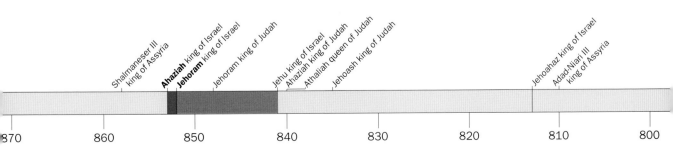

Shalmaneser III king of Assyria
Ahaziah king of Israel
Jehoram king of Israel
Jehoram king of Judah
Jehu king of Israel
Ahaziah king of Judah
Athaliah queen of Judah
Jehoash king of Judah
Jehoahaz king of Israel
Adad-Niari III king of Assyria

870   860   850   840   830   820   810   800

Now Ahaziah fell through the lattice in his upper chamber in Samaria, and lay sick; so he sent messengers, telling them, 'Go, inquire of Baal-zebub, the god of Ekron, whether I shall recover from this sickness'. But the angel of the LORD said to Elijah the Tishbite, 'Arise, go up to meet the messengers of the king of Samaria, and say to them, "Is it because there is no God in Israel that you are going to inquire of Baal-zebub, the god of Ekron?" Now therefore thus says the LORD, You shall not come down from the bed to which you have gone, but you shall surely die.' So Elijah went.... So he died according to the word of the LORD which Elijah had spoken. Jehoram, his brother, became king in his stead in the second year of Jehoram the son of Jehoshaphat, king of Judah, because Ahaziah had no son.

2 Kings 1:2-4, 17

It is the outcome of this self-contained unit (2 Kings 1:2-17) that raises a chronological problem. Ahaziah is said to be succeeded by his brother Jehoram in the second year of Jehoram, son of Jehoshaphat, the king of Judah. This latter king (also called Joram in the biblical account) probably acceded in 848 BC, and his second year would be 847/6 BC. On this chronology, Ahaziah's reign lasted for six or seven years, not the two years given at 1 Kings 22:5. Reconciling these discrepancies is very

Scenes from the life of Elijah, from a Bible illumination of the first half of the 13th century. In the penultimate roundel in the left-hand column, Elijah declares his fate to the injured Ahaziah. Next to this in the right-hand column, Elijah is taken up to heaven in a chariot, while Elisha receives his mantle.

complex, especially when, as in this case, the ancient Greek version of 2 Kings 1:17-18 differs from the traditional Hebrew version. According to the Greek (4 Kingdoms 1:18), Jehoram acceded in the 18th year of Jehoshaphat, i.e. 852, thus confirming the two-year reign of Ahaziah; but this should not be regarded as a simple and obvious solution to the difficulty. Later in this volume (p. 129) it will be suggested that the Israelite king Jehoram is in fact identical with the Judahite king of the same name. That, however, must remain for the section on Judah.

JEHORAM	
Born	Buried
? Samaria	Jezreel
Father	Bible references
Ahab	2 Kings 3:1–9:26
Son	
Unnamed	

JEHORAM

Jehoram did what was evil in the sight of the LORD though not like his father and mother.

2 Kings 3:2

Jehoram (he is also called Joram) was the son of Ahab and Jezebel. His reign spans several chapters, from 2 Kings 1:17 to 9:26, but as in the case of Ahab, much of this material is devoted to the prophet Elijah, and his successor Elisha. Various battles between the Israelite and Syrian kings are described, without the names of the kings being explicitly mentioned, and it is clear that these stories could come from the reigns of several kings. However, the picture that emerges is one of Syrian ascendancy over Israel, and of sieges of Samaria, the Israelite capital. In an explicit reference to Jehoram, it is said that he was seriously wounded fighting the Syrians at Ramoth-gilead (possibly Tell Ramith in Jordan). It should be remembered that Ahab, his father, was said to have been killed in battle at the same place, fighting the same enemy.

The one exception to the accounts of Israelite defensiveness is the story of the expedition against Mesha king of Moab, following his rebellion against Israel after Ahab's death. In the Bible (2 Kings 3), this is described as a resounding success, but the Moabite king's own account of his revolt in the Inscription of Mesha (p. 102), presents a quite different picture, claiming that 'I have triumphed over him [Omri's grandson] and over his house, while Israel has perished for ever!' It is, of course, possible that 2 Kings 3 describes a particular incident, while the Mesha Inscription records the outcome of the whole campaign to eliminate Israel from Moab. At any rate, the Mesha Inscription could hardly have been set up publicly if its claims were not at least partly true, and it should thus be allowed that Moab's rebellion against Israel was successful.

Jehoram's reign, then, in terms of its effects on Israel, was probably one of military setbacks at the hands of Syria and Moab. It seems also that there was growing internal opposition spearheaded by the prophetic groups led by Elisha. This would soon lead to a coup d'état, and to the destruction of Omri's dynasty by the prophetically-inspired Jehu. While recovering from his wounds sustained in the battle against the Syrians at Ramoth-gilead, Jehoram was killed by Jehu near the city of Jezreel. He had reigned for 12 years.

ELISHA

Elisha, from Abel-meholah (possibly Tell Abu Sus on the western side of the river Jordan almost due east of Jabesh-gilead) was appointed by Elijah as his successor (1 Kings 19:16, 19-21). He presided over prophetic groups on the margins of society, and established a reputation as a miracle worker. He was also deeply involved in the political affairs not only of Israel but of Syria too. It was at his instigation that Jehu overthrew the dynasty of Omri and Ahab, and that Hazael usurped the Syrian throne from Ben-hadad.

יֵהוּא Jehu

841–813 BC

The commander Jehu, a detail from an engraving by Gustave Doré.

JEHU	
Born	*Buried*
Unknown	Samaria
Father	*Bible references*
Jehoshaphat	2 Kings 9:1–10:36
Son	
Jehoahaz	

Then Elisha the prophet called one of the sons of the prophets and said to him, 'Gird up your loins, and take this flask of oil in your hand, and go to Ramoth-gilead. And when you arrive, look there for Jehu the son of Jehoshaphat, son of Nimshi; and go in and bid him rise from among his fellows, and lead him to an inner chamber. Then take the flask of oil, and pour it on his head, and say, "Thus says the LORD, I anoint you king over Israel."'

2 Kings 9:1-3

The driving is like the driving of Jehu the son of Nimshi; for he drives furiously.

2 Kings 9:20

Jehu was the founder of the fourth, and longest, dynasty of the northern kingdom, his descendants ruling until 747 BC. He was a commander in the Israelite army, and had probably been either a member of Ahab's bodyguard or in a sufficiently senior position to ride in a chariot close to Ahab (2 Kings 9:25).

While Jehoram was recuperating in his palace in Jezreel and the army was encamped against the Syrians at Ramoth-gilead, Jehu had himself proclaimed king, after which he proceeded to Jezreel where he killed Jehoram as well as the Judahite king Ahaziah, who was visiting Jehoram. Secular reasons for the coup can easily be suggested. If, as has been argued above (p. 109), Jehoram's reign saw the loss of territory in Moab as well as sieges of Samaria by the Syrian armies, it is understandable that an ambitious commander should take advantage of the absence of the wounded king from the battlefield to take over the army and proclaim himself king. However, the biblical account gives explicit religious reasons for Jehu's revolt. According to 2 Kings 9:1-13, the prophet Elisha instructed

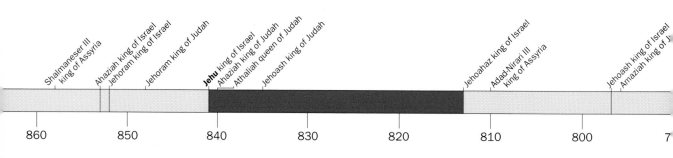

Jehu and the fate of Ahaziah, Jehoram and Jezebel, from the Bible Historiale by Guiart Desmoulins (1460/70).

(*Below*) An ivory plaque, depicting a Syrian. From Arslan Tash, Syria.

(*Below right*) 'The tribute of Jehu' – a detail from the Black Obelisk of Shalmaneser III (see p. 112).

one of his followers to travel to Ramoth-gilead, there to anoint Jehu as king. This was done privately, but when Jehu revealed to his fellow commanders what had happened, they rallied to his side. Thus Jehu's revolt is portrayed in the Bible as a prophetic revolution; and the account devotes much space to a graphic description of Jehu's elimination of the prophets of Baal and of their patron, Jezebel. The timing of the extirpation of Baalism and its wider consequences need closer examination.

Interpreting the biblical story

The records of the Assyrian king Shalmaneser III (858–824 BC) contain a description of an expedition in his 18th year (i.e. *c.* 840), directed primarily against Hazael king of Damascus. The Assyrian king claims to have killed 16,000 Syrian soldiers, to have captured 1,121 chariots and to have besieged Hazael in Damascus. At the end of the account Shalmaneser

The Black Obelisk of the Assyrian king Shalmaneser III. The 'tribute of Jehu' is in the second register from the top.

THE RECHABITES

The Rechabites are mentioned in the Bible in Jeremiah 35:1-11. Their founder, J(eh)onadab son of Rechab, is described in 2 Kings 10:15-17 as supporting the revolt of Jehu against the house of Ahab. They were forbidden by their founder to drink wine, plant vineyards or build houses and in Jeremiah their obedience to Jonadab is contrasted with the unfaithfulness of Judah towards God. According to some scholars the Rechabites perpetuated or revived a nomadic ideal of simplicity and were ardent followers of the God of Israel. While the fact that they lived in tents and abstained from wine does not necessarily mean that they were nomads (a problematic term in any case) they certainly adopted an alternative lifestyle that demonstrated their religious convictions.

asserts that 'At that time I received the tribute of the inhabitants of Tyre, Sidon, and of Jehu, son of Omri'. Jehu was not, of course, Omri's son, but the destroyer of his dynasty! Two reasons can be suggested as to why Jehu should want or need to send tribute to Shalmaneser: to prevent him from invading Israel, or as a request to him to invade Syria. The linking together of Tyre, Sidon and Israel suggests that these allies were requesting Shalmaneser to proceed against their common enemy Damascus. The tribute of Jehu, as pictured on the famous Black Obelisk of Shalmaneser III, consisted of silver, gold, various golden vessels, tin and a royal staff.

If this interpretation is correct, and Israel was still allied with Tyre and Sidon in 840, then perhaps Jehu had not yet proceeded against Jezebel and the prophets of Baal; for his murder of the princess of Sidon would presumably bring to an end any alliance with that city. Three years later the alliance may indeed have been ended: Shalmaneser records an expedition against Hazael in his 21st year (c. 837) and mentions tribute from Tyre, Sidon and Byblos, but not Israel.

Whenever Jehu eliminated Jezebel and the prophets of Baal, not to mention all the surviving members of Ahab's family (2 Kings 10:1-11), his actions severed links with Sidon and seriously weakened Israel internally. Further, the fact that Shalmaneser was unable to break the power of Hazael in Damascus and that the Assyrians then ceased to intervene in the region south of the Euphrates gave Hazael the chance to turn his attentions to Israel, with dire consequences. Hazael, as conceded in 2 Kings 10:32-3, took from Israel all its territory in northern Transjordan. A later passage (2 Kings 12:17) even records an expedition of Hazael against Gath and Jerusalem. This can only mean that Israel and Judah were powerless to prevent the Syrians from crossing the Jordan or from pressing from the north down through Israel.

Jehu's reign can thus be viewed in two different lights. As a protégé of the prophetic opposition to Omri and Ahab and a friend of the radical sect of the Rechabites (2 Kings 10:15-17), Jehu succeeded in ridding Israel of Omri's dynasty with its apparent indifference to justice and to prophetic ideals. Politically and militarily he paid a heavy price, one which the ordinary people also had to bear. He appears to have died peacefully.

יְהוֹאָחָז **Jehoahaz**
813–797 BC

יְהוֹאָשׁ **Jehoash**
797–782 BC

JEHOAHAZ	
Born	*Buried*
? Samaria	Samaria
Father	*Bible references*
Jehu	2 Kings 13:1-9
Son	
Jehoash	

JEHOAHAZ

There was not left to Jehoahaz an army of more than fifty horsemen and ten chariots and ten thousand footmen; for the king of Syria had destroyed them.

2 Kings 13:7

Jehu's son Jehoahaz merits nine verses in 2 Kings 13, yet these are more than usually informative. It is clear that the pattern of Israelite weakness in the face of Syrian dominance that had characterized Jehu's reign was continued into that of his son. Jehoahaz's army was reduced to ten chariots, 50 horsemen and 10,000 footmen (2 Kings 13:7), such was the extent of the Syrian victories. The biblical account attempts to soften this dismal picture by referring vaguely to a saviour who enabled the Israelites to escape from the Syrians and dwell in their homes (2 Kings 13:5), but in the absence of any concrete details this cannot be taken seriously. At best, it can be assumed that the 17-year rule of Jehoahaz was not continuously dominated by war, and that the Israelites enjoyed periods of uneasy peace of varying lengths. The fact that Israel's dire situation does not seem to have engendered any movements for revolt can be explained

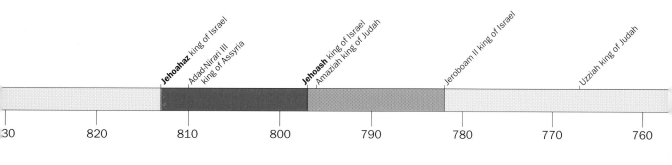

in two ways. Either the army was too weak and the people too weary to mount an effective opposition, or the prophetic groups still supported the dynasty of Jehu and rallied the people accordingly, in spite of their hardships.

JEHOASH

Jehoash came to Jerusalem, and broke down the wall of Jerusalem.

2 Kings 14:13

The Syrian commander Naaman dips himself seven times in the Jordan, as commanded by Elisha, to be cured of his leprosy. A painting by Cornelis Engebrechtsz (c. 1520).

The reign of Jehoahaz's son Jehoash (also called Joash) saw an upturn in the fortunes of Israel. Two stories enlarge the two brief annalistic accounts of his reign (2 Kings 13:10-19, 14:15-16). The first, in 2 Kings 13:14-19, is actually the story of the death of the prophet Elisha. On his deathbed, the prophet is visited by the Israelite king who is distressed at the imminent loss to the kingdom of a man regarded as a miracle worker. The prophet commands the king to take a bow and arrow and to shoot an arrow through the window towards the east. This symbolizes a divinely assisted victory over the Syrians. Next the king is commanded to strike the ground with the arrows. This he does three times, not knowing that each blow represents a victory over the Syrians. Elisha is therefore angry with him for thus limiting the number of Israelite victories.

The other story, in 2 Kings 14:8-14, is more concerned with the Judahite king Amaziah, and with the fate of Jerusalem, than with Jehoash. Nevertheless, it contains important information for reconstructing the latter's reign. A challenge is issued by the king of Judah to Jehoash to fight. Jehoash replies with one of the celebrated fables in the Old Testament, which compares Judah, likened to a thistle, to Israel which is seen as a cedar of Lebanon. In the ensuing encounter at Beth-shemesh (an important intersection between a main north–south route and a route eastwards to Jerusalem), Jehoash is victorious, Amaziah is captured, and the Israelite king is able to proceed to Jerusalem

JEHOASH	
Born	*Buried*
? Samaria	Samaria
Father	*Bible references*
Jehoahaz	2 Kings 13:10-19,
Son	14:15-16
Jeroboam	

where he destroys part of the city wall, plunders the temple and royal palace, and takes hostages back to Samaria.

Interpreting Jehoash's reign

In these two stories we can perhaps discern two parts to Jehoash's reign. In the first, the king was preoccupied with the Syrian threat which, with prophetic encouragement, he was gradually able to meet and overcome. He was assisted by external factors: one was the death of the powerful and aggressive Syrian king, Hazael; and the other was the revival of Assyrian power under Adad-nirari III (810–782 BC). According to one inscription Adad-nirari crossed the Euphrates in 805, besieged Damascus and received tribute from Hazael. Another inscription claims that Adad-nirari conquered Tyre, Sidon, Israel, Edom and Philistia – presumably an exaggeration. However, a massive exacting of tribute from Damascus is again detailed. Yet another inscription repeats details about the tribute from Damascus (with some variations), and adds that tribute was also received from Jehoash and from the Samarians, as well as from Tyre and Sidon. If this last Assyrian inscription describes an expedition in 802 BC, it could indicate that the dates normally given for the reign of Jehoash (797–782 BC) are wrong. Clearly, the Assyrian campaigns were directed primarily at the closer and more prosperous region of Syria rather than Israel. Jehoash will gladly have paid tribute to support an Assyrian campaign against Damascus.

With the Syrians once more under pressure from the north, and the death, whenever it occurred, of Hazael, Jehoash was able to recover from Damascus the territory lost by his father (2 Kings 13:24-5). How extensive this recovery was, and whether it extended to Transjordan, cannot be determined. At any rate, Jehoash was able to restore Israel's military strength to the point where he could take on and defeat the challenge of Amaziah of Judah. The second part of his reign was therefore probably one of consolidation. Freed from pressure from the north, Israel began to enjoy a period of peace and prosperity, from which Jehoash's son, Jeroboam II, would benefit greatly.

An ivory plaque showing a cow suckling a calf, part of the tribute paid by the king of Damascus to the Assyrian king Adad-Nirari III, as recorded in inscriptions. From Arslan Tash, Syria.

יָרָבְעָם Jeroboam II
782–747 BC

JEROBOAM II	
Born	*Buried*
? Samaria	? Samaria
Father	*Bible references*
Jehoash	2 Kings 14:23-29
Son	
Zechariah	

The seal of Shema, the servant of Jeroboam, from Megiddo, dating from the first half of the 8th century BC.

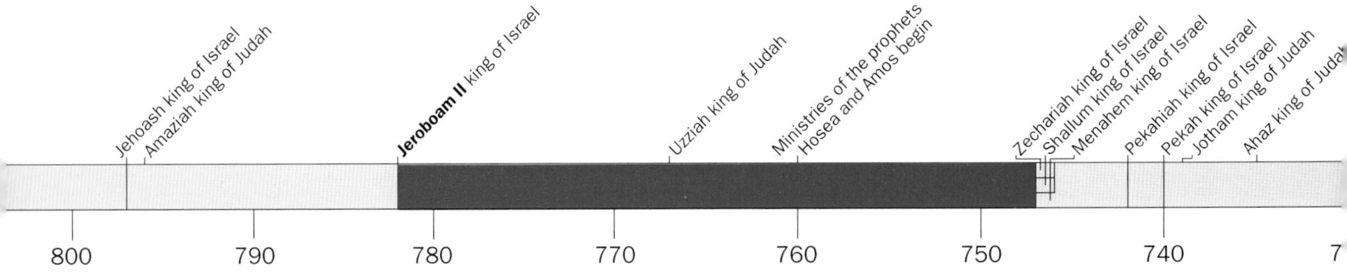

Jeroboam restored the border of Israel from the entrance of Hamath as far as the Sea of the Arabah.

2 Kings 14:25

A mere seven verses in the Bible are devoted to Jeroboam II, whose long reign was undoubtedly one of the most successful and prosperous in Israel's history. Although the Bible gives his reign as lasting for 41 years, most scholars reduce it by around five years because of other details in the biblical chronology, or suggest that Jeroboam ruled as co-regent for several years with his father Jehoash before the latter's death. The brief biblical account does list Jeroboam's achievements. He extended the northern border of Israel to the 'entrance of Hamath', by which is probably meant Lebo-hamath, modern Lebweh, north of Baalbek in Lebanon. He is also credited with capturing Damascus. In the other direction, his conquests extended to the 'Sea of the Arabah', by which is probably meant the Dead Sea, although it is not clear exactly what this implies.

Jehoash king of Israel
Amaziah king of Judah

Jeroboam II king of Israel

Uzziah king of Judah

Ministries of the prophets
Hosea and Amos begin

Zechariah king of Israel
Shallum king of Israel
Menahem king of Israel
Pekahiah king of Israel
Pekah king of Israel
Jotham king of Judah
Ahaz king of Judah

800   790   780   770   760   750   740   7

The Dead Sea – possibly what the biblical account refers to as the 'Sea of the Arabah' in its report of Jeroboam II's conquests. The sea's high concentration of salt is visible around the coastline.

The ministry of the prophet Amos

To this meagre, although impressive, information, can be added several passages from the book of the prophet Amos. Amos' ministry fell probably in the latter half of Jeroboam's reign, and the prophet's denunciations of the prosperity of the rich and powerful, the oppression of the poor and the shallowness of religious observance are generally held to reflect the social conditions of the time.

The prophet Amos, from the Bury Bible (c. 1135).

The book of Amos opens with a series of oracles against foreign nations, two of which are relevant to Jeroboam's reign. The first (Amos 1:3-5) accuses Damascus of having threshed Gilead with threshing sledges of iron, and foresees judgment coming upon Hazael and Damascus. Clearly, this refers to the bitter fighting between Syria and Israel in north Transjordan. If the judgment against Damascus is still in the future and if scholars are right to date Amos' ministry from about 760, then Jeroboam's conquest of Damascus must be dated after that year. The same logic holds with regard to the other passage (Amos 1:13-15), which condemns the Ammonites for their atrocities against Israelites in Transjordan. If Jeroboam conquered Ammon, it must have been after 760. However, certainty is not possible.

Another passage in Amos (6:13) implies that Israel had recently conquered Lodebar and Karnaim. That these places have symbolic names (meaning 'a thing of naught' and 'horns' respectively) is clear. But scholars have identified them with sites in northern Transjordan, in which case the implication again is that Jeroboam's conquests were towards the end of his reign.

The vision of luxury pictured by Amos includes the building of strongholds (presumably fortified cities), the provision of winter houses (in the warm Jordan or Jezreel valleys) and summer houses (in the cooler central hill country), the decoration of houses with ivory, the building of houses

HOSEA AND AMOS

The reign of Jeroboam II witnessed the rise of the first of the 'classical' prophets Hosea and Amos. Hosea's place of origin is not given. Amos was from Tekoa in Judah, although the fact that he prophesied in the northern kingdom, Israel, has led some scholars to look for a Tekoa in the northern kingdom. Their ministries began around 760–750 BC and lasted some 20 years. They thus covered the last years of Jeroboam's reign, and the chaos that followed his death. The importance of Amos for understanding the social conditions of the time is indicated in the section on Jeroboam. Hosea deals mostly with the religious abuses of the time, although he is critical of the revolution of Jehu 100 years earlier, whose descendant Jeroboam was. While Amos was primarily a prophet of judgment, Hosea laid more stress on God's love for Israel and on the divine longing for the people to turn back to him and not to follow foreign gods.

The prophet Hosea, from the French Bible Historiale by Guiart Desmoulins, 14th century.

of hewn stone and the planting of vineyards. While these may themselves not seem deserving of censure, the bad side of this prosperity is that merchants use false balances and measures of quantity, and landowners dispossess the poor and needy. Justice is corrupted, and bribes ensure the outcome of disputes in favour of the rich.

Amos also mentions an expectation of the imminent arrival of the 'day of the Lord' (5:18). It may well be that Israel's victories, the enlargement of territory and the prosperity that this new-found power brought, engendered the expectation that God was about to grant a permanent Golden Age to Israel. However, Amos warns that the day of the Lord, if it comes, will be darkness rather than light; and his whole message is one of impending disaster and judgment.

It is indeed the case that, within 25 years of Jeroboam's death his enlarged and prosperous kingdom had ceased to exist. That his prosperity and his kingdom's demise owed much to external factors cannot be denied. But a fool can make a disaster out of the most propitious circumstances; and if Jeroboam made the most of favourable conditions, then he was no fool, but an able and successful ruler by secular standards.

זְכַרְיָהוּ **Zechariah**
747 BC

שַׁלּוּם **Shallum**
747 BC

מְנַחֵם **Menahem**
747–742 BC

פְּקַחְיָה **Pekahiah**
742–740 BC

פֶּקַח **Pekah**
740–731 BC

הוֹשֵׁעַ **Hoshea**
731–722/1 BC

Tiglath-pileser III, from a wall painting from Tell Ahmar (Til Barsip), Syria.

In the days of Pekah King of Israel Tiglath-pileser king of Assyria came … and he carried the people captive to Assyria.

2 Kings 15:29

The fact that no fewer than six kings reigned during the last 25 years of the existence of the northern kingdom, Israel, contrasts starkly with the stability which preceded this period. Some of the reasons for the instability can be put forward with reasonable certainty. In 745 BC a new Assyrian king, Tiglath-pileser III, came to the throne, and began to extend his empire southwards towards Syria and Israel. The Israelite king Menahem is recorded in both the Assyrian and biblical records as having paid tribute; and no doubt the successful revolt against his son Pekahiah was carried out in the name of resistance to Assyria. Much about this period is obscure, however. Correlation between the biblical and Assyrian records is not straightforward, and the biblical information raises problems. For example, the length of Pekah's reign is estimated above as nine or ten years, whereas the Bible gives a figure of twenty. Similarly, the five years given for Menahem ignores the biblical figure of ten.

The last ruler of the dynasty of Jehu, Zechariah, reigned for only six months before being assassinated by Shallum who, in turn, was killed by

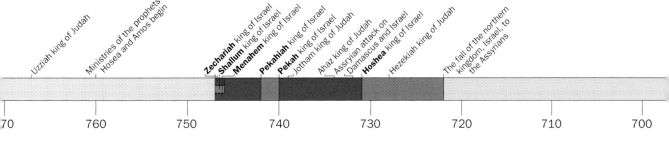

Uzziah king of Judah

Ministries of the prophets Hosea and Amos begin

Zechariah king of Israel
Shallum king of Israel
Menahem king of Israel

Pekahiah king of Israel
Pekah king of Israel
Jotham king of Judah

Ahaz king of Judah

Assyrian attack on Damascus and Israel

Hoshea king of Israel

Hezekiah king of Judah

The fall of the northern kingdom, Israel, to the Assyrians

70   760   750   740   730   720   710   700

THE LAST SIX KINGS OF ISRAEL	

ZECHARIAH
Father
  Jeroboam
	PEKAHIAH
	Father
	  Menahem

SHALLUM
Father
  Jabesh
	PEKAH
	Father
	  Remaliah

MENAHEM
Father
  Gadi
Son
  Pekahiah
	HOSHEA
	Father
	  Elah
	
	Bible references
	  2 Kings 15:8-30,
	  17:1-6

The prophet Isaiah, between night and dawn, from a Byzantine illuminated manuscript.

Menahem after reigning for just one month. Why these assassinations took place is not known. It has been suggested that Jabesh and Gadi, the names of the fathers of Shallum and Menahem (2 Kings 15:10, 14), actually refer to their places of origin, namely Jabesh-gilead and Gad. This would indicate that a group or groups from Transjordan took over the government of Israel, perhaps in order to safeguard the interests of that vulnerable region. Shallum and Menahem could have been rival officers in the army. A possible interpretation of a very difficult verse (2 Kings 15:16) is that, on his way from Transjordan to Samaria, Menahem sacked the old capital of Tirzah because it would not join his revolt and he is said to have ripped open the pregnant women in the city.

In 2 Kings 15:19-20 we read that Pul (Tiglath-pileser) came up against Israel and that Menahem paid a thousand talents of silver in tribute. In confirmation of this a fragmentary Assyrian annal also lists Menahem of Samaria as paying tribute. The biblical account informs us that the sum was raised by imposing a tax of 50 shekels on wealthy citizens. This undoubtedly unpopular move probably led to the assassination of Menahem's son Pekahiah after a reign of only one or two years (2 Kings 15:23). The assassin, Pekah, was supported by 50 Gileadites (2 Kings 15:25) and is described as Pekahiah's captain. His coup can be interpreted as a stand against subservience to the Assyrians.

From the records in 2 Kings we learn only that Pekah lost large parts of his territory to the Assyrians and that he was killed and succeeded by Hoshea (2 Kings 15:29-30). Other material enlarges this scant information. In Isaiah 7:1-9 there is an account of a coalition between Pekah and king Rezin of Damascus against king Ahaz of Judah. No reason is given for this hostile move, but it is not fanciful to suppose that the two kings were trying to force Ahaz to join them in a stand against the Assyrians.

Ignoring the advice of the prophet Isaiah (p. 136) to trust in God, Ahaz appealed to Tiglath-pileser for help. The Assyrian, whom we may imagine was more than happy to do so, moved against Damascus and Israel, probably around the period 734 to 732 BC. He captured Galilee and Transjordan, leaving only the Samaria hills to Israel. Tiglath-pileser's annals claim that:

Israel … all its inhabitants [and] their possessions I led to Assyria. They overthrew their king Pekah … and I placed Hoshea … as king over them. I received from them 10 talents of gold, 1,000 (?) talents of silver as their [tri]bute and brought them to Assyria.

This does not contradict the biblical record – Hoshea could have been the person through whom the people overthrew Pekah, and Tiglath-pileser could have confirmed him as king on payment of tribute. It certainly illumines the biblical account.

The reign of Hoshea is described in 2 Kings 17:1-6. It is said that he paid tribute to the new king Shalmaneser V but that he

THE FALL OF SAMARIA

The Bible

Against him came up Shalmaneser king of Assyria; and Hoshea became his vassal, and paid him tribute. But the king of Assyria found treachery in Hoshea; for he had sent messengers to So, king of Egypt, and offered no tribute to the king of Assyria, as he had done year by year; therefore the king of Assyria shut him up, and bound him in prison. Then the king of Assyria invaded all the land and came to Samaria, and for three years he besieged it. In the ninth year of Hoshea the king of Assyria captured Samaria, and he carried the Israelites away to Assyria, and placed them in Halah, and on the Habor, the river of Gozan, and in the cities of the Medes.

2 Kings 17:3-6

Assyrian inscriptions

... [I re]ceived from him. Israel ['Omri-Land' Bît Humria] ... all its inhabitants (and) their possessions I led to Assyria. They overthrew their king Pekah and I placed Hoshea as king over them. I received from them 10 talents of gold, 1,000 (?) talents of silver as their [tri]bute and brought them to Assyria.

Tiglath-pileser III

I surrounded and deported as prisoners 27,290 of its inhabitants, together with their chariots and the gods in whom they trusted. From them I equipped 200 chariots... while the rest I made to take up their lot within Assyria. I restored the city of Samaria and made it more habitable than before. I brought into it people from the countries conquered by my own hands. My official I set over them as district governor and reckoned them as people of Assyria itself.

Sargon, Nimrud Prism IV.25–41

A detail of a relief from the palace of Sargon II at Khorsabad, showing captives used as forced labour.

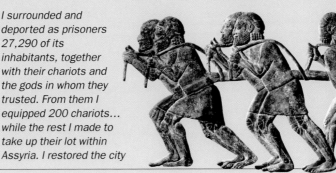

A seal inscribed 'Belonging to Abdi, servant of Hoshea'. Hoshea was the last king of the northern kingdom, Israel.

A relief from the palace of Sargon II at Khorsabad, northern Iraq. With his capture of Samaria, Sargon (left) brought to an end the existence of the northern kingdom, Israel. Here he is seen receiving men bearing offerings.

then rebelled against the Assyrians, possibly in league with Egypt, although attempts to identify king So of Egypt (2 Kings 17:4) have not met with agreement. A siege of the capital Samaria lasted three years before its capitulation – a tribute to the site chosen by Omri. The Assyrian king who ended over 200 years of the northern kingdom's existence was not Shalmaneser, however, but Sargon II, in 722/1. Assyrian records state that 27,290 Israelites were sent into exile. Whether or not this is true, the northern kingdom, Israel, was no more.

THE DIVIDED MONARCHY: JUDAH

Rehoboam
c. 931–914 BC

Abijam
c. 914–911 BC

Asa
c. 911–871 BC

Jehoshaphat
871–848 BC

Jehoram
848–841 BC

Ahaziah
841–840 BC

Athaliah
840–835 BC

Jehoash
835–796 BC

Amaziah
796–767 BC

Uzziah
c. 767–739 BC

Jotham
c. 739–734 BC

Ahaz
c. 734–728 BC

Hezekiah
c. 728–698 BC

Manasseh
698–643 BC

Amon
642–641 BC

Josiah
640–609 BC

Jehoahaz
609 BC

Jehoiakim
609–598 BC

Jehoiachin
597 BC

Zedekiah
597–587 BC

THE EXILE
587–539 BC

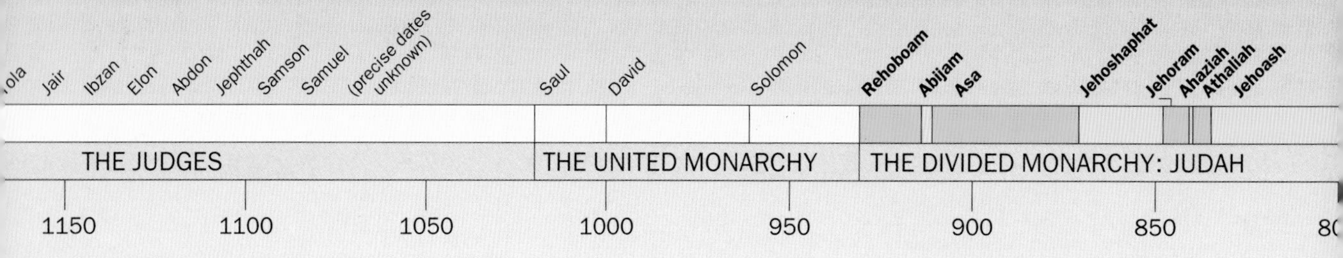

Tola Jair Ibzan Elon Abdon Jephthah Samson Samuel (precise dates unknown) Saul David Solomon Rehoboam Abijam Asa Jehoshaphat Jehoram Ahaziah Athaliah Jehoash

| THE JUDGES | THE UNITED MONARCHY | THE DIVIDED MONARCHY: JUDAH |

1150   1100   1050   1000   950   900   850   80

Rehoboam

Hezekiah

Manasseh

THE DIVIDED MONARCHY: JUDAH
c. 931–539 BC

IN CONTRAST TO THE NORTHERN KINGDOM, Israel, one dynasty, that of David, ruled in Judah for over 450 years. Succession was not trouble free, however: assassination or deposition of a king by a foreign ruler were not unknown. But the dynasty of David always overcame these setbacks until the Babylonian destruction of Jerusalem in 587 BC and the resulting disruption of political life in Judah eventually brought the line to an end.

Probably the main reason for such stability was the small size of Judah and the large size of Jerusalem in proportion. Although very little is known about the administration of Judah, it is reasonable to suppose that a form of control based on the army and court officials left scant opportunity for dissent, at any rate from the 8th century BC onwards. Also, because Judah was in effect a one-tribe state (it also included Benjamin, but this was hardly a factor) there was no inter-tribal rivalry as an incentive for dynastic change. To what extent religious factors played a part is difficult to ascertain. In its final form, the Old Testament makes much of Jerusalem as the chosen dwelling-place of God and the Davidic dynasty as the embodiment of an eternal covenant between God and the people. While it is not impossible that this ideology was a factor in Judah's stability, it may mask a degree of religious pluralism in pre-Exilic Judah. This would not have destabilized the dynasty – but it did criticize it. Probably, and paradoxically, this ideology, stressing the permanence of the Davidic dynasty, reached its developed form after the Exile, when Judah's political independence was already lost.

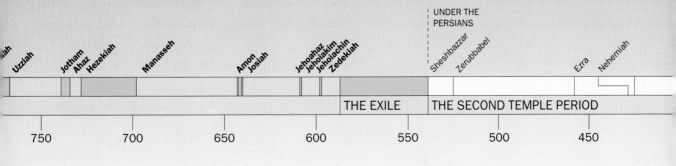

רְחַבְעָם **Rehoboam**
c. 931–914 BC

אֲבִיָם **Abijam**
c. 914–911 BC

אָסָא **Asa**
c. 911–871 BC

Rehoboam, a detail from the painted wooden ceiling of the church of St Martin, Graubuenden, Switzerland (*c.* 1130/40).

REHOBOAM	
Born	*Buried*
? Jerusalem	Jerusalem
Father	*Bible references*
Solomon	1 Kings 12:1-24,
Mother	14:21-31;
Naamah the	2 Chronicles 10:1-
Ammonite	12–12:16
Son	
Abijam	

REHOBOAM

Rehoboam spoke to them according to the counsel of the young men, saying, 'My father made your yoke heavy, but I will add to your yoke'.

1 Kings 12:14

Rehoboam, the son of Solomon and an Ammonite princess, Naamah (2 Kings 14:31), is portrayed as the king directly responsible for the division of the kingdom after Solomon's death. At a meeting with the northern tribes in the old northern capital of Shechem, Rehoboam refuses to lighten the burdens that Solomon's rule had imposed on the people and even threatens to increase them (1 Kings 12:1-15). Consequently, the ten northern tribes rebel. This story provides the sufficient cause of the division; that there were also necessary causes is clear from the biblical material itself. Jeroboam, the first king of the breakaway Israel, is encouraged by a prophet to rebel, thus indicating prophetic opposition to Solomon. Further, this prophet comes from Shiloh, the ancient northern sanctuary, whose personnel may well have looked askance at the new royal sanctuary of Jerusalem, with its temple designed by a non-Israelite. Jeroboam's call to his people, after he had

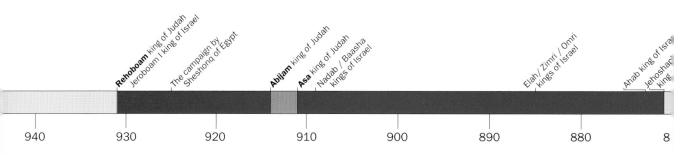

Rehoboam king of Judah
Jeroboam I king of Israel

The campaign by Sheshonq of Egypt

Abijam king of Judah

Asa king of Judah
Nadab / Baasha kings of Israel

Elah / Zimri / Omri kings of Israel

Ahab king of Isra
Jehoshap king

940   930   920   910   900   890   880   8

Rehoboam went to Shechem, for all Israel had come to Shechem to make him king. Then Jeroboam returned from Egypt. And they sent and called him; and Jeroboam and all the assembly of Israel came and said to Rehoboam, 'Your father made our yoke heavy. Now therefore lighten the hard service of your father and his heavy yoke upon us, and we will serve you'. He said to them, 'Depart for three days, then come again to me'. So the people went away. So Jeroboam and all the people came to Rehoboam the third day, as the king said, 'Come to me again the third day'. And the king answered the people harshly, and forsaking the counsel which the old men had given him, he spoke to them according to the counsel of the young men, saying, 'My father made your yoke heavy, but I will add to your yoke; my father chastised you with whips, but I will chastise you with scorpions'.

1 Kings 12:1, 2b-5, 12-14

Rehoboam meets the representatives of the northern tribes at Shechem (1 Kings 12:1-5), by Hans Holbein the Younger.

set up bull images at Bethel and Dan – 'Here are your gods [or: here is your God] O Israel, who brought you up out of the land of Egypt' (1 Kings 12:28) – could have been a re-assertion of the Exodus faith as opposed to the Judahite cult based on the royal dynasty in Jerusalem. The causes of the division were thus many, and not simply the result of Rehoboam's hard line.

An immediate question is why Rehoboam did not try to reunite the kingdom by force. Although Judah was much smaller than Israel, it presumably had a standing army that could have defeated Israel. Here the biblical material is contradictory. On the one hand, 1 Kings 12:21-24 relates that Rehoboam assembled an army precisely in order to reunite the kingdom, and that he decided not to proceed because of a prophetic warning. On the other, the annalistic note at 1 Kings 14:30 records that there was war between Rehoboam and Jeroboam continually. This latter information sounds the more plausible, and indicates that, in spite of a superior standing army, Rehoboam was unable to re-conquer the larger northern kingdom.

It is claimed in 2 Chronicles 11:5-11 that Rehoboam fortified a number of cities in Judah and Benjamin. Whether this can be supported by archaeology is disputed. Only a few of the cities have been, or can be, excavated, including Lachish and Azekah. However, it is not possible to distinguish between work possibly dating to the reign of Solomon, and what might have been done in the next generation. What is undisputed, however, is that the expedition of the Egyptian pharaoh Sheshonq I (the

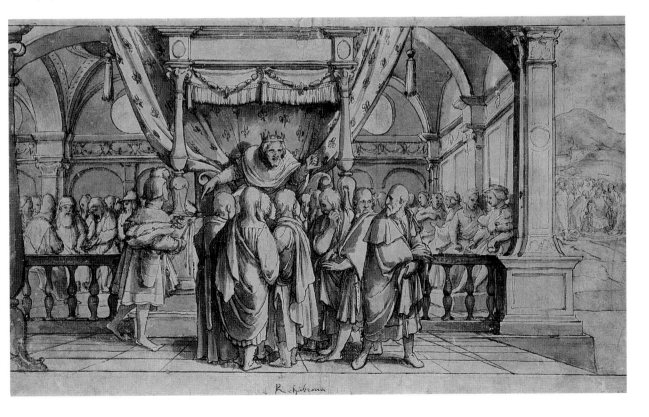

Rehoboam, from the Bible Historiale by Guiart Desmoulins, 14th century, French.

THE BOOKS OF CHRONICLES

Any account of the history of the kings of Judah from Rehoboam onwards has to decide what to do with the material in the two books of Chronicles. This is not a problem for the kings of Israel, since they are almost completely disregarded in Chronicles, leaving only the books of Kings as the source of biblical information about them. Chronicles, however, deals fully with many kings of Judah.

The reliability of Chronicles as an historical source has been a contentious issue for nearly 200 years. A standard view – recently challenged – is that the writer(s) of Chronicles used the books of Kings as a source.

The question then centres upon the material that is found in Chronicles but is not present in Kings. Is it based upon ancient archival material? Can it be verified by archaeology? Varying answers have been given, although there is general agreement that Chronicles is a late work, compiled around 400–350 BC. In what follows, attention will be drawn to additional material in Chronicles, and its historical reliability will be assessed in each case.

biblical Shishak) in 925 affected Judah (p. 95). Although Sheshonq probably did not come up against Jerusalem itself (contra 1 Kings 14:25 and 2 Chronicles 12:2), Rehoboam raided the temple and palace treasuries in order to pay tribute to avert the threat. Thus, his was an unsuccessful reign judged politically and materially. He inherited a small kingdom and died having lost at least two-thirds of it, as well as having handed over as tribute much of the wealth that Solomon had accumulated.

ABIJAM	
Born	*Buried*
? Jerusalem	Jerusalem
Father	*Bible references*
Rehoboam	1 Kings 15:1-8;
Mother	2 Chronicles 13:
Maacah	1-22

ABIJAM

The brief reign of Abijam highlights the difficulty of using the books of Kings and Chronicles as historical sources. Even his name is in dispute: in 2 Chronicles 13:1-22 it is given as Abijah. Then 2 Chronicles 12:20 and 13:2 disagree about Abijah's parentage. According to the first Abijah's mother was Maacah daughter of Absalom; according to the second it was Micaiah daughter of Uriel of Gibeah. The account in Kings, usually held to be the more reliable, is also problematic: 1 Kings 15:2 agrees that Abijam's mother was Maacah the son of Abishalom (*sic*), but then exactly the same parentage is ascribed to Abijam's son, Asa, at 15:10!

All we learn from the brief notice of Abijam in 1 Kings 15:1-8 is that he continued the war with Jeroboam. However, 2 Chronicles 13:1-22 records an encounter between Abijah and Jeroboam in which God gives the victory to Abijah, enabling him to take Bethel, among other towns, from Israel. If this is accepted, then Abijah pushed his boundary a little to the north; but the legendary nature of the story cannot be overlooked.

ASA	
Born	*Buried*
? Jerusalem	Jerusalem
Father	*Bible references*
Abijam	1 Kings 15:9-24;
Mother	2 Chronicles
Maacah	14:1–16

ASA

There are inconsistencies also in the accounts regarding Abijam's son Asa. The statement in 1 Kings 15:16 that there was war between Asa and

The wilderness of Judaea, the area to the west of the Dead Sea also known as the Judaean Desert.

the Israelite king Baasha 'all their days' is contradicted by 2 Chronicles 14:6 which describes a period of peace, because Asa was faithful to God. While both accounts record Asa's alliance with the king of Damascus against Baasha of Israel, 2 Chronicles 14:9-15 records an invasion by Zerah the Ethiopian, which Asa repelled. Attempts to identify Zerah with an Egyptian pharaoh have not proved convincing, and if there is any truth in this story, which has all the trappings of legend, it is probably that Asa defeated a nomadic group that had penetrated from the Negev to the Shephelah.

We have more substantive information concerning Asa's alliance with Damascus. Baasha, the king of Israel, had captured and fortified Ramah, probably the modern er-Ram, some 5 miles (9 km) north of Jerusalem. From here, he was able to disrupt Jerusalem's trade routes. As a means of gaining relief, Asa sent tribute to Ben-hadad of Damascus requesting him to attack the north of Israel and to divert Baasha's attention from Judah. The tactic was successful, pressure on Judah ceased, and Asa was able to dismantle the fortifications at Ramah.

An unusual, and presumably authentic, glimpse of the human figure behind the biblical account is the information in 1 Kings 15:23 that Asa suffered from diseased feet in old age.

יְהוֹשָׁפָט **Jehoshaphat**
871–848 BC

יְהוֹאָשׁ **Jehoash**
835–796 BC

יְהוֹרָם **Jehoram**
848–841 BC

אֲמַצְיָהוּ **Amaziah**
796–767 BC

אֲחַזְיָהוּ **Ahaziah**
841–840 BC

עֲתַלְיָה **Athaliah**
840–835 BC

JEHOSHAPHAT	
Born	*Buried*
? Jerusalem	Jerusalem
Father	*Bible references*
Asa	1 Kings 22:41-50;
Mother	2 Chronicles
Azubah	17:1–20:34
Son	
Jehoram	

JEHOSHAPHAT

Jehoshaphat made peace with the king of Israel.

1 Kings 22:44

Jehoshaphat is another king for whom we have widely differing accounts in 1 Kings and 2 Chronicles. The report in 1 Kings 22:41-50 is brief and contains two points of note: that Jehoshaphat made peace with Israel, and that an attempt to build a fleet of ships based in the Gulf of Aqaba came to nothing. Some amplification of the first is given by the earlier part of 1 Kings 22, where Jehoshaphat is described as an ally of the Israelite Ahab at the battle of Ramoth-gilead. In the section on Ahab (p. 105) the difficulties of reconstructing his reign have been pointed out, and the question of whether he died in battle, as claimed by 1 Kings 22:37, has been raised. Clearly, doubts about this narrative would also affect the role of Jehoshaphat. On the other hand, it is not unlikely that Judah became a vassal of Israel during Jehoshaphat's reign. Omri and Ahab had achieved a remarkable turn around in Israel's fortunes and had transformed it into a very powerful small kingdom, which dominated Moab. If Jehoshaphat did no more than 'make peace', this would certainly be on Israel's terms.

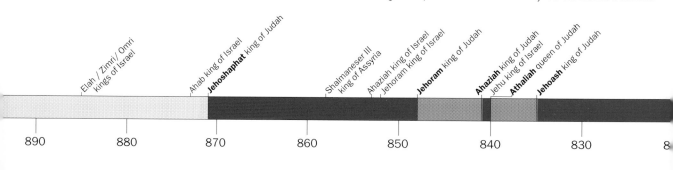

| 890 | 880 | 870 | 860 | 850 | 840 | 830 | 8 |

Now the rest of the acts of Jehoshaphat, and his might that he showed, and how he warred, are they not written in the Book of the Chronicles of the Kings of Judah? And the remnant of the male cult prostitutes who remained in the days of his father Asa, he exterminated from the land. ... Jehoshaphat made ships of Tarshish to go to Ophir for gold; but they did not go, for the ships were wrecked at Ezion-geber.

1 Kings 22:45-46, 48

In contrast, the material in 2 Chronicles 17–20 is more expansive. It describes Jehoshaphat as king of a powerful, well-fortified country, receiving tribute from Philistines and Arabs. At the end of this account he faces a coalition of forces from Moab and Ammon, which he meets and defeats in the region of Edom and Transjordan. Jehoshaphat is also credited with appointing judges to operate in all the fortified cities of Judah, as well as setting up a kind of central law court in Jerusalem. It is difficult, however, to know whether these claims rest on reliable sources.

Another reference to Jehoshaphat in 2 Kings 3:4-27 describes him as an ally of Jehoram of Israel in the latter's expedition against the king of Moab. Although not without difficulties, this is a further hint that Judah is at best a loyal ally of Israel, and at worst a vassal. Whatever the case, Jehoshaphat probably presided over a period in which Judah enjoyed the conditions that enabled Omri, Ahab and their immediate successors to develop trade links and economic prosperity. The maritime adventure in the Gulf of Aqaba, thwarted by a storm, would be consistent with this.

JEHORAM	
Born	*Buried*
? Jerusalem	Jerusalem
Father	*Bible references*
Jehoshaphat	2 Kings 1:17, 8:16-
Wife	24; 2 Chronicles
Athaliah	21:1-20
Son	
Ahaziah	

JEHORAM

On the face of it, accounting for the reign of Jehoram (also called Joram) should present no problems. A straightforward narrative in 2 Kings 8:16-24 covers his exploits, and there is an extended treatment in 2 Chronicles 21:1-17. According to these accounts, Jehoram acceded at the age of 32 and reigned for 8 years (848–841 BC), the most important incident being an abortive attempt to recover Edom after it revolted against Judah. The Chronicles version rather baldly adds that, on his accession, he killed his six younger brothers, 'and some of the officials of Israel' – presumably to secure his position. It also recounts that Judah was invaded by Philistines and Arabs, and that the invaders took captive all Jehoram's sons and wives, save for the youngest son Jehoahaz – a fact that is immediately contradicted by 2 Chronicles 22:1, which says that Jehoram was succeeded by his youngest son Ahaziah.

It has already been suggested in the section on Ahab, king of Israel (p. 105) that events from the time of Ahab's grandson, also called Jehoram, had probably been transposed to Ahab's reign, in order to make Ahab die a violent death. The critical problems of this period are extremely complex but several factors point to the possibility that, in addition to placing incidents from the reign of Jehoram into that of Ahab, the biblical material has failed to register that Jehoram of Israel and Jehoram of Judah were one and the same person. First, we have contemporary kings of

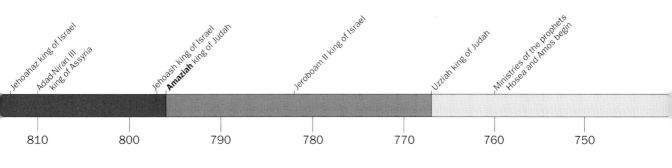

Judah and Israel with the same name. Second, unusually for a king of Judah, the notice at 2 Kings 8:17 fails to give the name of Jehoram's mother. Third, the Hebrew text at 2 Kings 8:16 reads:

> *In the fifth year of J[eh]oram son of Ahab king of Israel, Jehoshaphat being king of Judah, Jehoram son of Jehoshaphat king of Judah began to reign.*

Now the words 'Jehoshaphat being king of Judah' could, of course, be a scribal error, or they could mean that Jehoram began a co-regency with his father. However, they could also be interpreted as implying that Jehoram king of Israel usurped the throne of Judah, and united Israel and Judah under his personal rule. If this theory is correct, it has implications for the reigns of Jehoram king of Israel (p. 109), Jehoshaphat king of Judah (p. 128) and Ahaziah king of Judah (p. 130). Here we will follow the traditional picture, although the implications for Ahaziah will be indicated.

AHAZIAH	
Born	*Buried*
? Jerusalem	Jerusalem
Father	*Bible references*
Jehoram	2 Kings 8:25-29,
Mother	9:16, 27-29;
Athaliah	2 Chronicles 22:1-9
Son	
Joash	

AHAZIAH

Ahaziah's brief reign of one year is mentioned in 2 Kings 8:25-29, 9:27-29. While 2 Chronicles 22:1-9 superficially appears to repeat the Kings material plus theological embellishments, it contradicts 2 Kings 9:27-28 in one important respect. In Kings it is said that Jehu, having killed Jehoram king of Israel, pursued Ahaziah from Jezreel in the direction of Beth-haggan (possibly modern Jenin on the southern edge of the Jezreel valley), that Ahaziah was shot during the pursuit and that he then fled to Megiddo, where he died. According to 2 Chronicles 22:9, however, Ahaziah was hiding in Samaria before being caught and brought to Jehu, who had him put to death.

The introductory notice to Ahaziah's reign states that his mother was Athaliah (see below), a granddaughter of Omri (the Hebrew word for 'daughter' can also mean granddaughter), and that he was a son-in-law of the house of Ahab (2 Kings 8:26-7). If this is correct, then Jehoram his father must have married into the dynasty of Omri and Ahab, and *his* father, Jehoshaphat, must have approved. Yet while the biblical record is unanimous in its condemnation of the house of Omri and Ahab, it has nothing but praise for the uprightness of Jehoshaphat.

The problems of interpreting the biblical material at this point have already been outlined (p. 129) and the radical suggestion has been made that Jehoram of Israel and Jehoram of Judah were in fact the same person. If this is correct, then either Ahaziah did not exist, and has come into the tradition to maintain the separate identities of the two kings with the same name, or he was the son of Jehoram king of Israel. Is it only coincidence that Ahab's son was also called Ahaziah and that he reigned but briefly (1 Kings 22:51, 2 Kings 1:17)?

If Ahaziah existed, then the one thing known about him is that he joined Jehoram king of Israel in a battle against the Syrians at Ramoth-gilead, that he was wounded, and subsequently killed in Jehu's revolution against the house of Omri and Ahab.

ATHALIAH	
Born	*Buried*
? Samaria	Unknown
Father	*Bible references*
Ahab, king of Israel	2 Kings 11:1-20;
Husband	2 Chronicles
Jehoram	22:10–23:15
Son	
Ahaziah	

ATHALIAH

With the short reign of Athaliah we come to a *de facto* break in the Davidic dynasty. She was, according to 2 Kings 8:26, a daughter or granddaughter of Omri, and on the death of her son Ahaziah, she seized power and destroyed the royal house of Judah by killing all Jehoram's other sons save for the child Jehoash (also called Joash), who was concealed by Ahaziah's sister (2 Kings 11:1-3). In 2 Chronicles 22:11 the sister is named as Jeho-shabe-ath and we learn that she was married to the priest Jehoiada.

How was Athaliah able to seize and maintain power for six years? If Ahaziah's sister was married to the leading priest, then Athaliah would surely have needed supporters outside the immediate royal and priestly circles. Did she rely on the soldiers of the royal household, the very ones who apparently overthrew her six years later? Had this elite been supplied by the royal house of Israel as part of their control over Judah? Was Athaliah the wife not of Jehoram king of Judah, but of Jehoram king of Israel who, as suggested above, may have deposed Jehoshaphat and personally combined the thrones of Judah and Israel?

The violent death of Queen Athaliah (2 Kings 11:16), as depicted by Gustave Doré.

Whether or not there is anything in this scenario, we can propose the following sequence of events. After Jehoram (and Ahaziah if he existed) were killed by Jehu, Athaliah seized power in Jerusalem supported by the Israelite bodyguard that had been put there either when Jehoram deposed Jehoshaphat or when Israel took control of Judah during the reign of Omri or Ahab. Jehu was unable to follow up his own seizure of power in Israel by pressing on to Jerusalem, because he had almost immediately to face the threat posed by Shalmaneser III (see p. 112). Athaliah was thus able to hold on to power. But with the destruction of the dynasty of Omri and Ahab by Jehu, her bodyguard no longer had a loyalty to Samaria, and was eventually persuaded to take part in the coup against her. Because of her attempt to destroy the royal house of Judah, it is not clear whom Athaliah expected to succeed her. Perhaps hers was simply an act of survival, having seen all her family in Samaria wiped out by Jehu.

JEHOASH	
Born	*Son*
? Jerusalem	Amaziah
Father	*Buried*
Ahaziah	Jerusalem
Mother	*Bible references*
Zibiah of Beer-	2 Kings
sheba	11:1–12:21; 2
	Chronicles 25:1-28

JEHOASH

And Jehoash did what was right in the eyes of the LORD all his days, because Jehoiada the priest instructed him.

2 Kings 12:2

Jehoash (also Joash, and not to be confused with Jehoash of Israel), having survived Athaliah's attempt to destroy the royal house of Judah, made possible the palace revolution that ousted Athaliah and restored the rule of the Davidic dynasty. Again we have two versions of events: an account of the coup is given in 2 Kings 11:4-21, while the parallel report in 2 Chronicles 23:1-21 greatly exaggerates the proceedings. What in Kings is a clandestine operation becomes in Chronicles a national movement of whose existence Athaliah could hardly have been unaware.

The method of the coup was simple. On an appointed day the entire palace and temple guard was to assemble in the temple and protect the seven-year-old boy Jehoash while the priest Jehoiada crowned and anointed him as king. When Athaliah discovered what was happening she was arrested, taken outside the temple and killed. There followed a destruction of the temple of Baal, whose worship Athaliah had encouraged, and the enthronement of Jehoash.

Four pieces of information are given in the sources about Jehoash. First, his mother's name was Zibiah of Beer-sheba (2 Kings 12:1). This immediately arouses speculation that Jehoash was a distant member of the royal family rather than a direct descendant. Much depends on whether it is accepted that Jehoram of Israel had also taken over the throne of Judah (see p. 130). Second, Jehoash presided over a refurbishment of the temple. Third, he suffered an invasion from Hazael of Damascus which, while not directly threatening Jerusalem, induced Jehoash to use the temple treasury to pay tribute to Hazael. Finally, he was assassinated by two of his servants (2 Kings 12:19-21).

The version in 2 Chronicles 24:15-22 elaborates on the last two points by claiming that Jehoash killed Zechariah the son of the priest Jehoiada, that the invasion by Hazael was brought about by God, and that Jehoash was severely wounded in the encounter. As always, it is hard to know what to make of the Chronicles material. It may be correct to link the assassination with Jehoash's decision to pay tribute to Hazael, and he may have been the victim of a group that favoured resistance. But this is only speculation.

AMAZIAH	
Born	*Buried*
? Jerusalem	Jerusalem
Father	*Bible references*
Jehoash	2 Kings 14:1-22;
Mother	2 Chronicles
Jeho-addin of	25:1-28
Jerusalem	
Son	
Azariah (Uzziah)	

AMAZIAH

Jehoash was succeeded by his son Amaziah. His reign coincided with the beginnings of a period which saw Judah and Israel freed from interference from Damascus and Assyria, and expanding their own spheres of influence. Inevitably, they clashed. After he had secured power, Amaziah avenged the murder of his father (2 Kings 14:5). His attempt to extend his influence southwards brought victory over the Edomites in the Valley of Salt. Identifications of this unknown location vary from an area east of Beer-sheba to the plains to the south of the Dead Sea. Presumably Amaziah's move had strategic and economic motives, such as the acquisition of minerals.

Having thus met with success against Edom, Amaziah issued a challenge to Jehoash of Israel (2 Kings 14:8-14). This was certainly ill judged. Ignoring Jehoash's warnings (p. 114), Amaziah insisted on an encounter at Beth-shemesh, and was defeated and captured. His freedom was dearly bought – it required both a heavy tribute and the destruction of a stretch of the wall of Jerusalem.

Like his father, Jehoash, Amaziah was assassinated. In 2 Chronicles 25:27 this unfortunate fate is attributed to his unfaithfulness to God, and Chronicles adds details such as that he hired mercenaries from Israel. He had reigned for 25 years.

Amaziah, king of Judah, issued a challenge to Jehoash, king of Israel. Jehoash replied by comparing Judah to a thistle (2 Kings 14:9-10). From a mid-15th century English manuscript.

עֻזִּיָּה **Uzziah (Azariah)**
c. 767–739 BC

יוֹתָם **Jotham**
c. 739–734 BC

אָחָז **Ahaz**
c. 734–728 BC

An inscription dating from the 1st century BC in Aramaic, recording the relocation of the bones of king Uzziah: 'The bones of Uzziah King of Judah were brought here, and must not be reopened'.

UZZIAH	
Born	*Son*
? Jerusalem	Jotham
Father	*Buried*
Amaziah	Jerusalem
Mother	*Bible references*
Jecoliah of	2 Kings 15:1-7;
Jerusalem	2 Chronicles 26:1-
	22

UZZIAH

The LORD smote the king, so that he was a leper to the day of his death.

2 Kings 15:5

The reign of Uzziah is yet another that presents many puzzles for the historian of ancient Israel, and these begin with his name. In 2 Kings 15:1-7, usually regarded as the primary historical source, he is named throughout as Azariah. The name Uzziah occurs only once in Kings, at 15:13, in a synchronism with the reign of the Israelite Shallum. In 2 Chronicles 26:1-22, his name throughout is Uzziah; and it is this name that is found in the introductions to prophetic books such as Isaiah, Hosea and Amos. Also, the well-known passage that describes the call of Isaiah (Isaiah 6:1-13) begins 'In the year that king Uzziah died'. Various attempts, none totally convincing, have been made to explain the two names; for example, that the name used was Azariah until the king contracted 'leprosy' (a malignant, but curable skin disease is meant by the Hebrew word) after which it was Uzziah.

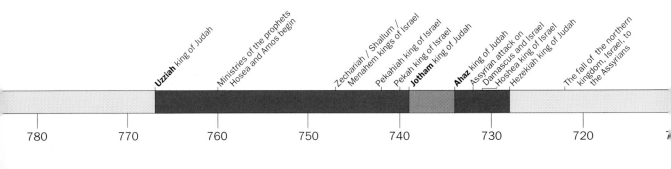

Uzziah king of Judah

Ministries of the prophets Hosea and Amos begin

Zechariah / Shallum / Menahem kings of Israel

Pekahiah king of Israel

Pekah king of Israel

Jotham king of Judah

Ahaz king of Judah

Assyrian attack on Damascus and Israel

Hoshea king of Israel

Hezekiah king of Judah

The fall of the northern kingdom, Israel, to the Assyrians

780　　　770　　　760　　　750　　　740　　　730　　　720

Another question concerns the length of the king's reign. The biblical record (2 Kings 15:2) allots him 52 years, while the figure used here is just under 30 years. All scholars agree that Uzziah cannot have ruled alone for 52 years – there is simply not enough chronological space. Accordingly, one or two periods of joint rule are envisaged by those who defend the figure of 52. One proposal is that, after Amaziah's defeat by Jehoash (p. 133), Uzziah was made co-regent. However, this does not fit well with the information at 2 Kings 14:21, according to which Uzziah was 16 years old when he acceded. Even if we take this to mean that he was 16 when he was made co-regent, it has to be asked why a recently defeated nation should feel that one so young could lead them. Another proposal is that after Uzziah contracted 'leprosy', his son Jotham took over effective government, as stated in 2 Kings 15:5, and that the years credited to Jotham's reign should run concurrently with those of Uzziah.

Yet another problem is that while the account in 2 Kings 15 is brief and does not record any events of his reign, 2 Chronicles 26 is expansive. Victories against the Philistines, Arabs and Ammonites are mentioned, as are building works in Jerusalem and provisions for the extension of agriculture; the army is also said to have been re-equipped. The account of how Uzziah contracted 'leprosy' is elaborated and is attributed to divine punishment when Uzziah tried to offer incense in the temple. He was resisted by the chief priest whose name, confusingly in view of Uzziah's other name, was Azariah.

The remains of the royal palace at Ramat Rahel provide some of the best evidence of palace architecture in Judah. The 'proto-Aeolic' capital (*above right*) and ornamental balustrade with dwarf palmette columns, as well as the fine ashlar masonry walls, may date from the 8th century BC.

As always it is difficult to assess the accuracy of the material in Chronicles. The claims are generalized, and cannot in the nature of things be tested by archaeology. On the other hand, the period of Uzziah's undisputed rule was one of peace and prosperity for both Israel and Judah, and it would be surprising if there had not been consolidation and expansion. It was once thought that Uzziah is mentioned in the records of Tiglath-pileser III under the name 'Azriau (Azariah) of Iuda', with the implication that Uzziah had a considerable army. However, the text concerned is not well preserved and current opinion is that Uzziah is not attested.

JOTHAM

JOTHAM	
Born	*Son*
? Jerusalem	Ahaz
Father	*Buried*
Uzziah	Jerusalem
Mother	*Bible references*
Jerusah daughter of	2 Kings 15:32-38;
Zadok	2 Chronicles 26:1-22

As mentioned above, Jotham may have begun to reign during the latter part of his father's life, although here we reckon their reigns consecutively. The notice at 2 Kings 15:32-38 records only that Jotham built the upper gate of the temple in Jerusalem. We learn from 2 Chronicles 27:1-9 that he undertook extensive building work on part of the city wall, and that he exacted tribute from the Ammonites. He is also credited with building cities in Judah's hill country and towers on the wooded hills. If the material exclusive to Chronicles is accepted, it implies the extension of centralized power from Jerusalem over the remainder of Judah.

AHAZ

AHAZ	
Born	*Buried*
? Jerusalem	Jerusalem
Father	*Bible references*
Jotham	2 Kings 16:1-20;
Son	2 Chronicles 28:1-27
Hezekiah	

With Ahaz we are faced with the problem that the exact limits of his reign are difficult to fix. On the basis of 2 Kings 16:2 two ways of fitting this period into the time available are possible. One is to assume that his father Jotham died before Uzziah and that Ahaz therefore had a co-regency with his grandfather Uzziah. Alternatively we can assume that Ahaz succeeded Jotham, who was sole ruler, to begin his reign in 733/2 and to extend it to 715. Implications arising from this for the reign of his son Hezekiah will be discussed below (p. 138). All that can be said here is that the dates for the reign given above are approximate. However, it is certain that Ahaz was on the throne at the latest by 734/3 BC because he was involved in incidents that are attested in extra-biblical sources.

According to 2 Kings 16:5-9 Ahaz was besieged in Jerusalem by Rezin king of Damascus and Pekah king of Israel. It is usually assumed that the two kings wished to force Ahaz to join a coalition against the Assyrian king Tiglath-pileser III, and although there is no direct evidence for this it is not an unreasonable inference. This incident also features in Isaiah (7:1-17) where the prophet advises Ahaz to stand firm against his enemies and to trust in God's deliverance. Ahaz instead appealed for help to Tiglath-pileser and became, in effect, an Assyrian vassal. The Assyrian king responded by attacking Damascus and Israel. As a result the former probably became an Assyrian province while to Israel only a rump of land around Samaria remained. The Assyrian attack probably

A clay seal impression with the inscription 'Belonging to Ahaz [son of] Yehotam king of Judah'. It originally sealed a papyrus document as the marks of the strings are preserved on the reverse. Traces of a fingerprint on its left edge may even belong to Ahaz himself.

took place in 732, and one outcome was that the people of the northern kingdom deposed Pekah (p. 120). It is possible that Ahaz's payment of tribute to Tiglath-pileser is mentioned in the latter's annals, if the reference to Ja-u'-ha-zi of Ja-u'-da-i is correctly linked to Ahaz. A description in 2 Kings 16:10-18 of various alterations to the temple and its worship that Ahaz ordered following his submission to Tiglath-pileser implies that Assyrian practices were introduced into the Jerusalem cult.

A much fuller account appears in 2 Chronicles 28:1-27. What in 2 Kings is a siege of Jerusalem by the rulers of Samaria and Damascus becomes a major defeat for Ahaz with much loss of life and the taking of hostages and booty. However, the captives and booty are returned by the leaders of Israel following the intervention of a prophet, Oded. Ahaz's appeal to Tiglath-pileser is mentioned, but the Assyrian king is said to have oppressed rather than helped Ahaz. Ahaz's religious practices are presented in an extremely bad light, implying that he even allowed child sacrifice, among other abominations.

We can view Ahaz as a pragmatist who had to deal with a threat to the very existence of his country: the combined forces of Damascus and Israel were easily capable of defeating him. By appealing to Assyria for help he preserved the separate identity of Judah even if there was a price to pay, in terms of tribute and the official cult.

A detail from a relief showing Tiglath-pileser III in a chariot, from his palace at Nineveh.

חִזְקִיָּה Hezekiah

c. 728–698 BC

Hezekiah: a detail from an English
13th-century illuminated manuscript.

HEZEKIAH	
Born	*Buried*
? Jerusalem	Jerusalem
Father	*Bible references*
Ahaz	2 Kings
Mother	18:1–20:21;
Abi, daughter of	2 Chronicles
Zechariah	29:1–32:33
Son	
Manasseh	

Hezekiah rebelled against the king of Assyria and would not serve him.

2 Kings 18:7

Hezekiah's reign saw one of the most turbulent and important periods in Judah's history, culminating in an invasion in 701 BC by the Assyrian king Sennacherib. If the significance of his reign is clear, unfortunately its dates are not. There are at least two ways of dating the reign, depending on how synchronisms with Assyrian records are used, and whether the reigns of Hezekiah's predecessors are expanded or compressed.

The sources

Two synchronisms with Assyrian records are relevant. In 2 Kings 18:9, the siege of the Israelite capital Samaria is said to have begun in Hezekiah's fourth year. Since that siege began in 724 BC according to Assyrian records, this would date Hezekiah's accession to 728 BC as indicated above. However, 2 Kings 18:13 dates Sennacherib's invasion of Judah to Hezekiah's 14th year. Since we know from Assyrian records that the invasion took place in 701 BC, by this reckoning Hezekiah would have acceded in 715 BC, and some dating systems follow this, giving his dates as 715–687/6 BC. This, in turn, allows more 'room' in the latter part

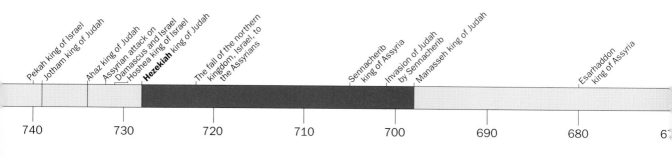

Pekah king of Israel
Jotham king of Judah
Ahaz king of Judah
Assyrian attack on
Damascus and Israel
Hoshea king of Israel
Hezekiah king of Judah
The fall of the northern
kingdom, Israel, to
the Assyrians
Sennacherib
king of Assyria
Invasion of Judah
by Sennacherib
Manasseh king of Judah
Esarhaddon
king of Assyria

740   730   720   710   700   690   680   6

MICAH

Micah came from the city of Moresheth (possibly modern Tell el-Judeideh) in southern Judah and was active prophesying against Samaria before its fall in 722/1 BC. He possibly also prophesied against the preparations for resisting the Assyrian invasion of Judah in 701 BC under king Hezekiah.

Many scholars argue that only chapters 1 to 3 of Micah can be connected with the prophet, although this is probably too minimal a view. Micah was bitterly critical of the abuse of religious and political power in Jerusalem, probably during the reign of Hezekiah, and also prophesied the destruction of Jerusalem (Micah 3:9-12).

The prophet Micah preaching, an engraving by Gustave Doré.

of the 8th century for the reigns of Ahaz, Jotham and Uzziah. A further feature of the later dating is that it has made possible the theory (not accepted here) that Sennacherib invaded Judah twice, and that the account in 2 Kings 8:13–19:37 conceals two invasions, one in 701 and the other a decade later.

The material in 2 Kings 18:1–20:21 is almost entirely concerned with the Assyrian invasion of 701; and it also appears with only very minor variations in Isaiah 36:1–39:7 (except for the 'psalm' at Isaiah 38:9-20 which has no parallel in 2 Kings). Material also pertinent to Hezekiah's reign is found in Isaiah chapters 1 and 20. In 2 Chronicles 29:1–32:33 Hezekiah is credited with a religious reformation in Jerusalem in which he cleansed the cult, reorganized the temple personnel and worship, and staged a national celebration of the Passover, which included worshippers from the northern kingdom of Israel. As so often, it is difficult to assess the additional material in Chronicles, and in what follows, it will not be incorporated.

The early years of the reign

When Hezekiah came to the throne, Judah was a vassal of Assyria, following his father's appeal for help to Tiglath-pileser III. The latter's death in 727 provided the space for tentative steps towards independence, and in the northern kingdom prompted an outright rebellion by king Hoshea. This was punished by Shalmaneser V, whose successor, Sargon II, captured Samaria in 722/1. One of the immediate results of this was that refugees from the former northern kingdom moved southwards. Excavations in Jerusalem have uncovered a late 8th-century wall on the upper part of the western hill of Jerusalem that indicates the expansion of population at that time.

Hezekiah probably gained much more than refugees from the former Israel, however. Among those fleeing must have been scribes, priests and representatives of prophetic groups, bringing with them the distinctive records, traditions and religious outlook of their own kingdom. Suddenly, Judah became the spiritual heir of the northern kingdom, and new religious energies were released which certainly led to the reformation described briefly in 2 Kings 18:3-4, even if not necessarily on the scale claimed in 2 Chronicles. A reference in 2 Kings 18:4 to the destruction by Hezekiah of a bronze serpent made by Moses, to which offerings had been made, may relate to a cult object brought from the north.

On the political front, Hezekiah sought to strengthen his control over the whole of Judah as well as areas occupied by the Philistines. This must have involved intrusion into the affairs of local communities and may have provided opportunities for exploitation by officials and nobles from Jerusalem. The prophet Micah, who came from the provincial town of Moresheth (possibly today's Tell el-Judeideh) was sharply critical of the appropriations of land for military and administrative purposes and in a bitter denunciation of Jerusalem foretold the city's destruction (Micah 3:9-12).

ISAIAH

Isaiah son of Amoz was born around 765 BC and called to be a prophet in the year of the death of king Uzziah (Azariah) of Judah (?739 BC; Isaiah 6:1-8). His earliest surviving words concern the Syro-Ephraimite crisis of 734/3 when the kings of Damascus and the northern kingdom, Israel, threatened to attack Jerusalem (Isaiah 7:1-2). His last words are probably to be dated to the invasion of Judah by the Assyrian king Sennacherib in 701 BC. Other prophetic words can be dated to crises in 711 and 705 involving threats from or resistance to Assyria. He appears to have had easy access to the kings of Judah, and his message was that Judah should rely on God rather than human alliances. Although Isaiah chapters 1 to 39 are called First Isaiah, material that can be attributed to the prophet is found mainly in chapters 1 to 10 and scattered through chapters 14, 18, 20 and 28 to 30.

Isaiah moves the sun back by ten degrees as a sign to the sick Hezekiah from God that Jerusalem will be saved from the Assyrians.

War with Assyria

From about 715 BC onwards attempts were made to build an anti-Assyrian coalition with support from Egypt. This was apparently opposed by the prophet Isaiah who publicly went about naked and bare-foot as a sign that Egypt and Ethiopia would be defeated (Isaiah 20:1-6). In 711 BC Sargon II attacked and captured the city of Ashdod for its opposition to Assyrian rule. From 705 BC, following Sargon's death, Judah joined in a rebellion against Assyria, which was severely punished by Sennacherib's invasion of 701 BC.

Sennacherib's own account records that Hezekiah had imprisoned king Padi of Ekron, a loyal Assyrian vassal, before the Assyrian army proceeded to subdue the towns in the coastal plain of Judah, including Ashkelon and Joppa. An Egyptian force was met and defeated at Eltekeh (not identified for certain, but in the coastal plain region). Sennacherib then turned to Judah and claims to have captured 46 walled settlements and to have driven out over 200,000 inhabitants. The Assyrian conquest of one of these, Lachish, has been

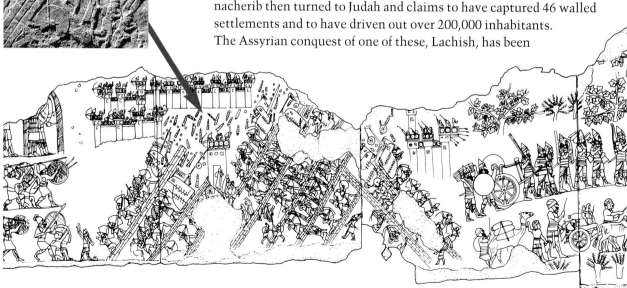

SENNACHERIB'S CAMPAIGN

The biblical account

In the fourteenth year of King Hezekiah Sennacherib king of Assyria came up against all the fortified cities of Judah and took them. And Hezekiah king of Judah sent to the king of Assyria at Lachish, saying, 'I have done wrong; withdraw from me; whatever you impose on me I will bear.' And the king of Assyria required of Hezekiah king of Judah three hundred talents of silver and thirty talents of gold. And Hezekiah gave him all the silver that was found in the house of the LORD, and in the treasuries of the king's house. At that time Hezekiah stripped the gold from the doors of the temple of the LORD, and from the doorposts which Hezekiah king of Judah had overlaid and gave it to the king of Assyria.

2 Kings 18:13-16

The Assyrian account

As to Hezekiah the Jew, he did not submit to my yoke, I laid siege to 46 of his strong cities, walled forts and to the countless small villages in their vicinity, and conquered (them) by means of well-stamped (earth-) ramps, and battering-rams brought (thus) near (to the walls) (combined with) the attack by foot soldiers, (using) mines, breaches as well as sapper work. I drove out (of them) 200,150 people, young and old, male and female, horses, mules, donkeys, camels, big and small cattle beyond counting, and considered (them) booty. Himself I made a prisoner in Jerusalem, his royal residence, like a bird in a cage. ... Hezekiah himself ... did send me, later, to Nineveh, my lordly city, together with 30 talents of gold, 800 talents of silver, precious stones, antimony, large cuts of red stone, couches (inlaid) with ivory, nîmedu-chairs (inlaid) with ivory, elephant-hides, ebony-wood, boxwood (and) all kinds of valuable treasures, his (own) daughters, concubines and female musicians.

The siege of Lachish was recorded in a relief in the palace of Sennacherib at Nineveh, as seen in this drawing. The left-hand scene shows the attack on the city, with a detail of the inhabitants leaving. In the centre and detail below, the captives are led away.

Many jar handles bearing the seal impression 'for the king' have been found in Judah and beyond. They are dated to the time of Hezekiah, and include a scarab or a 'flying scroll' and the name of one of four places (that on the right is 'Hebron'), indicating administrative centres.

made famous by the reliefs, now housed in the British Museum, of the assault and capitulation of the city, and by recent excavations at Lachish itself which have uncovered both Sennacherib's siege ramp and the counter-ramp thrown up by the desperate inhabitants.

Sennacherib also besieged Jerusalem but was not able to capture it. Hezekiah had prepared the city's fortifications well, and may have constructed the so-called Warren's Shaft, which gave access from inside the city to the Gihon spring which was outside the city wall (2 Kings 20:20 and 2 Chronicles 32:30). Whether or not he did construct this shaft, it was certainly available to him, and he therefore had no need to construct the Siloam Tunnel (often also called Hezekiah's Tunnel) which brought the water from outside the city on the eastern side to the western side of the city.

If Jerusalem did not fall, this was partly because Hezekiah paid tribute to Sennacherib (2 Kings 18:14-16) and had to suffer a reduction in the size of his kingdom, as Sennacherib gave parts of it to vassals in the coastal plain and Shephelah regions. On the other hand, the biblical writers saw the hand of God in Sennacherib's failure to capture Jerusalem, and devoted much space to Hezekiah's heart-searching at the time and his consultation with the prophet Isaiah, who urged him not to surrender Jerusalem (2 Kings 18:17–19:37).

Supposing the dates accepted for Hezekiah's reign are correct, then he died within three years of his humiliation, leaving his son Manasseh to preside over a long period of Assyrian domination of Judah. However, his reign had seen important developments, especially in the uniting of the northern and southern traditions and some of their personnel. This would leave a permanent mark on the character of Old Testament religion and literature.

The Siloam Inscription was discovered in 1880 at the southern end of the tunnel of the same name in Jerusalem. The inscription records how two parties of miners met, tunnelling from opposite directions. According to the text, it was only when they heard each other at work that the teams realized they were so close.

The Siloam Tunnel, which can be waded through today, is about 1,750 ft (533 m) long. It conducted water from the Gihon spring, Jerusalem's only reliable water source which was outside the city walls, into the western part of ancient Jerusalem. Its height varies because some sections had to be cut from solid rock while others involved enlarging existing fissures.

Jerusalem's complex water supply systems: all drew water from the Gihon Spring.

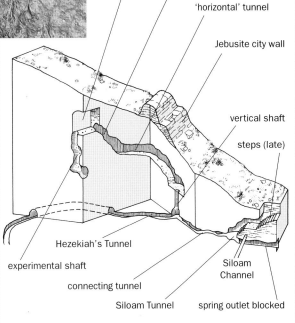

vaulted chamber (late)

vertical stepped tunnel

'horizontal' tunnel

Jebusite city wall

vertical shaft

steps (late)

Hezekiah's Tunnel

experimental shaft

connecting tunnel

Siloam Channel

Siloam Tunnel

spring outlet blocked

THE WATER SYSTEMS OF JERUSALEM

The standard view of Jerusalem's complex system of water supply is that in pre-Davidic Jebusite Jerusalem access from inside the city to the Gihon spring was via a vertical stepped and a horizontal tunnel which led to a vertical shaft from which buckets could be lowered to a pool created by the spring. It has been suggested that David captured Jerusalem by sending troops up this shaft. In the 8th century BC, Hezekiah blocked up the 'Siloam Channel' that let water run down outside the eastern walls of the city and constructed a tunnel that directed the waters in a south-westerly direction to the western side of the spur on which the city stood. This is known as Hezekiah's Tunnel, and it is said to have been built to help the city withstand the siege of Jerusalem by the Assyrians in 701 BC. Early in 1999 discoveries were made in the Old City that may require the revision of many accepted ideas. The vertical shaft and its tunnels may in fact date from after the time of David and the position of the walls in Hezekiah's time is disputed.

מְנַשֶּׁה **Manasseh**
698–643 BC

אָמוֹן **Amon**
642–641 BC

A detail of a clay seal impression from
Judah, possibly showing king Manasseh.

MANASSEH	
Born	*Buried*
? Jerusalem	Jerusalem
Father	*Bible references*
Hezekiah	2 Kings 21:1-18;
Mother	2 Chronicles 33:1-
Hephzibah	20
Son	
Amon	

MANASSEH

*Manasseh shed very much innocent blood, till he had filled Jerusalem
from one end to another.*

2 Kings 21:16

Manasseh's long reign of 55 years, which most experts in biblical
chronology accept without difficulty, is treated in 2 Kings 21:1-18. The
account is one of unrelieved condemnation, and he is portrayed as a religious syncretist whose offences against God were so extreme that God
decided to bring the kingdom of Judah to an end. Initially 2 Chronicles
33:1-20 follows the tone of Kings, but then records Manasseh's repentance after he was taken as a captive to Assyria. This repentance led to a
prayer for forgiveness (the Prayer of Manasseh in the Apocrypha is a later
attempt to supply the content), in response to which Manasseh was
restored to Jerusalem where he undertook building works and suppressed
some of the offensive cultic practices that he had earlier introduced.

Light from Assyrian records is shed on Manasseh's reign in the form of
two references, one from the time of Esarhaddon (680–669 BC) and the
other of Ashurbanipal (668–*c*. 632 BC). Manasseh is listed among 12 kings

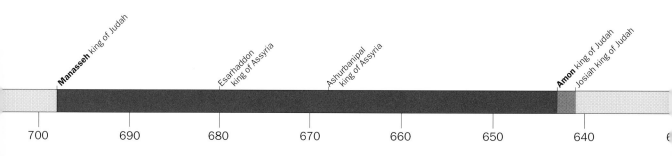

Manasseh king of Judah		Esarhaddon king of Assyria		Ashurbanipal king of Assyria			Amon king of Judah / Josiah king of Judah

700   690   680   670   660   650   640

Ashurbanipal, king of Assyria, feasting in a garden with his queen Ashursharrat. Detail of a relief from the North Palace at Nineveh.

from the seacoast who, together with ten kings from islands, provided Esarhaddon with materials for building works in Nineveh. In Ashurbanipal's records Manasseh appears in a similar list of 'seashore' kings who assisted an Assyrian invasion of Egypt.

Evaluating the reign of Manasseh involves deciding how far to trust the information about his repentance in 2 Chronicles. If this is ignored, then Manasseh's reign emerges as one of complete subservience to Assyria, accompanied by religious syncretism and social injustice. The groups who encouraged Hezekiah's religious reforms would have been driven underground, awaiting more favourable circumstances. If, on the other hand, Manasseh did institute a modest reformation towards the end of his reign, the changes brought about by his grandson Josiah would not have been as radical as our first scenario would entail. Defenders of at least that part of the Chronicles version which speaks of Manasseh's Assyrian captivity link it either to the rebellion (652–648 BC) of Shamash-shumukin of Babylon against Ashurbanipal, or the rebellion of Ashdod at the beginning of Ashurbanipal's reign, as occasions when Manasseh might have wavered in his loyalty and been punished.

AMON

Manasseh was succeeded by his son Amon, whose reign of two years receives only eight verses in 2 Kings 21:19-26, while 2 Chronicles 33:21-25 is even shorter. We are told only that he was evil, as his father was (Chronicles adds that he did not humble himself as his father had done) and that he was killed in the royal palace by his servants.

Two details call for comment; first, his age at accession is given as 22, which means that Manasseh, who was 67 when he died, must have fathered him when he was around 45. It seems incredible that Manasseh should have waited so long before seeking to produce an heir, and questions are inevitably raised about possible earlier offspring and their fate. Secondly, Amon's mother is said to have come from a family in Jotbah. While opinions differ as to Jotbah's exact location, it is generally held to have been in Galilee. If so, was Manasseh, as an Assyrian vassal, able to wield influence in Assyrian provinces that formerly had been the northern kingdom, Israel? Does the comparatively late date of Amon's birth (c. 664 BC) point to a time of incipient Judahite independence when tentative steps were taken towards reintegrating the former northern kingdom? Unfortunately, these can only remain as questions.

AMON	
Born	*Son*
? Jerusalem	Josiah
Father	*Buried*
Manasseh	Jerusalem
Mother	*Bible references*
Meshullemeth,	2 Kings 21:19-26;
daughter of Haruz	2 Chronicles 33:21-
of Jotbah	25

יֹאשִׁיָּהוּ Josiah

640–609 BC

King Josiah, a detail from a French engraving.

JOSIAH	
Born	*Son*
? Jerusalem	Jehoahaz
Father	*Buried*
Amon	Jerusalem
Mother	*Bible references*
Jedidah, daughter	2 Kings
of Adaiah of	22:1–23:30;
Bozkath	2 Chronicles
	34:1–35:27

Before him there was no king like him ... nor did any like him arise after him.

2 Kings 23:25

Following Amon's assassination, the 'people of the land' – usually taken to mean the wealthy landowners – placed his eight-year-old son Josiah on the throne. If the biblical figures can be trusted, Amon's promptness in providing an heir (he would have been around 15 when he fathered Josiah, given that he died aged 24) contrasts with Manasseh's rather less urgent approach (p. 145). Three main events dominate the accounts of his reign in 2 Kings and 2 Chronicles: the discovery of the 'book of the law' in the temple in Josiah's 18th year (622 BC); the subsequent reformation culminating in a national celebration of the Passover; and Josiah's death at Megiddo in 609 BC. In each case, Chronicles has a slightly different slant.

The discovery of the law book raises many questions. Did it inaugurate the reformation or, as 2 Chronicles 34:3 implies, was it part of a reformation already in progress? Secondly, was the book of law 'planted' or had it been concealed in the temple for safety (perhaps during Manasseh's reign), and was it accidentally discovered after being forgotten? Third, what was its content? Various answers have been given to this last

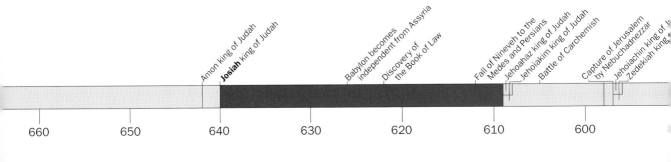

Amon king of Judah
Josiah king of Judah
Babylon becomes independent from Assyria
Discovery of the Book of Law
Fall of Nineveh to the Medes and Persians
Jehoahaz king of Judah
Jehoiakim king of Judah
Battle of Carchemish
Capture of Jerusalem by Nebuchadnezzar
Jehoiachin king of Judah
Zedekiah king of Judah

660   650   640   630   620   610   600

question, but the most enduring is that it contained part of what we know as Deuteronomy. The reason for this is that the reforms carried out by Josiah and described in 2 Kings 23:1-24 can be paralleled from Deuteronomy 12–13, 16, 29. Their main thrust is that there is only one legitimate sanctuary where sacrifice to God can be offered. However, since 2 Kings in its final form was produced by writers influenced by or representing the theology expressed in Deuteronomy, we should not necessarily regard 2 Kings 23 as an independent source, against which the Deuteronomy material can be checked.

The national celebration of the Passover raises the question of how it was celebrated prior to Josiah's time. Josiah's closing of all cult centres other than Jerusalem and the insistence that sacrifice could only be offered in the temple there meant that the Passover could no longer be a local family festival with the lamb killed at a local sanctuary, or even killed by a lay head of the family; but we have no information about how the local observances might have been carried out, or where. Was the Passover an observance from the former northern kingdom brought southwards after 721 BC?

The wider picture

Bronze kneeling statue of the Egyptian pharaoh Necho II. An ally of the Assyrians, Necho was coming to their aid when he defeated and killed Josiah at Megiddo in 609 BC.

Josiah's death is most easily dealt with, and, paradoxically, it provides the key to his life. Josiah's reign coincided with the disintegration of the Assyrian empire, a process accompanied by the assertion of Egyptian independence under Psammetichus I (664–610 BC), the unsuccessful rebellion of Shamash-shumukin of Babylon (652–648 BC) followed by the gaining of Babylon's independence from Assyria in 626 BC, shortly before the discovery of the law book in the Jerusalem temple. From this point, Assyria's fortunes went rapidly downhill. Babylon gained the upper hand, while Assyria also had to contend with attacks from the Medes. Nineveh, the Assyrian capital, fell in 612 BC and in 609 BC the Assyrian army made a last stand at Haran, hoping to recapture that city. The new Egyptian ruler, Necho II (610–595 BC), as an ally, went to Assyria's aid. The anti-Assyrian Josiah tried to prevent Necho's passage at the strategic site of Megiddo, but was defeated and killed there in 609 BC.

In the light of these events, Josiah's reign can be reconstructed as follows. As Assyrian power collapsed, Judah was able to reassert its independence, and this involved both expansion within the former northern kingdom and a religious reformation. We need not doubt the sincerity of this reformation. Religious groups in Jerusalem, influenced by prophetic teaching and probably including guardians of the traditions of the former northern kingdom, abolished pagan practices and, in the laws set out in Deuteronomy, sought to introduce social and legal reforms aimed at relieving poverty and curbing the absolute power of the king. There is evidence that Assyrian treaty forms binding smaller states to obedience to Assyria were adapted to express Judah's exclusive loyalty to God.

THE PASSOVER

The instructions about observing the Passover are given in Exodus 12: each household in Egypt is to take a lamb without blemish, one year old; it is to be killed on the 14th day of the month and its blood is to be daubed on the two door posts and lintel of the house; the lamb is then to be eaten roasted with bitter herbs and unleavened bread, while the participants are shod with sandals and hold a staff. The purpose of the daubed blood is to make the angel whose task it is to kill first-born children and cattle to 'pass over' the tents of the Israelites. Linked with Passover is the feast of unleavened bread in which no leaven is to be present in any house for 14 days.

The account in Exodus 12 evidently reflects later practices, and the instructions are not without difficulties. For example, why did the houses of the Hebrews need to be identified so that they would be spared when in earlier plagues Egyptian property was affected while that of the Israelites was spared (Exodus 9:1-7, 22-26)?

One popular view of the origin of the Passover which attempts to explain the ritual of blood daubing is that it was originally a rite used by shepherds when they moved from their winter pasturage in the desert regions to wells in the more civilized areas in the dry summer. They would kill a lamb and daub its blood on the entrance to their tent to ward off the dangers that would await them when they moved. Whatever its origins, Passover came to be linked to the agricultural festival of unleavened bread and it commemorated the Israelite deliverance from Egypt at the Exodus. In the reign of Josiah the closure of all sanctuaries except for Jerusalem made Passover into an official national festival because only in Jerusalem could the Passover lamb be killed (Deuteronomy 16:1-8). Prior to this time, although there is no direct evidence, Passover was probably celebrated locally by families in parts of the northern kingdom, Israel.

The Passover ceremony as depicted in a Hebrew liturgical manuscript of 1466.

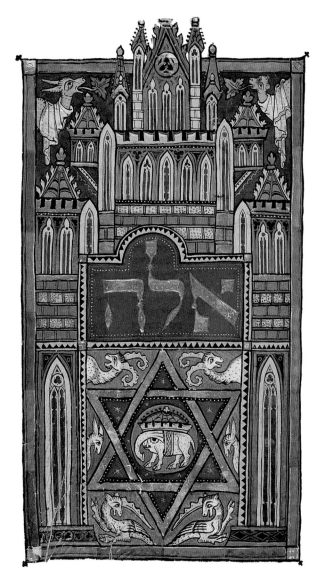

Title-page of Deuteronomy from a 13th-century German illuminated manuscript. The 'book of the law' discovered during the reign of Josiah may have contained part of what we know as Deuteronomy.

But if the reformation was sincere, it had the effect of greatly centralizing power in Judah, even if, according to Deuteronomy 17:14-20, the king's power was diminished. Making Jerusalem the only legitimate place of sacrifice and closing local sanctuaries represented a degree of control over the affairs of Judah from Jerusalem on a scale greater than ever before. In addition, the traditions of Judah and Israel, increasingly in written form, were shaped by the outlook of a religious group that interpreted the successes and failures of previous generations in terms of their faithfulness or otherwise to the recognition of Jerusalem as the sole legitimate sanctuary. Ironically, Judah's end was soon to mirror that of Assyria. The euphoria of independence and enlargement of territory during Josiah's reign evaporated after his death as Judah faced up to the two major powers of Egypt and Babylon. Judah's independent existence would now last for only two more decades.

יְהוֹאָחָז **Jehoahaz**
609 BC

יְהוֹיָקִים **Jehoiakim**
609–598 BC

יְהוֹיָכִין **Jehoiachin**
597 BC

צִדְקִיָּהוּ **Zedekiah**
597–587 BC

A fragment of a painted pottery jar showing a king, possibly Jehoiakim, seated on his throne; from Ramat Rahel, late 7th/early 6th century BC.

JEHOAHAZ TO JEHOIACHIN	
JEHOAHAZ	*Buried*
Born	Jerusalem
? Jerusalem	
Father	**JEHOIACHIN**
Josiah	*Born*
Mother	? Jerusalem
Hamutal, daughter of	*Father*
Jeremiah of Libnah	Jehoiakim
Buried	*Mother*
Egypt	Nehushtah,
	daughter of
JEHOIAKIM	Elnathan of
Born	Jerusalem
? Jerusalem	*Buried*
Father	Babylon
Josiah	
Mother	*Bible references*
Zebidah, daughter	2 Kings
of Pediah of Rumah	23:31–24:17;
Son	2 Chronicles 36:1-
Jehoiachin	10

Pharaoh Necho made Eliakim the son of Josiah king in the place of Josiah his father, and changed his name to Jehoiakim.

2 Kings 23:34

JEHOAHAZ TO JEHOIACHIN

Josiah was succeeded by his son Jehoahaz, a move initiated once more by the 'people of the land'. However, the Egyptian ruler Necho II had other plans. He set up his headquarters at Riblah (modern Ribleh near the Lebanon–Damascus border), a strategic site on the river Orontes controlling the main route from the Mediterranean to the interior of Syria and Mesopotamia. From here he deposed Jehoahaz after three months, replacing him with his half-brother, Eliakim, whom Necho named Jehoiakim. Jehoahaz was taken to Egypt, where he died. If the Rumah where Jehoiakim's mother came from is correctly located in lower Galilee, it indicates attempts by Josiah to forge links with families in the former northern kingdom.

Jehoiakim's reign is dealt with in 2 Kings 23:35–24:7, which briefly describes his transfer of allegiance from Necho, to whom he paid heavy tribute, to the Babylonian Nebuchadnezzar. The background to this was

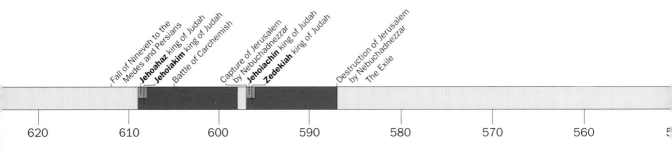

Fall of Nineveh to the Medes and Persians
Jehoahaz king of Judah
Jehoiakim king of Judah
Battle of Carchemish
Capture of Jerusalem by Nebuchadnezzar
Jehoiachin king of Judah
Zedekiah king of Judah
Destruction of Jerusalem by Nebuchadnezzar
The Exile

620   610   600   590   580   570   560

no doubt the battle of Carchemish (modern Jerablus on the Euphrates) in 605 BC when the crown prince Nebuchadnezzar decisively defeated the Egyptians, an event alluded to in Jeremiah 46:2. After succeeding his father as king in the same year, Nebuchadnezzar began to bring Syria and Palestine under his control. In 604 he captured Ashkelon – possibly the occasion on which Jehoiakim changed his allegiance. At about the same time Jeremiah caused a scroll that he had dictated to be read at a public assembly (Jeremiah 36:9-10). In this Jeremiah forecast that Nebuchadnezzar would destroy the land of Judah; Jehoiakim had it burnt piece-by-piece when it was read to him. In 602 BC Nebuchadnezzar engaged the Egyptian army somewhere near the border of Egypt. The outcome was indecisive, and could have been seen as a setback for the Babylonians. Possibly this caused Jehoiakim to rebel against Nebuchadnezzar (2 Kings 24:1 would just support this view) and it now became only a matter of time before Judah experienced the full force of Babylonian power.

In 597 BC Nebuchadnezzar came up against Jerusalem, capturing it on 16 March of that year. According to 2 Kings 24:6 Jehoiakim died before the city's capture, leaving his son Jehoiachin to make the surrender.

Jeremiah and the siege of Jerusalem, by Master Hugo, the Bury Bible (c. 1135).

However, 2 Chronicles 36:6-7 says that Jehoiakim was taken in fetters to Babylon together with vessels from the temple. Whatever the truth, Jehoiachin was certainly taken as a captive to Babylon together with his family and officials. According to 2 Kings 24:14 Nebuchadnezzar further exiled administrators, soldiers and craftsmen, leaving only the poorest people of the land. The numbers taken into exile were either 10,000 or 17,000, depending on whether or not the figures of 10,000 and 7,000 in 2 Kings 24:14 and 16 are taken as inclusive of each other. Jehoiachin would spend the next 36 years as a prisoner in Babylon. His release in 560 BC is recorded in 2 Kings 25:27, and his name appears in Babylonian records as a recipient of provisions. Nebuchadnezzar placed on the throne the full brother of Jehoahaz, Mattaniah, changing his name to Zedekiah.

ZEDEKIAH	
Born	*Buried*
? Jerusalem	? Babylon
Father	*Bible references*
Josiah	2 Kings
Mother	23:31–25:7;
Hamutal, daughter	2 Chronicles 36:11-
of Jeremiah of	14
Libnah	

ZEDEKIAH

Zedekiah's eleven-year reign is covered briefly in 2 Kings 24:18–25:7 (cf. 2 Chronicles 36:11-14), the main information being that Zedekiah rebelled against Nebuchadnezzar in his ninth year, thus provoking the onslaught that would lead to the destruction of Jerusalem and its temple in 587 BC. Further light is shed on this period by the book of Jeremiah and the Lachish ostraca. The book of Ezekiel is also relevant, since Ezekiel was a priest who had been exiled in 597 BC. From these sources we can piece together the following picture.

Although the exile of 597 BC was a catastrophe for Judah, hopes ran high both in Babylonia and Jerusalem that the setback was temporary. Among the exiles, Ezekiel urged that the cultic and moral behaviour in Jerusalem was so offensive to God that there would be no hope of restoration until Jerusalem had been destroyed. In Judah, Jeremiah opposed the expectation that the temple vessels taken to Babylon in 597 BC would soon be returned and that Jehoiachin would be restored to the throne (Jeremiah 28:1-4). Jeremiah's response was to write to the exiles in Babylonia urging them to prepare for a long stay of 70 years (Jeremiah 29:1-15). It is clear that Jeremiah was not an isolated proponent of the view that Babylon's ultimate triumph was inevitable and was even part of God's plan for the renewal of the people of Israel. Supporting him was the family of Shaphan, who had been involved in the discovery of the book of the law in the temple in 622 BC (2 Kings 22:3-8). Of Shaphan's sons, Elasa

Ezekiel's prophecy of the destruction and restoration of the nation is graphically depicted in this wall painting from the synagogue at Dura-Europos in modern Syria, *c.* AD 245.

The call of Jeremiah: the illuminated initial of the book of Jeremiah, by the Master of the Leaping Figures, Winchester Bible (1140–1160).

The second side of Letter 4 of the Lachish letters, discovered in 1935 and dated to shortly before the destruction of Jerusalem in 587 BC. The fragment contains the words 'we cannot see Azekah', indicating that this city had fallen and is no longer signalling by means of fires and smoke.

took Jeremiah's letter to the exiles in Babylonia (Jeremiah 29:3), Ahikam protected Jeremiah when he was threatened with death for saying that Jerusalem would be destroyed (Jeremiah 26:24), and Gemariah provided the chamber in the temple where Jeremiah's scroll was first read (Jeremiah 36:10). Opposing the family of Shaphan was that of the state-secretary Elishamah. These opposing families would assert themselves after the destruction of Jerusalem.

Jerusalem was besieged in 589/8 BC and Jeremiah was imprisoned for weakening the morale of the people (Jeremiah 38:4). The Babylonian army invaded the whole of Judah to the point where only Azekah and Lachish remained of the fortified cities (Jeremiah 34:7). The Lachish ostraca, messages written on pieces of pottery to Lachish from a military outpost during the invasion, record the moment of the fall of Azekah: 'Let [my lord] know that we are watching for the signals of Lachish for we cannot see Azekah' (Letter 4). With the fall of these cities, and the breaching of the wall of Jerusalem by the Babylonians in 587 BC, Zedekiah tried unsuccessfully to escape from the city. He was captured and taken as a prisoner to Nebuchadnezzar at the latter's headquarters at Riblah (p. 150). Having been forced to witness the execution of his sons, he was blinded and taken as a prisoner to Babylon. There is no record of when or how he died.

In 597 BC the Babylonians had spared Jerusalem and the temple. They now destroyed both. Evidence of this destruction has been found in recent excavations in the city of David. It was followed by another deportation of population to Babylon (2 Kings 24:11-12), though probably on a smaller scale than that of 597. Jerusalem and the temple lay in ruins and the line of the kings of Judah was at an end.

(Opposite above) A fragment of a clay tablet from Babylon dating to 592 BC, containing lists of rations handed out to captives, including 'Jehoiachin, king of Judah'.

(Opposite right) The beginning of the biblical book of Lamentations, bemoaning the destruction of the Temple and Jerusalem; from Germany, 14th century.

(Below) A lion made up of glazed bricks from the Processional Way from the Temple of Marduk through the Ishtar Gate, from the time of Nebuchadnezzar. The Ishtar Gate had similar decorations in the form of bulls and dragons.

A reconstruction of the Ishtar Gate in Babylon, built by Nebuchadnezzar in c. 580 BC.

THE EXILE (587–539 BC)

Judah has gone into exile because of affliction and hard servitude.

Lamentations 1:3

The period from the destruction of Jerusalem in 587 BC to Cyrus' defeat of the Babylonians in 539 BC, followed by his edict permitting the repatriation of exiles and the rebuilding of the temple in Jerusalem, is usually called the Exile. However, organized life in Judah did not cease; it is simply that we have very little information about it.

The major biblical source for the period is Jeremiah 39:11–43:7, but this covers only the initial period of the Exile. Following Jerusalem's destruction, the Babylonians set up a Judahite administration at Mizpah (Tell en-Nasbeh) in the territory of Benjamin, a few miles north of Jerusalem. Gedaliah, of the family of Shaphan (p. 153) was appointed as governor. There rallied to him the 'leaders of the forces in the open country' (Jeremiah 40:7), who presumably were commanders of regular and/or voluntary soldiers who had taken refuge in inaccessible places when fortified cities such as Lachish and Azekah fell to the Babylonians. There is also reference to Judahites who were in Moab and among the Ammonites and in Edom and in other lands (Jeremiah 40:11).

What the numbers of those remaining amounted to and how Judah was administered, we do not know. That some kind of worship continued in the ruins of the temple is indicated by Jeremiah 41:4-5, which speaks of men arriving from Shechem, Shiloh and Samaria to offer grain and incense at the temple. Otherwise, it is not unreasonable to assume that village dwellers got on with producing basic foodstuffs, probably with little interference from any central administration. Further, there may have been some redistribution of property. Some villagers may have been displaced from southern Judah by Edomites, while others occupied land formerly belonging to wealthy, and now exiled, landowners.

Village life was probably untouched by the events in Mizpah that ended Gedaliah's governorship. The rivalry between the families of Shaphan and Elishamah (p. 153) flared up when a

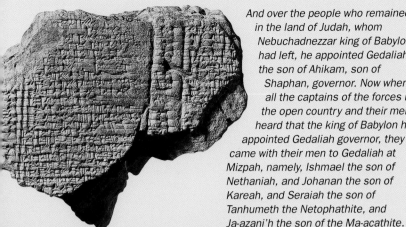

And over the people who remained in the land of Judah, whom Nebuchadnezzar king of Babylon had left, he appointed Gedaliah the son of Ahikam, son of Shaphan, governor. Now when all the captains of the forces in the open country and their men heard that the king of Babylon had appointed Gedaliah governor, they came with their men to Gedaliah at Mizpah, namely, Ishmael the son of Nethaniah, and Johanan the son of Kareah, and Seraiah the son of Tanhumeth the Netophathite, and Ja-azani'h the son of the Ma-acathite.

And Gedaliah swore to them and their men, saying, 'Do not be afraid because of the Chaldean officials; dwell in the land, and serve the king of Babylon, and it shall be well with you'. But in the seventh month, Ishmael the son of Nethaniah, son of Elishama, of the royal family, came with ten men, and attacked and killed Gedaliah and the Jews and the Chaldeans who were with him at Mizpah. Then all the people, both small and great, and the captains of the forces arose, and went to Egypt; for they were afraid of the Chaldeans.

2 Kings 25:22-26

grandson of Elishamah killed Gedaliah and fled to Ammon. The leadership was now assumed by Johanan son of Kareah but, fearing Babylonian reprisals, he and his supporters fled to Egypt, taking with them an unwilling Jeremiah. This was possibly in 582 BC, the occasion of the third deportation of population to Babylon (cf. Jeremiah 52:30). The next 40 years are a blank regarding events in Judah.

Of those who were deported from Jerusalem and Judah in 597, 587 and 582 BC, some were resettled in the region between Babylon and Erech, beside the canal joining these two cities called in Ezekiel 1:1 the river Chebar. The king (Jehoiachin) and the other notables were taken to Babylon and imprisoned. Those exiles who established themselves in Babylon found themselves in a city whose buildings, canals and gardens epitomized a civilization far more powerful than that of Judah, and whose religion may have therefore seemed superior to that of the Jerusalem temple. On the other hand, if the Exile was a disaster for Judah's political life it was a creative period for its religion. It is from this time on that scholars use the words Jewish and Judaism, indicating that the

people began to organize themselves as a religious community which emphasized its identity by stressing sabbath observance and circumcision. It was also now that the process began in earnest to shape traditions into what was to become the Old Testament, producing one of its major prophets, Deutero-Isaiah, whose words are contained in Isaiah 40–55 and who taught that the God of Israel was the only God, the creator and the lord of Judah's history. The sufferings of the people would soon be over, for God was stirring up his servant the Persian king Cyrus, who would defeat Babylon and allow the people to return to Jerusalem and Judah.

THE SECOND TEMPLE PERIOD

Under the Persians

Sheshbazzar
539–? BC

Zerubbabel
525–? BC

Ezra
? 458–428 BC

Nehemiah
445–425 BC

Under the Ptolemies
333–c. 200 BC

Under the Seleucids
c. 200–166 BC

The Hasmonaean Dynasty

Judas Maccabeus
166–161 BC

Jonathan
161–143 BC

Simon
143–135 BC

John Hyrcanus
135–104 BC

Aristobulus I
104–103 BC

Alexander Jannaeus
103–76 BC

Alexandra Salome
76–67 BC

Aristobulus II
67–63 BC

Hyrcanus II
63–40 BC

Antigonus
40–37 BC

Herod the Great
37–4 BC

Archelaus
4 BC–AD 6

Herod Antipas
4 BC– AD 39

Philip
4 BC–AD 34

Herod Agrippa
AD 37–44

The Roman Period
63 BC–AD 70

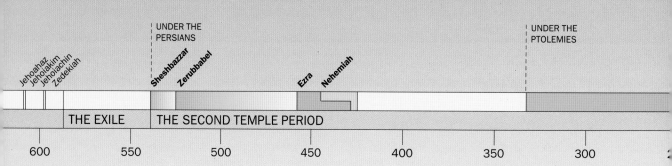

Ezra

Herod the Great

Herod Antipas

Herod Agrippa

THE SECOND TEMPLE PERIOD

Under the Persians 539–333 BC
Under the Ptolemies 333–*c.* 200 BC
Under the Seleucids *c.* 200–166 BC
The Hasmonaean Dynasty 166–37 BC
The Roman Period 63 BC–AD 70

THE TERM 'SECOND TEMPLE' is traditionally used to designate the period from the return of the Jews from Babylon and the rebuilding of the temple in Jerusalem to the final destruction of the temple by the Romans in AD 70. Like many such designations it is an over-simplification. Although the return is dated from 539 BC, the second temple was not completed until nearly 25 years later, in 515 BC. Further, this building did not stand unaltered for 585 years. It was captured and desecrated by the Seleucids in 168/7 BC, for example, and then re-dedicated in 164 BC by the Jews. Again, during Herod the Great's reign, it was refurbished and rebuilt on such a scale as to make it in effect a new building. It is also likely that there were other repairs, alterations and improvements of which no record has survived. Thus the term 'Second Temple' is useful shorthand for a period rather than an accurate description of a building.

For all that the Second Temple period is closer to us in time, much less is known about it compared with, say, the 8th century BC.

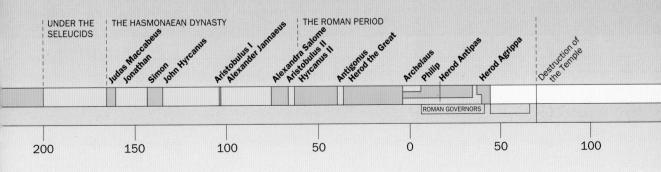

UNDER THE SELEUCIDS | THE HASMONAEAN DYNASTY | THE ROMAN PERIOD

Judas Maccabeus · Jonathan · Simon · John Hyrcanus · Aristobulus I · Alexander Jannaeus · Alexandra Salome · Aristobulus II · Hyrcanus II · Antigonus · Herod the Great · Archelaus · Philip · Herod Antipas · Herod Agrippa · Destruction of the Temple

ROMAN GOVERNORS

200   150   100   50   0   50   100

שֵׁשְׁבַּצַּר Sheshbazzar
539–(?) BC

זְרֻבָּבֶל Zerubbabel
525–(?) BC

SHESHBAZZAR	
Father	identified with
Exiled king	Sheshbazzar
Jehoiachin if	*Bible references*
Shenazzar of 1	Ezra 1:8, 5:14-16
Chronicles 3:18 is	

ZERUBBABEL	
Father	*Bible references*
Shealtiel son of	Ezra 3:1-9, 4:1-3,
Jehoiachin (but	5:1-2; Haggai 1–2;
Pedaiah son of	Zechariah 4:6
Jehoiachin acc. to	
1 Chronicles 3:19)	

In the first year of Cyrus king of Persia, … the LORD stirred up the spirit of Cyrus king of Persia so that he made a proclamation throughout all his kingdom and also put it in writing: 'Thus says Cyrus king of Persia … whoever is among you of all his people … let him go up to Jerusalem … and rebuild the house of the LORD'.

Ezra 1:1-3

The fortunes of the Jews were radically altered by the fall of the Babylonian empire in 539 BC to Cyrus king of the Medes and Persians. Cyrus issued a general decree allowing exiles to return home and for temples to be rebuilt. Whether or not this was a more liberal religious policy than that of the Babylonians, it does seem to have enabled a more formal social and religious life to be organized in Jerusalem and Judah.

Edicts of Cyrus are recorded in 2 Chronicles 36:23 and Ezra 1:2-4 which specifically order the rebuilding of the Jerusalem temple, and even if there are good reasons for doubting their genuineness they certainly accord with Cyrus' policy set out in the so-called Cyrus Cylinder. Ezra 1:5-11 details 5,400 vessels of gold and silver made up of voluntary donations by Jews and the vessels of the first temple that were given into the charge of Sheshbazzar, who is described as 'the prince of Judah' (Ezra 1:8).

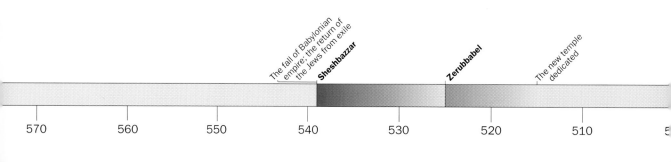

Clay cylinder with a cuneiform text of the Persian king Cyrus, decreeing religious toleration and the re-establishment of sanctuaries destroyed by the Babylonians.

Ezra 2 lists 42,360 returnees not counting 7,337 servants and 200 singers. Exactly who Sheshbazzar was or what official position he held, if any, is not clear. Some scholars link him with Shenazzar who, in 1 Chronicles 3:18, is listed as a son of the last king of independent Judah, Jehoiachin.

From these descriptions in Ezra 1–2 we might expect that, with so much money and so many returnees, not to mention the royal command to rebuild the temple, the operation would begin immediately and be finished rapidly. However, the book of Haggai and Zechariah 1–8 give a quite different picture. Haggai 1:1-6 records a prophetic oracle addressed in 520 BC (the second year of the reign of king Darius) to Zerubbabel, governor of Judah, which chides the people for saying that the time has not yet come to rebuild the Lord's house. What more encouragement could they possibly need, if the material in Ezra 1–2 is authentic?

The likelihood is that the list of returnees in Ezra 2 dates from a later period and that the author of Ezra, writing 200 years after the events, put together an account that greatly exaggerated the extent of the return. Haggai's picture of a small and struggling community debating whether it has the means to rebuild the temple is much more convincing.

In both Haggai and Zechariah 1–8 the leader of the newly re-established community is Zerubbabel son of Shealtiel. In 1 Chronicles 3 Shealtiel is given as a son of king Jehoiachin and Zerubbabel is identified as the son of Pedaiah, Shealtiel's brother. Whatever the truth, this seems to indicate that Zerubbabel had some connection with the former royal family of Judah. Zerubbabel is said to have laid the foundations of the temple (Zechariah 4:9) and Haggai (1:14-15) records that Zerubbabel, Joshua the high priest and the people worked on the temple in 520 BC.

The rebuilding of the temple in Jerusalem, as a massive, communal effort, envisaged by Gustave Doré. The new temple was not completed and dedicated until 515 BC.

THE PERSIANS

From 539 to 333 BC Judah was part of the empire created by Cyrus the Great (559–530 BC) and his successors. The Persians had occupied what today is a small part of southern Iran for some 400 years before Cyrus began to extend his power, defeating first the Medes whose kingdom included most of modern Iran and part of Turkey, and then the kingdom of Lydia (modern western Turkey). In 539 BC Cyrus invaded Babylon, taking the capital without a fight, after which he gave permission for exiles to return home and for sanctuaries destroyed by the Babylonians to be rebuilt. The Bible (Isaiah 45:1; Ezra 1:1-4) describes Cyrus as God's anointed servant through whom the Babylonian Exile was ended. Cyrus' son Cambyses (539–522 BC) added Egypt to the Persian empire, while Darius I (521–486 BC) extended the empire into Europe and the province of the Indus. Darius reorganized the empire into administrative provinces called satrapies and rebuilt Susa as the administrative capital. The official language of the empire was Aramaic. Aramaic, and its script, gradually replaced Hebrew and its Phoenician script in Judah. Parts of the books of Ezra and Daniel are in Aramaic.

A coin from the Persian period with the name Yehud, the Persian name for the province of Judah. The Phoenician script is still used here.

By the time of the completion and dedication of the temple in 515 BC as described in Ezra 6:13-18, no mention is made of Zerubbabel or Joshua. It has often been claimed that behind Zechariah 6:9-14 lies a possible attempt to crown Zerubbabel that was firmly stamped on by the Persian authorities, and which resulted in an alteration to the original text of this passage. Zechariah is ordered to make crowns and to set them on the head of Joshua the high priest. Joshua is designated as 'the Branch', the one who shall build the temple and beside whose throne there shall be a priest. It certainly looks possible that 'the Branch' was originally intended to be Zerubbabel and that Joshua would be the priest beside his throne, and that the text had to be altered following Zerubbabel's demise, however and whenever that came about.

The prophet Haggai (*above*), from the French Bible Moralisée (1230) and the prophet Zechariah in the Sistine Chapel, by Michelangelo (1509). Both prophets urged the post-Exilic community in Jerusalem to rebuild the temple.

עֶזְרָא **Ezra**
?458–428 BC

נְחֶמְיָה **Nehemiah**
445–425 BC

Ezra, by Gustave Doré.

EZRA AND NEHEMIAH	
EZRA	NEHEMIAH
Father	*Father*
Seraiah (a	Hacaliah
descendant of	*Bible reference*
Aaron)	Nehemiah
Bible references	
Ezra 7, 10;	
Nehemiah 8	

'I, Artaxerxes the King make a decree to all the treasurers in the province Beyond the River: whatever Ezra ... requires of you, be it done with all diligence ...'

Ezra 7:21

From the dedication of the second temple (515 BC) to the earliest possible time of Ezra (458 BC) there is a gap in our knowledge of nearly 60 years. What happened in Judah in the intervening period can only be speculated upon. Even if there was only a small and steady return of exiles from Babylon, tensions would have arisen between the peasant farmers who had remained behind and the returnees, some of whom would have claimed back their land. It is also likely that an attempt to rebuild the walls of Jerusalem was frustrated by the authorities in Samaria, possibly to the point of forceful intervention and material damage.

On the face of it, the information in the books of Ezra and Nehemiah breaks this silence and gives us our first glimpse of life in Judah in the second half of the 5th century BC. According to Ezra 7:1-28, Ezra was a priest who, in the seventh year of the Persian king Artaxerxes (458 BC if this is Artaxerxes I (465–423 BC)), journeyed from Babylonia to Jerusalem, with the king's authority, to teach and enforce the law of God.

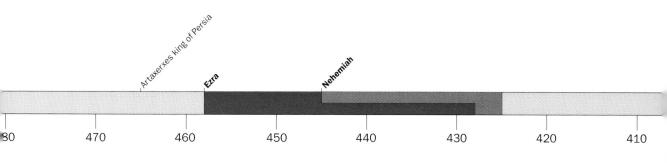

Artaxerxes king of Persia

Ezra

Nehemiah

80   470   460   450   440   430   420   410

FESTIVAL OF BOOTHS

The Festival of Booths or Tabernacles was part of the autumn celebration of the harvest of grapes, figs and other fruits in ancient Israel (Leviticus 23:39). In the Bible the festival is linked to the story of the wilderness wanderings as a reminder to the Israelites that they lived in booths (tents) during their journey from Egypt to Canaan (Leviticus 23:42-3). In the late Second Temple Period the official ceremonies included prayers for rain accompanied by the pouring of water. In modern Jewish observance families construct and spend seven nights in booths built on balconies or in gardens through whose roof the stars are visible. The booths contain examples of the food which sustained the Israelites during their journeyings.

A German 19th-century wooden booth.

'This Ezra went up from Babylonia. He was a scribe skilled in the law of Moses...' (Ezra 7:6). In this detail from the Codex Amiatinus (Italian, 11th century) Ezra is shown as a scribe, as described in the Bible, surrounded by his books.

Ezra's main task was to compel men who had married foreign women to divorce them so that their foreign religious practices would not lead the people away from God (Ezra 9–10). Ezra also commanded the observance of the festival of booths and of the sabbath, and the reorganization of the offerings of the temple; he also read the law in the presence of the people (Nehemiah 8:9–10:39).

Nehemiah journeyed to Jerusalem in the twentieth year of Artaxerxes (445 BC if this is Artaxerxes I). His work involved rebuilding the walls of Jerusalem which were broken down, requiring men who had married foreign wives to divorce them, enforcing the sabbath, and reorganizing the temple worship and its offerings (Nehemiah 1–4, 12–13).

Nehemiah inspecting the condition of the walls of Jerusalem secretly at night (Nehemiah 2:11-16), by Gustave Doré. There may have been opposition to his work of rebuilding the community.

A diagram showing the extent of Jerusalem at the time of Nehemiah. The black lines indicate the present walls of the old city. The city was much smaller than it had been in the 7th century BC, and was perhaps the same size as it had been in the 10th century BC.

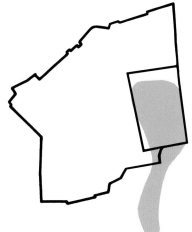

It is impossible to ignore the astonishing overlap between the work of Ezra and Nehemiah. If, in 458 BC, Ezra required foreign wives to be divorced, the sabbath to be observed and the temple offerings to be properly organized, why did Nehemiah need to repeat precisely these tasks 13 years later at the most, or even sooner if, as can reasonably be assumed, Ezra was in Jerusalem for longer than a year? Why did Nehemiah find the walls of the city broken down? Had Ezra not noticed this, or had the walls been destroyed between Ezra's death or departure from Jerusalem and Nehemiah's arrival? Because of these difficulties, it has been suggested by some experts that Ezra arrived in Jerusalem not in the reign of Artaxerxes I, but in the seventh year of Artaxerxes II (404–359 BC), that is, in 398 BC. In this view, Nehemiah's reforms of 445–423 BC had failed and needed to be repeated by Ezra a generation later. Another view is that the text of Ezra 7:7 is corrupt, and that it should read that Ezra came to Jerusalem in the 27th year of Artaxerxes. If this was the first Persian king of that name, the year would be 438 BC, and the work of Ezra and Nehemiah would have overlapped.

These difficulties raise some of the most acute critical problems in the whole of the Old Testament. The view taken here is that the letters found in Ezra 4–5 and dated to the reign of Darius (522–486 BC) are misplaced, and deal with the unsuccessful attempts of the Jews in Jerusalem to rebuild the walls prior to Nehemiah's arrival. Further, the author of the book of Ezra knew little about Ezra apart from his name, and based his account of Ezra's mission on the details of Nehemiah's work in the book of Nehemiah. The latter was then edited (8:1) to make the two men contemporaries, with the priestly Ezra preceding the layman Nehemiah. The substantive point is that the Ezra material tells us nothing that is not also found in the book of Nehemiah.

Looking beyond the biblical evidence

Fortunately, extra-biblical material comes to our aid in elucidating this period and Nehemiah's work. An Aramaic papyrus found at the Jewish colony of Elephantine on the Upper Nile and dated to 407 BC – apparently a copy of a letter sent to the 'governor of Judah' – requests permission for a temple to be rebuilt there following its destruction by Egyptians in 410 BC. From this papyrus it becomes evident both that the 'governor of Judah' was one Bagoas and that the high priest in Jerusalem was called Johanan, and also that a similar letter has been sent to Delaiah and Shelemaiah, the sons of Sanballat, the governor of Samaria. Some of these names are found in the book of Nehemiah. Sanballat is portrayed as the opponent of Nehemiah (Nehemiah 4:1-9) while Johanan may be the Johanan whose father, Eliashib, earned Nehemiah's displeasure because of his closeness to another 'enemy' of Nehemiah, Tobiah the Ammonite (cf. Nehemiah 4:1-9, 12:22-3, 13:4-9).

Combining the information from this papyrus with the book of Nehemiah, the following picture can be tentatively reconstructed. Prior

ELEPHANTINE PAPYRUS

To our lord Bagoas, governor of Judah, your servants Yedoniah and his colleagues, the priests who are in the fortress of Elephantine. ... Now, your servant Yedoniah and his colleagues depose as follows: In the month of Tammuz in the 14th year of King Darius, ... the priests of the god Khnub, who is in the fortress of Elephantine, conspired with Vidaranag, who was commander-in-chief here, to wipe out the temple of the god Yaho from the fortress of Elephantine. ... We have also sent a letter before now,

when this evil was done to us, (to) our lord and to the high priest Johanan. ... We have also set the whole matter forth

in a letter in our name to Delaiah and Shelemiah, the sons of Sanballat the governor of Samaria.

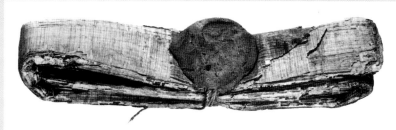

A papyrus letter, rolled and sealed on the outside ready for despatch, from the site of Elephantine in Egypt.

to Nehemiah's arrival, Judah was governed from Samaria and enjoyed strong links with powerful families in Transjordan, such as that of Tobiah. Judah was thus open to cultural, economic and religious influences from its immediate wider environment. Nehemiah's mission was to break these links and to establish a much more self-conscious community, with Jerusalem gaining enhanced political importance in the process. This he achieved in the face of fierce opposition from both Tobiah and Sanballat the governor of Samaria, a fact that makes his autobiographical account of events one of the most arresting in the Old Testament.

How far he had the general support of the people is difficult to say. Certainly, the insistence that men should divorce their 'foreign' wives, if put into effect, must have produced considerable social tension, if not distress. A crucial question is what were Nehemiah's motives? Was he driven by religious fervour, believing that his actions would result in divine blessing? Was he instead a kind of nationalist in exile, whose self-awareness of belonging to a displaced minority drove him to insist that his homeland should represent his ethnic group in the fullest possible purity? Were there class interests behind his reorganization of Jerusalem and Judah, with the stress on the need to prove one's descent as a Jew being a cloaked way of restoring land to families that had lost it when they were exiled to Babylon? No certain answers can be given.

We can, however, suggest an answer to the question of how long Jerusalem and Judah enjoyed the political independence that Nehemiah established. Not for very long, it seems, to judge from the papyrus from Elephantine, according to which Samaria was still an important factor in Judah's government. From the end of Nehemiah's activity to the end of the Persian period (c. 425–333 BC) there is no hard information about Jewish leaders or governors in Judah. All we can discern is the general point that the chief or high priest in Jerusalem was regarded by the Persian authorities as the head of the community.

UNDER THE PTOLEMIES (333–200 BC)

After Alexander son of Philip, the Macedonian, who came from the land of Kittim, had defeated Darius, king of the Persians and the Medes, he succeeded him as king ... And after Alexander had reigned twelve years, he died. Then his officers began to rule each in his own place. They all put on crowns after his death, and so did their sons after them for many years; and they caused many evils on the earth.

1 Maccabees 1:1, 7-9

If there is scant information about Jewish leaders in the Persian period, there is even less for the period 333–200 BC. As one authority has put it, 'all we have are a few fragments – a keyhole here and there for a brief glimpse into what is otherwise closed. We are attempting to reconstruct the mosaic of third-century Jewish history from a few odd pieces' (L.L. Grabbe, *Judaism from Cyrus to Hadrian*, 1992, vol.1, p. 205).

The background to the period is the defeat of the Persians by Alexander the Great. Following the battle of Issus (southern Turkey) in 333 BC, Alexander proceeded southwards towards Egypt, forcing the capitulation of cities such as Tyre and Gaza on the way. There is a legend that Alexander also visited Jerusalem; all we can safely assume is that Judah capitulated voluntarily. Samaria revolted in 331 BC after having earlier surrendered, and was severely punished.

In the aftermath of Alexander's death in 323 BC, an extremely complex struggle for power among his generals began, which lasted for over 40 years, resulting in the establishment of the Ptolemaic dynasty in Egypt and the Seleucid dynasty in Syria. During the wars between the generals and their descendants, Palestine was the scene of many battles, although to what extent Jerusalem and the

(Above) Alexander the Great (on the left) and the fleeing Darius, king of the Persians (right), in details from a mosaic depicting the battle of Issus. Alexander marched on virtually unopposed to Egypt, where he identified himself with the god Ammon, as seen on many of his coins. On this example (below), the obverse of a gold medallion from Abukir, he is shown with the ram's horns of the god.

Judaean hill country were affected we cannot say. According to one source, Ptolemy I (self-proclaimed king 305–282 BC but ruler from 323 BC) captured Jerusalem on a sabbath.

Some of the fragments from this period mention a Hezekiah, a chief or high priest of the time of Ptolemy I, and, in the latter part of the period two high priests named Onias (II) and Simon (II) emerge, who seem to have been pro-Seleucid. Whether or

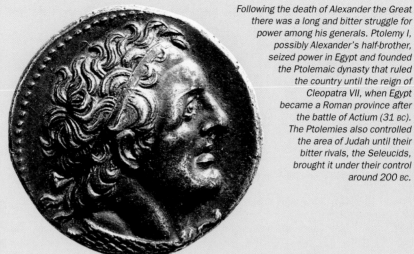

Following the death of Alexander the Great there was a long and bitter struggle for power among his generals. Ptolemy I, possibly Alexander's half-brother, seized power in Egypt and founded the Ptolemaic dynasty that ruled the country until the reign of Cleopatra VII, when Egypt became a Roman province after the battle of Actium (31 BC). The Ptolemies also controlled the area of Judah until their bitter rivals, the Seleucids, brought it under their control around 200 BC.

A reconstruction of the façade of the palace of Hyrcanus at Iraq el-Amir in Jordan. According to Josephus (Antiquities 12:4:6–10), Hyrcanus was the youngest son of Joseph, who belonged to the Tobiad family who were tax-farmers under the Ptolemies. Hyrcanus fled to Transjordan following a family feud and built himself a magnificent palace c. 200 BC. He took his own life when the Seleucid Antiochus IV acceded in 175 BC.

not their Greek names are significant, there is evidence for the penetration of Greek language and culture into Judah by this time. Another fragment of information concerns the Tobiad family based in Transjordan (p. 165): we learn that Joseph and his son Hyrcanus gained the tax-farming rights for Palestine under the Ptolemies. The general impression is that, apart from the need to pay taxes, the rural population of Judah was left to its own devices to produce olive oil and wine which could be exported and exchanged for cereals. That situation would change after 200 BC.

Antiochus III, on the obverse of a silver tetradrachm.

(Below and opposite above) Evidence of the upheavals in Palestine following the death of Alexander the Great (323 BC) is furnished by the massive fortifications that were built at Samaria at that time, including this magnificent tower.

UNDER THE SELEUCIDS (200–166 BC)

[There] came forth a sinful root, Antiochus Epiphanes, son of Antiochus the king; he had been a hostage in Rome. He began to reign in the one hundred and thirty-seventh year of the kingdom of the Greeks.

1 Maccabees 1, 10

Around 200 BC the Seleucid king Antiochus III (223–187 BC) succeeded in wresting control of Judah from the Ptolemies and incorporated it into his empire. Initially, this transfer brought benefits to Judah in the form of tax concessions in return for support for Antiochus among sections of the aristocracy. By 168 or 167 BC, however, this honeymoon was over to the extent that Judaism had been banned and the Jews were in revolt against the Seleucids. The reasons for this breakdown are not well understood, such is the paucity and polemic of the available sources. Blame has been fastened upon Antiochus IV Epiphanes (175–164 BC) for allegedly wanting to impose a uniform religion on his subjects and for thus proscribing Judaism; alternatively the culprits have been identified as the 'usurping' high priests Jason and Menelaus, who allegedly 'hellenized' Judaism and thus provoked a revolt of Jews faithful to the traditional observance of Judaism.

Of causes that can be listed, the following are possibly necessary ones: the founding of Greek cities in Judah after 200 BC, including the transformation of Jerusalem into a Greek city at Jason's request in 175 BC; the external difficulties of

Antiochus IV Epiphanes, whose ambitions to extend his empire, especially to Egypt, brought him into conflict with Rome, and drained his funds to a desperately short level; the division in Jerusalem between pro-Ptolemaic and pro-Seleucid factions; and the power struggles between the rivals Jason and Menelaus. These factors became a potentially explosive mixture as Jason and Menelaus each bribed their way to power as high priest, offering ever-increasing sums to the financially hard-pressed Antiochus, fought against each other, and even sold temple vessels. This final act was more likely than any other to provoke outrage amongst 'ordinary' Jews. Antiochus may well have proscribed Judaism in an attempt to suppress the rivalries that were producing civil war in Jerusalem, at a time when his humiliation by the Romans in 168 ended his hopes of conquering Egypt and called for tough action within his own territory. He therefore raided the treasury of the Jerusalem temple. Whatever the reasons for Judaism's temporary suppression and the revolt that opposed it, the outcome was a revival of Jewish political independence which lasted for over a century and which enlarged Judah's borders to their greatest ever extent.

(Right) The notorious Antiochus IV Epiphanes, who banned the practice of Judaism, on a silver coin of c. 170 BC. It is possible that he proscribed the religion simply to bring to an end the troublesome feuding between rivals for the position of high priest.

(Below) The 'hellenization' of Judaism and Jewish society, such as exercising in public (1 Maccabees 1:14-15), aroused much ill feeling against the high priests Jason and Menelaus among traditionalist Jews in Jerusalem.

Ἰούδας Μακκαβαῖος **Judas Maccabeus**
166–161 BC

Ἰωανάθης **Jonathan**
161–143 BC

Σίμων **Simon**
143–135 BC

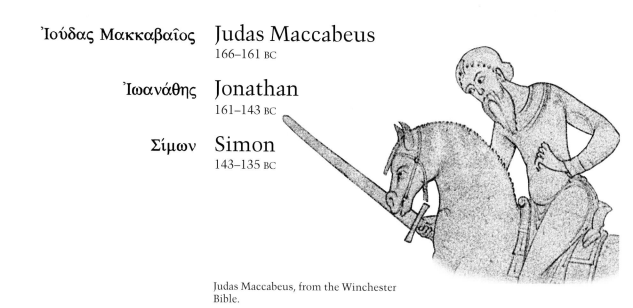

Judas Maccabeus, from the Winchester Bible.

Mattathias answered … 'Even if all the nations that live under the rule of the King obey him … I and my sons and my brothers will continue to live by the covenant of our ancestors'.

1 Maccabees 2:19-20

According to 1 Maccabees 2 active opposition to the decree of Antiochus IV banning Judaism came from a priest of the village of Modein: Mattathias. He is said to have killed a Jew in his village who was about to offer an unclean sacrifice and thus apostasize from Judaism. He then killed the king's officer who was enforcing the proscription of Judaism. Mattathias and his family became the focus of armed opposition to the Seleucids, and three of his sons, Judas, Jonathan and Simon, became successively the founders and leaders of what is called the Hasmonaean dynasty, the name being based on that of Mattathias' great-grandfather, Asamonaios.

Initially the movement was simply an attempt to reverse the suppression of Judaism – that is, it stood for freedom of religion within the Seleucid empire. However, it gradually developed into a movement for full independence, and met with varying degrees of success, depending on the broader politics of the Seleucid empire, until 142 BC when Simon was granted the status of ruler of an independent Judah.

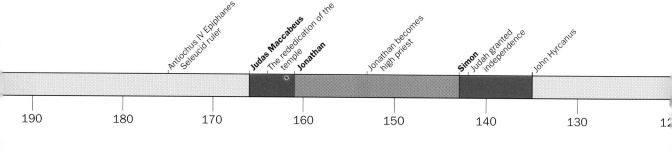

Antiochus IV Epiphanes Seleucid ruler

Judas Maccabeus

The rededication of the temple

Jonathan

Jonathan becomes high priest

Simon

Judah granted independence

John Hyrcanus

190   180   170   160   150   140   130   12

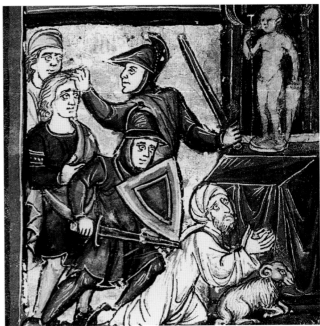

Scenes from the events which led to the Maccabean revolt: Jews are assaulted and oppressed by the soldiers of Antiochus IV; from the Arsenal Bible (1250–54).

JUDAS MACCABEUS

Following a Seleucid massacre of Jews who had refused to fight on the sabbath, Mattathias and his followers determined that they would actively defend themselves even on the sabbath. Judas Maccabeus then gathered a small army and won successive victories over a series of unfortunate Seleucid generals, before Antiochus despatched a large army under Ptolemy, Nicanor and Gorgias, amounting to 40,000 infantry and 7,000 cavalry. However, Judas engaged some of the forces of Gorgias at Emmaus and this pre-emptive attack disheartened the remainder of the Syrian army. A year later Judas defeated a force of 65,000 with only 10,000 men at Beth-zur. This victory enabled Judas to proceed to Jerusalem where the temple was cleansed and rededicated in 164 BC, an event of great significance. Judas' next moves were against the Idumaeans in southern Judah, the Ammonites in Transjordan, and the enemies of the Jews living in Gilead.

Despite these successes, a thorn in the flesh of the Jews remained – the fortress or fortified quarter in Jerusalem called the Akra which contained a Syrian garrison. When Judas besieged this it provoked a larger Syrian attack on Jerusalem, which practically succeeded when the Jews were tricked into accepting a truce. Two commanders, Bacchides and Nicanor, now concentrated on defeating Judas. Nicanor failed spectacularly and was killed in a battle near Beth-horon that has been celebrated ever since in Judaism. Bacchides was more wary. After an initial sortie which confirmed Alcimus, the Seleucid choice, as high priest, Bacchides defeated and killed Judas in the region of what is today el-Bireh on the road from Jerusalem to Ramallah.

JUDAS MACCABEUS	
Born	*Bible references*
Modein	1 Maccabees 3–9;
Father	2 Maccabees 8–15
Mattathias	
Buried	
Modein	

Scenes from the wars of the Maccabees, as portrayed in the Arsenal Bible (1250–54). Judas Maccabeus won several battles against the Seleucid army, though the numbers of the defeated enemies were probably exaggerated in the Bible.

Understandably, the material in 1 Maccabees lionizes Judas, whereas the historical reality is more likely that Judas won victories against much smaller forces than those claimed. In 1 Maccabees, Menelaus (p. 168) is not mentioned; but according to 2 Maccabees 11:29 he remained as high priest in Jerusalem after the suppression of Judaism and was in communication with the Seleucid rulers in Antioch. This suggests that support for Judas was by no means universal in Judah, and also

HANNUKAH

Hannukah, a Hebrew word meaning 'dedication', is a festival celebrating the occasion in December 164 BC when Judas Maccabeus purified and rededicated the temple in Jerusalem following its desecration by Antiochus IV Epiphanes (1 Maccabees 4:36-59). Because 1 Maccabees 4:50, 56 refers to the lighting of lamps and to celebrations lasting for eight days, modern observances of the festival includes lighting an additional candle each day until eight burn on the eighth day.

The kindling of the Hannukah lights, from an Italian Hebrew manuscript of 1470. This festival commemorates the cleansing and rededication of the temple in 164 BC.

raises questions about the nature of Antiochus' defilement of the temple. Although 2 Maccabees 6:2 states that the Jews were compelled to call the temple in Jerusalem the temple of Olympian Zeus, there is no reliable evidence that any idol was set up in it, and Zeus may have been simply the Greek name for an essentially Syrian cult. It is even possible that the capture and rededication of the temple was more an inner-Jewish dispute than one between Jews and Syrians, with Judas' movement opposing Menelaus. Certainly, after Menelaus had been executed by Antiochus V because of alleged treason, his successor as high priest, Alcimus, was hostile to Judas, if we are to believe 1 Maccabees 7:21-5 and 2 Maccabees 14. Thus the course of events and their background are likely to have been more complex than is indicated in 1 and 2 Maccabees, although the bravery and inspired leadership of Judas cannot be denied. Also, whatever the exact status of the temple between 168/7 and 164, Judas' capture and cleansing of it was, and has remained, a high point in Jewish history.

The wars of the Maccabees as depicted in an 10th-century illuminated manuscript. The revolt was begun by a priest, Mattathias; three of his sons in turn led the fight and were the founders of the Hasmonaean dynasty.

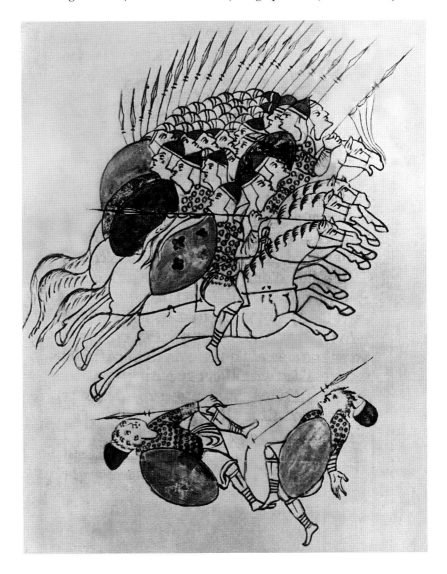

JONATHAN	
Born	*Bible references*
Modein	1 Maccabees 9–13
Father	
Mattathias	
Buried	
Baskama	

JONATHAN

Judas, who was Mattathias' third son, was succeeded by the fifth son, Jonathan. His leadership falls into two distinct periods. In the first, from about 161 to 153 BC, Jonathan was initially on the defensive and pursued by Bacchides. For some at least of the 'ordinary' Jews, there was no need for further struggle, since there was a high priest, Alcimus, and the ban on Judaism had been lifted. Later in this first period a truce was agreed between Bacchides and Jonathan (1 Maccabees 9:70-3) and the latter was able to consolidate his position, assisted by the fact that Alcimus had died in around 160 BC.

In the second period (153–143 BC) the struggle for the Seleucid throne between Demetrius I (162–150 BC) and Alexander Balas (150–145 BC) brought advantages to Jonathan. Both rivals vied for his support, with Alexander emerging the winner. His promises enabled Jonathan to assume the vacant high priesthood in 153 BC. Further advantages accrued from yet more struggles for the Syrian throne from 147 BC. Demetrius II (145–140 and 129–125 BC), son of Demetrius I, attempted to take the throne from Alexander Balas. Having succeeded, he was opposed by Alexander's son Antiochus VI (145–142 BC) and the latter's guardian, Tryphon. First Demetrius II and then Antiochus VI sought Jonathan's support in return for favours. As a result, Jonathan was able to extend his rule over cities such as Ashdod, Joppa, Gaza and Ekron, and parts of Samaria and Galilee.

Jonathan's end came when he was tricked and captured by Tryphon at Beth-shean. He was killed by Tryphon in 143 BC and was succeeded as commander and high priest by Mattathias' second son, Simon.

SIMON	
Born	*Bible references*
Modein	1 Maccabees
Father	13–16
Mattathias	
Son	
John Hyrcanus	

A silver shekel with a cup, above which is the Hebrew letter 'aleph' meaning '[year] one'. The letters around the edge read 'shekel of Israel'. The coin has been linked to Simon, but probably belongs to the First Jewish Revolt (AD 66/67).

SIMON

Like Jonathan, Simon benefited from the struggle for the Syrian throne. In 142 BC Tryphon assassinated his ward Antiochus VI and assumed the throne. The deposed Demetrius II was still bent on recovering his power, and since Tryphon had killed Jonathan, Simon had no doubt where his loyalty lay. He supported Demetrius, who in turn granted independence to Simon and Judah. The 170th year of the Seleucid era (142 BC) became the 'first year of Simon the great high priest and commander and leader of the Jews' (1 Maccabees. 13:42). Simon finally succeeded in removing the Syrian garrison in the Akra in Jerusalem.

When Demetrius II was taken prisoner by the Parthians, his brother took his place in the struggle against Tryphon, designating himself as Antiochus VII (139–129 BC). Simon assisted him against Tryphon but turned against him when Antiochus failed to recognize his independence. Simon's life ended when he was assassinated by Ptolemy, the Jewish governor of Jericho, at a banquet in that city. Ptolemy's aim was to kill Simon and his sons, and to seize power himself. However, John, who was to succeed Simon as John Hyrcanus, escaped.

| Ἰωάννης | # John Hyrcanus |
| | 135–104 BC |

| Ἀριστόβουλος | # Aristobulus I |
| | 104–103 BC |

| Ἀλέξανδρος | # Alexander Jannaeus |
| | 103–76 BC |

JOHN HYRCANUS	
Father	three others
Simon Maccabeus	*References*
Sons	Josephus,
Aristobulus,	*Antiquities* 13:7:4
Alexander	to 13:10:7
Jannaeus, and	

JOHN HYRCANUS

Hyrcanus having taken the high-priesthood that had been his father's ... made an expedition against Ptolemy.

Josephus, *Antiquities* 13:8:1

On his accession as high priest and commander, John Hyrcanus tried unsuccessfully to punish Ptolemy for his assassination of Simon, his father, and then found himself in turn under attack from Antiochus VII, who succeeded in dismantling the defences of Jerusalem. By a mixture of bribery (he is said by Josephus in *Antiquities* 13:9:4 to have raided David's tomb for funds), cunning and possibly with support from the Romans, Hyrcanus came to an agreement with Antiochus, after which further struggles for the throne of Syria left him free to consolidate his rule and extend his territory. The extensions included Idumaea in southern Judah, whose inhabitants he is said to have converted forcibly to Judaism, Samaria and Shechem in the north, and cities in the ancient territory of Moab, including Madeba.

Hyrcanus proved to be a capable and tough ruler, whose leadership provoked opposition from the Jewish sect, the Pharisees, according to

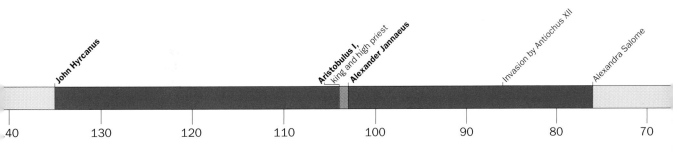

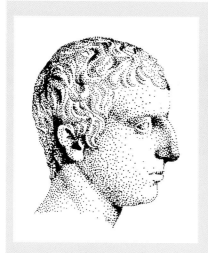

JOSEPHUS

Josephus Flavius (AD 37/8–after 100), the son of Matthias, was born into a wealthy priestly family from Jerusalem, and after studying with Pharisees, Sadducees and Essenes became a Pharisee with Stoic sympathies. From around AD 66 he was governor and military commander of Galilee. Following the outbreak of the first Jewish Revolt and the subsequent Roman moves to crush it he surrendered to the Roman commander Vespasian in AD 67. He is said to have prophesied that Vespasian would become the Roman emperor and for the remainder of the revolt he accompanied the Roman troops. He was later granted Roman citizenship and died in Rome. His two best-known works, *The Jewish War* (AD 79/81) and *The Antiquities of the Jews* (AD 93–4) are valuable sources for the history of the first Jewish Revolt and the Hasmonaean and Roman periods. Josephus' aim in writing was to present Judaism as a noble and civilized religion which was not well represented by those who had instigated and led the revolt against Rome.

Josephus. However, all opposition was vigorously suppressed, and, unlike his father and two uncles, he died a peaceful death.

ARISTOBULUS I

ARISTOBULUS I	
Father John Hyrcanus	*Reference* Josephus, *Antiquities* 13:11:1-3

Aristobulus, intending to change the government into a kingdom ... put a diadem on his head.

Josephus, *Antiquities* 13:9:1

Two points can be made about the brief, one-year reign of Aristobulus I, who was the eldest son of John Hyrcanus. First, and significantly, he took the title of king, and thus formally became the first priest-king of the Jewish people, although his predecessors had been kings in all but name.

Second, he extended his kingdom's territory into Iturea in southern Lebanon. As with his father's treatment of the Idumaeans, he is said to have required the newly conquered subjects to accept Judaism. On his death, he was succeeded by his brother Alexander Jannaeus.

ALEXANDER JANNAEUS

During his long reign of 27 years Alexander succeeded in extending the territory of Judah to include the coastal plain south of Mt Carmel, and Moab and northern Transjordan. But this success was not achieved without conflict, defeat and alliances. His attempt to take Akko in the coastal plain north of Mt Carmel was frustrated by Ptolemy IX of Egypt, while his forays into Transjordan brought him into conflict with the Nabataean kingdom in the south of that area, and its king, Aretas III. Alexander also had to face an invasion by Antiochus XII in *c.* 86 BC. However, he overcame these setbacks and increased Judah's territory to its greatest extent yet.

THE NABATAEANS

The Nabataeans were probably descended from the Qedar Arabs mentioned in the Bible (Jeremiah 49:28) and in Persian sources of the late 6th century BC. By the 2nd century BC they had established a kingdom in Transjordan and 2 Maccabees 5:8 mentions a king Aretas. Their wealth and power depended upon control of trade routes from Arabia to the Mediterranean and Red seas and Mesopotamia. In the 1st century BC the kingdom had to reckon with Roman power as well as with that of the Jewish Hasmonaean kings, and in 14 BC a sister of king Herod married the Nabataean chief administrator. Under Aretas IV (9 BC–AD 40) the Nabataean kingdom reached as far north as Damascus. After the death of king Rabel II (AD 70–106) the kingdom became a Roman province. The famous Urn Tomb, Palace Tomb and Corinthian Tomb at Petra probably date from the end of the Nabataean royal period.

Rock-cut buildings at Petra, the Nabataean capital: (right) the Khazneh (treasury), probably a tomb, and (below) Ed-Deir (the monastery).

A map showing the growth of the kingdom of Judah under successive Hasmonaean rulers.

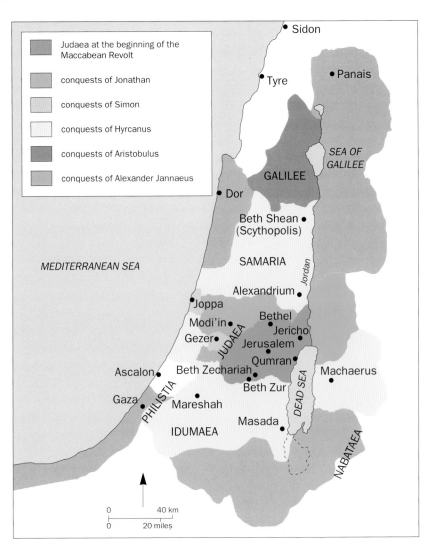

■	Judaea at the beginning of the Maccabean Revolt
■	conquests of Jonathan
■	conquests of Simon
■	conquests of Hyrcanus
■	conquests of Aristobulus
■	conquests of Alexander Jannaeus

Sidon

Tyre

Panais

SEA OF GALILEE

Dor

GALILEE

Beth Shean (Scythopolis)

MEDITERRANEAN SEA

SAMARIA

Jordan

Alexandrium

Joppa

Modi'in

Bethel

Gezer

Jericho

JUDAEA

Jerusalem

Qumran

Ascalon

Beth Zechariah

Machaerus

DEAD SEA

Beth Zur

Gaza

Mareshah

Masada

PHILISTIA

IDUMAEA

NABATAEA

0   40 km
0   20 miles

ALEXANDER JANNAEUS

Father
John Hyrcanus
Sons
Hyrcanus,
Aristobulus
Buried
Jerusalem

References
Josephus,
Antiquities 13:12:1
to 13:15:6

Alexander was not only occupied in conflicts externally, but at home he also encountered considerable opposition. It is often assumed that this was from the Pharisees, a group who sought to promote the strict obervance of Jewish ritual law, although it is unlikely that they provided the sole resistance. The group centred at Qumran, thought by many scholars to be the Essenes mentioned by Josephus (see p. 180), were also opponents, and some scholars have seen a reference to Alexander in the mention of the 'furious young lion' who 'hangs men alive' in the Commentary on Nahum among the Dead Sea Scrolls found in Cave 4 at Qumran.

While the figures of opponents whom Alexander Jannaeus killed may be exaggerated – there is a reference, for example, to 6,000 who were killed following a demonstration at which Alexander was pelted with citrous fruit while officiating at the Feast of Tabernacles – the overall picture conveyed by our main source, Josephus, is certainly one of a turbulent reign.

THE HASMONAEAN DYNASTY (166–37 BC)

Aristobulus (104–103 BC) used the title of king, and thus became the first explicit high priest and king of Judah, although royal status had previously become associated with the high priesthood. Other Hasmonaean rulers included John Hyrcanus (135–104 BC), a vigorous leader who greatly expanded his territory, and Alexandra Salome (76–67 BC) under whom the Jewish sect the Pharisees flourished. The dynasty ended in disharmony, however, as Alexandra's two sons, Aristobulus II and Hyrcanus II fought each other, and the Romans intervened in 63 BC to incorporate Judaea into their empire. Hasmonaean rule now limped on, however, under Roman auspices until Herod the Great brought it decisively to an end.

For the ordinary people of Judah the Hasmonaean dynasty was a mixed blessing. Some wanted only religious freedom, not political independence, especially when the latter meant that the Hasmonaean rulers acquired the characteristics of petty oriental kings.

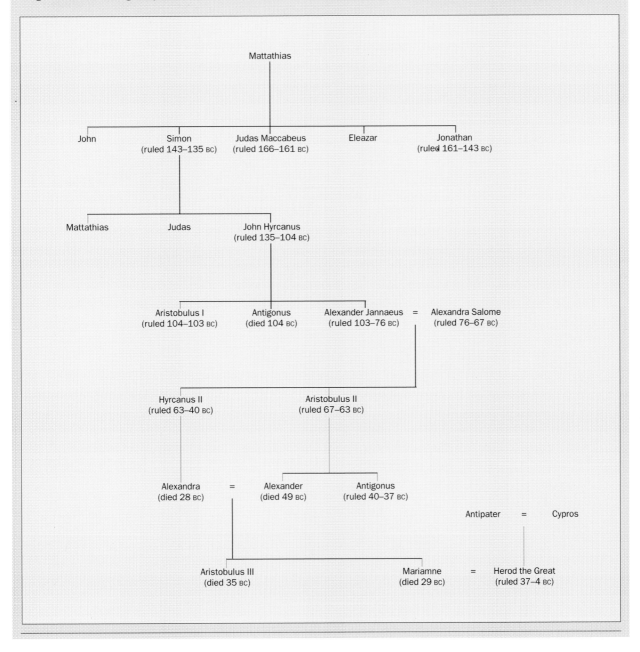

QUMRAN AND THE DEAD SEA SCROLLS

The accidental discovery in 1946/7 of ancient scrolls in a cave at the northern end of the western side of the Dead Sea, has been heralded as one of the greatest archaeological discoveries of the 20th century. It has also turned out to be a continuing cause of debate and something of an academic scandal. The following up of the initial discoveries was hampered by the deteriorating situation at the end of the British mandate in Palestine and the Israeli-Arab war of 1948. However, by the mid-1950s, 11 caves containing scrolls had been found and ruins at Khirbet Qumran had been excavated. One of the caves, Cave 4, was situated at the end of the promontory on which the buildings of Khirbet Qumran stood, and so the scrolls were linked with these buildings. The first cave that had been found was a mile (1.3 km) from the buildings. The scrolls included copies of books of the Old Testament and other Jewish writings, as well as documents that seemed to relate to a religious community that had lived at Qumran during the period roughly 150 BC to AD 68. By the late 1950s a scholarly consensus had emerged which identified the Qumran community with a sect called, by Jewish historians such as Josephus, Essenes. It was thought that this sect had been founded by followers or descendants of Onias III, the high priest who had been deposed around 170 BC in the events leading up to the banning of Judaism by Antiochus IV (p. 168). They had withdrawn to the desert in order to study and observe the Jewish law, and they regarded themselves as the true representatives of Judaism. One commentary (on the book of the prophet Habakkuk) mentioned how a member, or possibly the founder, of the community, the Teacher of Righteousness, had been persecuted by the Wicked Priest. Some experts identified the Wicked Priest with Judas Maccabeus' successor Jonathan, who assumed the high priesthood in 153 BC.

It was not their content, however, that caused the scrolls to become an academic scandal. Rather it was because, following the speedy publication of the original discoveries, little progress was made in publishing the many fragments found in Cave 4. Forty years after the discovery of the first scrolls, the scholars responsible for publishing the Cave 4 fragments were still not allowing other scholars to have access to them, and rumours abounded of a conspiracy on

(Opposite above) Yigael Yadin (1917–1984), a leading Israeli archaeologist and an expert on the Dead Sea Scrolls; he was responsible for obtaining and publishing the Temple Scroll.

(Opposite below) Cave 4 at the end of the promontory on which Khirbet Qumran stands.

(Right) The interiors of Cave 1, where the initial discoveries were made, and Cave 4, after the removal of the many hundreds of manuscript fragments.

(Bottom) The Temple Scroll opened at columns 57 (left) and 56 (right). Dated to the 2nd century BC, it describes and legislates for the construction of the temple, its personnel, rituals and festivals.

the part of church and Jewish authorities to suppress material embarrassing to their religions. Happily, all the material has now been made available, both to scholars and the general public. Although the consensus established in the 1950s is currently being reviewed and challenged, there seems to be no doubt that some, at least, of the material discovered near Qumran relates to a community that lived there immediately before and after the beginning of the Christian era, and which greatly enlarges our knowledge of the Judaism of the time. Attempts to link Jesus with the Qumran community have, however, been unconvincing.

Part of the Isaiah scroll from Qumran. Copies of every book of the Bible except Esther have been found among the manuscripts discovered at Qumran.

Ἀλεξάνδρα Σαλώμη

Alexandra Salome
76–67 BC

Ἀριστόβουλος

Aristobulus II
67–63 BC

Ὑρκανός

Hyrcanus II
63–40 BC

Ἀντίγονος

Antigonus
40–37 BC

A bronze coin of Hyrcanus II. The inscription reads: 'Jehohanan the high priest and the council [or community] of the Jews'.

THE LAST HASMONAEANS

ALEXANDRA SALOME	HYRCANUS II
Husband	*Father*
Alexander Jannaeus	Alexander Jannaeus
Sons	
Hyrcanus,	ANTIGONUS
Aristobulus	*Father*
	Aristobulus II
ARISTOBULUS II	*Buried*
Father	Antioch(?)
Alexander Jannaeus	
Mother	*References*
Alexandra Salome	Josephus,
Sons	*Antiquities* 13:16:1
Alexander,	to 14:9:5
Antigonus	
Buried	
Jerusalem	

Alexandra when she had taken the fortress, acted as her husband had suggested to her ... and put all things into the power of the Pharisees.

Josephus, *Antiquities* 13:16:1

Alexander Jannaeus was succeeded not by his eldest son Hyrcanus but by his widow, Alexandra. The reason given by Josephus (*War* I : 5:1) is that Alexandra was known to have disapproved of her husband's cruelty, and that this would favourably dispose the people to her. Josephus further says (*Antiquities* 13:15:5) that Alexander told his wife to give as much power as possible to the Pharisees. Both reasons for Alexandra's succession seem odd from a modern historical standpoint.

If Hyrcanus was not allowed to become king, he was installed as high priest; but his younger brother Aristobulus proved to be more able and ambitious. While the Pharisees were given power under Alexandra, they also aroused resentment among the people, and their opponents rallied so much to the support of Aristobulus that when Alexandra died, Hyrcanus allowed his younger brother to take the throne while he remained high priest. However, he was then persuaded that this had been a bad move, and with the support of the Nabataean ruler Aretas III, Hyrcanus besieged Aristobulus in Jerusalem. Affairs in Judah were now affected by

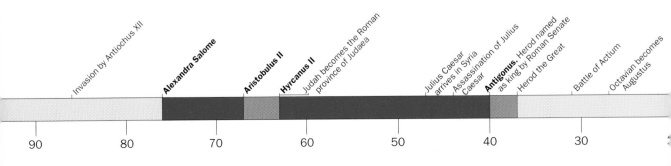

Invasion by Antiochus XII — Alexandra Salome — Aristobulus II — Hyrcanus II — Judah becomes the Roman province of Judaea — Julius Caesar arrives in Syria — Assassination of Julius Caesar — Antigonus, Herod named as king by Roman Senate — Herod the Great — Battle of Actium — Octavian becomes Augustus

90 80 70 60 50 40 30

A bust of Pompey the Great who, in 63 BC, incorporated Judah into the Roman empire.

events in Rome, and the ambitions of Pompey, who, in 66 BC, was given unlimited authority by the Roman Senate to expand Roman domination in the East. Rome had been trying to undermine the Seleucid state for more than a century, and Pompey now set about completing the task, sending his legate to Damascus in 65 BC. Hyrcanus and Aristobulus both appealed to the legate for help and he decided in favour of Aristobulus, in the process using threats to force Hyrcanus' supporter, the Nabataean king Aretas, to withdraw from besieging Jerusalem. Pompey arrived in Syria in 64/3 BC, where he received three delegations from the Jews, one each from the rival brothers and one from a third group, possibly the Pharisees, which asked for the Hasmonaean monarchy to be abolished. When Aristobulus pre-empted Pompey's decision and installed himself in Jerusalem, Pompey marched in anger into Judah. Jerusalem was captured after a siege, and Pompey entered the city and the temple, including the Holy of Holies, but did not otherwise desecrate it. In 63 BC Judah became the Roman province of Judaea, ending the independence that had nominally been gained under Simon in 142 BC. Aristobulus was taken as a hostage to Rome.

This was not the end of the rivalry between Hyrcanus and Aristobulus, however. Power struggles in Rome between Pompey and Julius Caesar, and later Mark Antony and Octavian left their mark on Judaea. Caesar appears to have supported Aristobulus but to have accepted Hyrcanus when Aristobulus unexpectedly died. A Parthian invasion of the area in 40 BC in support of Aristobulus II's son Antigonus, led to Hyrcanus being taken prisoner and Antigonus replacing him as high priest. He did not last long, though: he was beheaded on Mark Antony's orders in Antioch in 37 BC. However, out of this chaos another star was already rising – that of Herod. Herod's father Antipater had been appointed governor of Idumaea by Alexander Jannaeus and had become the power behind Hyrcanus. Out of the shambles of the end of the Hasmonaeans, Herod would produce a period of unparalleled brilliance.

THE PHARISEES

Readers of the New Testament are familiar with 'the scribes and the Pharisees', a group or groups who opposed Jesus and accused him of breaking the law, especially that concerning the sabbath. Elsewhere in the New Testament we learn that Paul had been brought up as a Pharisee, that he had been zealous in his observance of the Jewish law and that, in contrast to the priestly and aristocratic party of the Sadducees, he believed in the resurrection of the dead.

The New Testament is, in fact, one of the major early sources of information about the Pharisees, albeit a source that opposed Pharisaism and presented a negative picture of the movement. The origins of the Pharisees are obscure, and the meaning of their name is disputed. Thus, for example, it is not known whether 'Pharisee' was originally a contemptuous name given by opponents, or one that was adopted by the group themselves. Suggested meanings for the term include 'separated ones', 'abstainers [from luxuries, etc.]' and 'interpreters [of the Jewish law]'. It is generally agreed that

the Pharisees were a non-priestly movement originating some time before 150 BC, whose aim was to encourage the whole nation to observe the ritual purity required of priests in the Jewish law. To this end they studied, interpreted and taught the law, and were fiercely critical of the policies of Hasmonaean rulers such as Alexander Jannaeus, and later, of Herod the Great. They organized themselves in local groups. After the destruction of Jerusalem by the Romans in AD 70 they became the backbone of emerging Rabbinic Judaism.

‘Ηρῴδης Herod the Great
37–4 BC

Herod the Great, as depicted in a mosaic from the Kariye Çamii in Istanbul, Turkey.

HEROD THE GREAT	
Born	*Sons*
Idumaea	Antipater III,
Father	Alexander,
Antipater	Aristobulus IV,
Wives	Salampsio, Cyprus,
Doris of Jerusalem,	Herod, Philip,
Mariamne (daughter	Archelaus, Antipas,
of Alexander, son of	Philip
Aristobulus II),	*Buried*
Mariamne (second	Herodium
wife of that name),	*References*
Malthace, Cleopatra	Josephus,
of Jerusalem	*Antiquities* 14:9:1
	to 17:8:3;
	Matthew 2:1-16

Agrippa ... came into Judaea: whereupon Herod omitted nothing that might please him. He entertained him in his new-built cities, and showed him the edifices he had built, and provided all sorts of the best and most costly dainties for him and his friends, and that at Sebaste and Caesarea, about that port that he had built, and at the fortresses which he had erected at great expense, Alexandrium, and Herodium, and Hyrcania.

Josephus, *Antiquities* 16:2:1 on the visit of Marcus Agrippa, friend of Augustus in 15 BC

No Jewish king has left a greater mark on the appearance of his land than Herod the Great, and visitors to the Holy Land today will see more first-hand evidence of his work than of any other ruler before or since. It is true that in Jerusalem only the foundations of his temple can be seen, supporting buildings of later generations; but travellers have only to go from Jerusalem to the Mt of Olives to glimpse in the distance the strange conical hill of Herod's summer palace and presumed place of burial at Herodium. Masada by the Dead Sea or Caesarea on the Mediterranean coast both provide ample opportunities to view Herod's handiwork, while other Herodian remains can be seen at Tulul abu

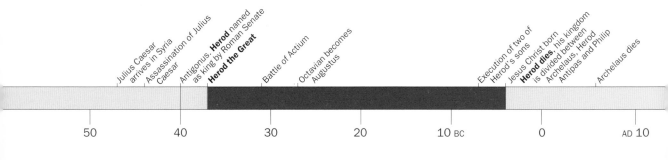

Julius Caesar arrives in Syria
Assassination of Julius Caesar
Antigonus, **Herod** named as king by Roman Senate
Herod the Great
Battle of Actium
Octavian becomes Augustus
Execution of two of Herod's sons
Jesus Christ born
Herod dies, his kingdom is divided between Archelaus, Herod Antipas and Philip
Archelaus dies

50   40   30   20   10 BC   0   AD 10

el-Alayiq near Jericho, Machaerus on the eastern side of the Dead Sea and Samaria in the heart of the northern highlands. It might be thought that such extensive projects could only have been carried out by a ruler who enjoyed peace and prosperity; yet Herod's rule began among the turmoil and intrigues of the last Hasmonaean priest-kings and the struggles of aspirants to pre-eminence in Rome. And once he had secured his power, intrigues within his own family led to brutal executions of those closest to him.

(*Above*) Despite Herod's reputation for cruelty and arrogance, he respected Jewish laws by not including his portrait on his coins, and no known portrait of Herod survives. The reverse of this bronze coin of Herod reads, in Greek letters, '[Of] king Herod'.

(*Right*) The great rock of Masada. Herod left his family here for safety when he fled to Rome seeking Roman support. He later built this palace there.

(*Below*) A ground view of Herodium, Herod's summer residence.

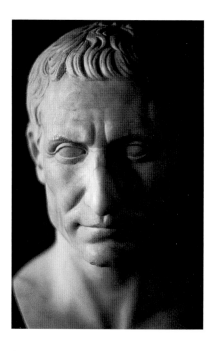

Herod's rise to power

Herod came from Idumaea, the part of southern Judah that had been occupied by Edomites, and which John Hyrcanus had converted to Judaism (whether forcibly or not being a matter of debate, see p. 175). Herod was regarded as a Jew by everyone except the Jews in Judaea, and although this rejection pained him and he tried to show sensitivity to Jewish practices by not, for example, having his image on his coins, he did much to further the cause of a Hellenized and outward-looking Judaism. His father, Antipater, was adviser to Hyrcanus II who, in league with the Nabataean king Aretas III, was advancing upon Jerusalem in an attempt to oust Aristobulus when the Romans intervened in the region under the leadership of Pompey in 63 BC. From this date until Pompey's defeat by Julius Caesar in 48 BC and the latter's arrival in Syria in 47 BC, Hyrcanus was high priest. Caesar confirmed him in this position and, more importantly, granted Antipater Roman citizenship, installing him as procurator of Roman Judaea. Antipater then appointed his elder son Phasael as 'strategos' (head of administration) in Judaea and Peraea, and Herod as 'strategos' in Galilee.

(*Above*) A bust of Julius Caesar. By appointing Herod's father Antipater as procurator of Roman Judaea, Caesar played an important part in Herod's rise to power.

(*Right*) Herod the Great and a soldier, in a mosaic from the Chora Monastery (Kariye Çamii) in Istanbul dating from the first quarter of the 14th century.

Moves by influential Jews in Jerusalem to oust Herod from this position after he had executed a bandit and his gang failed, but uncertainty prevailed following the assassination of Caesar in 44 BC. When Caesar's assassins were defeated by Mark Antony and Octavian in 42 BC, Herod was adroitly able to gain Antony's favour. A new threat, however, presented itself in the form of Antigonus the youngest son of Aristobulus II. Backed by the Parthians, Antigonus marched on Jerusalem, captured Hyrcanus and rendered him unfit to be high priest by cutting off his ears. Herod's brother Phasael committed suicide and Herod fled, leaving his close family and other relatives on the impregnable rock of Masada, at that stage a Hasmonaean fortress.

Herod reached Rome and having secured the support of Antony, Octavian and the Senate, was appointed king of Judaea. The year was 40 BC; but he was king in name only, not in territory. After the Romans had driven the Parthians from Syria Herod was able to begin the conquest of his country, beginning with the port of Joppa in 39 BC and culminating in the capture of Jerusalem two years later. His effective rule thus began in 37 BC.

Herod rebuilt Samaria, naming it Sebaste, the Greek rendering of Augustus, in honour of the Roman emperor Augustus (Octavian). Here, the remains of the basilica can be seen.

HEROD THE BUILDER

Many of Herod's remarkable building projects were realized in the short period of just 12 years between 25 and 13 BC. But before Mark Antony's suicide in the aftermath of the battle of Actium he had already constructed a fortress in Jerusalem at the north of the temple called, appropriately, the Antonia. Many of Herod's later buildings were also named in honour of his Roman patrons. Other Herodian buildings in Jerusalem included a theatre and a hippodrome, neither of which has been located, and a palace at the top of the western hill of Jerusalem. The crowning work, however, was the rebuilding of the temple, begun around 20 BC (see p. 192).

When Herod came to the throne, Judaea's only natural harbour was Joppa. In 22 BC Herod began perhaps his most ambitious project: he constructed a city on the coast 35 miles (56 km) north of Joppa, with an impressive harbour, temple, baths and a theatre that is still used today. He named his new city Caesarea. Herod built his great breakwater and harbour using the latest techniques borrowed from the Romans, including hydraulic cement. These structures are now submerged, but still visible is the aqueduct that brought water from the Mt Carmel region 5½ miles (9 km) away. After Herod's death the city would become the seat of the Roman governors and would eventually have over half a million inhabitants before its fall to the Muslims in AD 638. It was also the city in which the Christian apostle Paul was imprisoned before his journey to Rome.

Another great project was the improvement of the city of Samaria, the old capital of the northern kingdom, Israel, built by Omri and destroyed by the Assyrians in 722/1 BC. Herod renamed the city Sebaste, the Greek equivalent of Augustus – the title granted to Octavian in 27 BC. Herod also built a temple

dedicated to Augustus in the city, as well as a theatre and hippodrome.

Herodium, the strange conical hill visible near Jerusalem, was built around 23 to 20 BC. Its circular shape, punctuated by four round towers at the four points of the compass, housed a courtyard, domestic quarters and a bath house. Below the hill, Lower Herodium occupied an area of around 35 acres (over 14

(Above) A great feat of engineering: the aqueduct that brought water to the city of Caesarea was 5½ miles (9 km) long.

An aerial view of Herodium, clearly showing its strange conical shape. Herod built this around 23 to 20 BC, and it originally had four round towers at the points of the compass. It served as Herod's luxurious summer palace and reputedly also as his tomb, though this has never been found.

sunken garden and a swimming pool (where Aristobulus was drowned), while the northern bank boasted a large paved hall, courtyards and a bath house. It was here that Herod died, of an unknown illness, in 4 BC.

Probably the best known of Herod's buildings is his palace at Masada, the great rock in the Judaean desert. Herod had appreciated its value as a fortress when it afforded sanctuary to his family during his flight to Rome and it remained strongly fortified. He also ensured its water supply in case of siege by building cisterns and an aqueduct. The private terraces of his palace on the north-eastern tip, with their bath house, concealed staircase and painted murals, compete with the magnificent mosaics in the throne room for the admiration of visitors today.

hectares), with rows of buildings and living quarters for the officers who administered the local area. Because of its height the hill palace enjoyed cool breezes even during the hottest months, and it was Herod's summer palace.

His winter palace, where he died in 4 BC, was at Tulul abu el-Alayiq, near Jericho, spanning the wadi Qilt as it flows towards the river Jordan. On the southern side of the wadi were a

(Left and above) Herod had been so impressed by the merits of Masada as a fortress when he left his family there for safety in 40 BC, that he later built himself a large palace on the rock. It consists of various structures, including this series of rooms on descending terraces at the north-eastern tip. He decorated the interiors with magnificent mosaics and murals (above).

(Opposite right) The remains of the winter palace Herod built for himself near Jericho, spanning the wadi Qilt as it flows towards the river Jordan. On the southern side of the wadi were a sunken garden and a swimming pool, the traces of which have recently been found by archaeologists. On the northern bank were a lavish paved hall, courtyards and a bath house. Herod died here in 4 BC.

A potentially disastrous problem occurred in 31 BC when Octavian defeated Herod's supporter Mark Antony at the battle of Actium. Fortunately, Herod had been occupied fighting the Nabataeans in Transjordan and had therefore not fought with Antony, to whom he owed some favours. On hearing the outcome of the battle, Herod journeyed to Rhodes to seek an audience with Octavian. Having laid down his crown before the Roman ruler, Herod received it back with the promise of support, and from then on proved to be a loyal vassal of Octavian. His first test came in 30 BC when Octavian moved for the final confrontation with Mark Antony that resulted in the latter's suicide. After his victory over Cleopatra, Octavian restored to Herod's kingdom towns in the coastal plain and Transjordan that Antony had given to Cleopatra.

An orgy of executions

Before Herod had been proclaimed king he had married Mariamne, the granddaughter of Hyrcanus, thus allying himself with the Hasmonaeans. However, it was not a Hasmonaean that Herod appointed to be high priest, but an unknown priest from Babylon named Hananel. Not surprisingly, this incensed the Hasmonaeans, and after pressure from his mother-in-law Alexandra and his wife Mariamne, Herod was persuaded in 35 BC to depose Hananel from a post meant to be held for life, in favour of Mariamne's 17-year-old brother Aristobulus. Such intriguing by the Hasmonaeans who surrounded him inflamed Herod's suspicious nature and resulted in a series of brutal murders. Less than a year after his appointment as high priest, Aristobulus was drowned on Herod's orders at a banquet in Jericho. In 30 BC Hyrcanus II, who had returned from exile in Babylon and was aged 80, was executed. More shockingly, Mariamne was executed a year later on the probably unfounded suspicion of adultery and of wanting to poison Herod. The execution of Mariamne's mother Alexandra followed in 28 BC when she plotted against Herod during a brief but serious bout of illness he suffered. There would be a similar orgy of executions at the end of Herod's reign, when two of his and Mariamne's sons, Alexander and Aristobulus, were executed in 7 BC on suspicion of involvement in a plot to assassinate their father.

In the midst of these intrigues Herod appointed and then deposed a series of high priests until finally, in 23 BC, he appointed Simon, the father of the second Mariamne whom Herod married. Simon remained in office until the year of Herod's death. The account in Matthew's Gospel (2:16-17), relating how Herod had all baby boys aged two and under in Bethlehem killed when he heard of the birth there of the 'king of the Jews', is certainly not out of character, whether or not it is historical.

Conclusion

Herod was an astute and successful politician. His alliance with Rome assured the survival of an enlarged, distinctive Jewish state for over 100 years, and also benefited the Jewish community in other parts of the Roman empire. To achieve this he not only destroyed the Hasmonaean

The Massacre of the Innocents (Matthew 2:16), by the workshop of Giotto (c. 1266–1337) in the chapel of San Francesco, Assisi. It is not known whether this event in fact took place, but it is not out of character that Herod should have ordered the killing of children to remove a perceived threat to his rule.

house into which he had married, he also diminished the power of the high priesthood by abolishing its lifelong tenure and he marginalized the aristocracy. The Sanhedrin, a court in Jerusalem drawn from the local elite and with tax, administrative and military responsibilities, became powerless, and Herod surrounded himself with those who favoured Greek culture. Greek became the official language of the state.

Not surprisingly, these policies only stored up hostility against Herod and Rome from within his kingdom. Although he was able to contain the opposition, the resentment boiled over during the reigns of his sons, culminating in the Jewish revolts against Rome in AD 66 to 73. Among the ironies of his reign two in particular stand out: his rebuilt temple, only made possible by the peace and wealth afforded by the Pax Romana, was destroyed by the Romans in AD 70, while Masada, the symbol of Herod's achievements as a client king within the Roman empire, became the place where the Jewish revolt against Rome ended in tragic but glorious failure.

HEROD'S TEMPLE

In characteristically ambitious fashion, Herod envisaged his new temple on a much grander scale than that rebuilt after the Exile which was now probably too small. He extended the foundations of the temple platform to the south and built a huge wall in the Tyropean valley on the western side of the spur on which the temple stood. These massive stones, some 3 ft (90 cm) high, with their characteristic 'rims' can still be seen today at the Western or Wailing Wall of Jerusalem. Of Herod's magnificent temple, built of marble and gold, however, nothing remains. By the time of Herod's death work on the temple was still in progress and it was not finally completed until AD 62 to 64, not long before its destruction by the Romans in AD 70.

(Right) This tiny limestone sundial, 2 in (5 cm) high, is the only known surviving object from Herod's temple. It was found in the debris of the temple's destruction.

(Below) An artist's conjectural reconstruction of Herod's temple. All that in fact remains today are the massive supporting walls of the enlarged platform on which the temple stood.

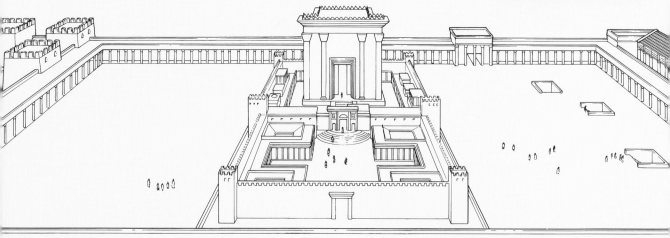

Ἀρχέλαος	**Archelaus** 4 BC–AD 6
Ἀντιπᾶς	**Herod Antipas** 4 BC–AD 39
Φίλιππος	**Philip** 4 BC–AD 34
Ἀγρίππας	**Herod Agrippa** AD 37–44

A bronze coin of Herod Agrippa I, with his portrait.

HEROD'S HEIRS

ARCHELAUS	Jerusalem
Father	*Wife*
Herod	Salome
Mother	*Buried*
Malthace	Bethsaida (Julias)?
Wives	
Mariamne, Glaphyra	HEROD AGRIPPA
Buried	*Father*
Vienne in Gaul(?)	Aristobulus IV
	(son of Herod)
HEROD ANTIPAS	*Mother*
Father	Berenice
Herod	*Wife*
Mother	Cyprus II
Malthace	*Son*
Wives	Agrippa
Daughter of	*Buried*
Nabataean king	Caesarea(?)
Aretas IV, Herodias	*References*
	Josephus,
PHILIP	*Antiquities* 17:8:4
Father	to 19:8:2; Mark
Herod	6:14-29; Luke 23:6-
Mother	12; Acts 12:1-5, 20-
Cleopatra of	23

A bronze coin of Herod Archelaus.

On Herod's death the Roman emperor Augustus divided his kingdom into three parts, having heard submissions from rival contenders among Herod's surviving sons. Archelaus was given Judaea, Idumaea and Samaria, Antipas received Galilee and Peraea (southern Transjordan) while Philip was in charge of a region comprising roughly the area north of the Yarmuk valley and east of the Jordan valley, with southern Syria.

Archelaus' rule was nasty, brutish and short. Although he inherited his father's fondness for building projects, his mode of governing was erratic and arbitrary, and his attitude to marriage caused offence when he unlawfully married the widow of his executed half-brother Alexander. Such was his misrule that a delegation was sent from Judaea and Samaria to Rome. On hearing their complaints Augustus deposed Archelaus and placed his territory under direct Roman rule with its own governor.

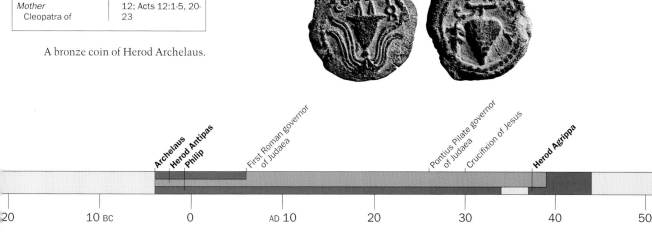

Herod Antipas – the Herod mentioned in the New Testament in connection with John the Baptist and the adult Jesus of Nazareth – was also a builder, and was responsible for the construction of Tiberias on the shores of the Sea of Galilee, named in honour of the Roman emperor. In order to secure his Transjordanian territory he married the daughter of Aretas IV, the Nabataean king. Antipas is best known for his part in the arrest and execution of John the Baptist, whose preaching in Antipas' territory of Peraea no doubt raised the spectre of political revolt. The New Testament (Mark 6:18) claims that Antipas' hostility to John was due to the latter's condemnation of Antipas' marriage to Herodias, the wife of his brother Philip; but it is generally agreed that Mark is incorrect, and that Herodias was married not to Philip but to Antipas' half-brother Herod Philip, son of Herod the Great's second wife of the name Mariamne. To confuse matters further, the young woman who danced in front of Antipas and who demanded John the Baptist's head is named in the best reading at Mark 6:22 as Herodias, not Salome, which name does not appear in this context in Mark. Herodias did, however, have a daughter called Salome, who later married the tetrarch Philip. Whatever the tangles of this narrative, the New Testament and Josephus agree that Herod imprisoned and executed John, Josephus giving the place of execution as the eastern fortress of Machaerus.

According to the Gospels, Antipas believed that Jesus of Nazareth was John the Baptist raised from the dead (Mark 6:14-16). Jesus was technically one of Antipas' subjects and Luke records an interview between them after Jesus' arrest in Jerusalem, where Antipas had travelled to observe the Passover (Luke 23:6-12). According to Luke, Jesus said nothing in reply to Antipas' questions.

Antipas' wish to marry Herodias and to divorce the daughter of the Nabataean king Aretas naturally soured relations, and in AD 36 Aretas attacked and defeated Antipas. Because the lost territory ultimately belonged to Rome, the order went out that Vitellius the governor of Syria should march against Aretas. However, the death of the emperor Tiberius in AD 37 resulted in the cancellation of the mission.

Philip was Herod the Great's third heir. By all accounts, his was a peaceful, moderate and just rule, distinguished by the building of two cities, Caesarea Philippi, at the source of the river Jordan with its famous shrine to Pan, and Bethsaida, named Julias after Augustus' daughter, Julia. The latter site has not been identified for certain. When Philip died in AD 34 his territory was put under Roman administration and then granted to Herod Agrippa in AD 37.

The dance of Salome before Herod Antipas, with the head of John the Baptist; a German altar painting of 1480. From Mark (6:17-19) it appears that it was Herodias who wanted John killed as he had condemned her marriage to Herod Antipas.

For Herod had sent and seized John, and bound him in prison for the sake of Herodias, his brother Philip's wife; because he had married her. For John said to Herod, 'It is not lawful for you to have your brother's wife.' And Herodias had a grudge against him, and wanted to kill him. But she could not, for Herod feared John, knowing that he was a righteous and holy man...

Mark 6:14-20

The sun god Helios, from a mosaic found in a synagogue in Tiberias, dating from the 4th century AD.

Caesarea Philippi was named after Augustus Caesar (Octavian) and Philip, Herod the Great's son, who adorned the town. It was the site of a shrine to the Greek god Pan, and its earlier name Paneas survives in modern name Banias.

A bust of the Roman emperor Caligula (AD 37–41). Caligula gave Herod Agrippa the territories of Philip and Herod Antipas.

In Rome, Tiberius was succeeded by Caligula (AD 37–41), whose favour had been cultivated by Herod Agrippa who was both the nephew and brother-in-law of Antipas. Agrippa was, in fact, in prison on Tiberius' orders when Caligula became emperor, and he was released and given the territory of the recently deceased Philip, with the title of king. This enraged Antipas' wife Herodias, if not Antipas himself, because Agrippa as a young man had lived well beyond his means, had run up huge debts, and had been helped financially by Antipas. Now the prodigal was a king, and Antipas wanted the same status. Showing little gratitude, Agrippa accused Antipas of disloyalty to Caligula, and when Antipas travelled to Rome to request his elevation to monarchy, Caligula deposed him, and gave his territory to Agrippa.

Caligula was assassinated in AD 41, and Agrippa played a part in the accession of Claudius, in return for which he was confirmed as ruler of the former territories of Philip and Antipas, to which were added Judaea and Samaria. Thus the entire kingdom of Herod the Great was at last under the rule of a descendant of Herod as king, and indeed Agrippa's territory was more extensive than that of his grandfather.

Agrippa's most conspicuous achievement was the enlargement of the area of Jerusalem to the north of the temple and the building of the so-called third wall, although the Roman authorities did not allow the project to be completed. He appears in the New Testament in connection with the execution of James and the arrest and imprisonment of Peter (Acts 12:1-14). His death is related in Acts 12:20-23, and attributed to an angel of God who struck him down because the people hailed him as semi-divine. According to Josephus (*Antiquities* 19:8:2) he died in

Christ before Pilate and Christ before Herod Antipas, by Duccio, Maestà altarpiece, Siena (1308–11). Jesus was technically a subject of Herod Antipas and Luke records that Christ was brought to the king to be interviewed, but made no reply. The Roman governor of Judaea, however, had ultimate authority and so Jesus was also brought before Pilate. From the biblical account it seems Pilate would have preferred to let Jesus go, but to keep order he condemned him to death by crucifixion.

When Pilate heard this, he asked whether the man was a Galilean. And when he learned that he belonged to Herod's jurisdiction, he sent him over to Herod, who was himself in Jerusalem at that time. When Herod saw Jesus, he was very glad, for he had long desired to see him, because he had heard about him, and he was hoping to see some sign done by him. So he questioned him at some length; but he made no answer. The chief priests and the scribes stood by, vehemently accusing him. And Herod with his soldiers treated him with contempt and mocked him; then, arraying him in gorgeous apparel, he sent him back to Pilate. And Herod and Pilate became friends with each other that very day, for before this they had been at enmity with each other.

Luke 23:6-12

Caesarea, having been taken ill while wearing a garment made of silver and being hailed by the people as superior to a mortal.

Thus ended the dynasty of Herod; for while Agrippa had a son who could have succeeded him, the emperor Claudius decided to divide the kingdom once more, and to place Judaea under direct Roman rule. Yet even this must be slightly qualified. Agrippa's brother Herod was given Chalcis to rule over, a province controlling the Beqar valley in Lebanon, and when he died in AD 49, Agrippa's son succeeded to this territory, later receiving various additions, including (in AD 53) the former territory of Philip. Agrippa II and his wife Berenice appear in Acts 25:13–26:32 in connection with Paul's trial before the Roman governor Festus in Caesarea in around AD 60.

For most of the last 60 years of Judaea's existence, before the revolt against Rome (AD 66–73) which resulted in the destruction of the Second Temple (AD 70), Judaea was a Roman province, technically under the governor of Syria but with its own prefect or procurator. In many cases, only the names of the prefects are known, and the dates are not certain. In the first phase (AD 6–41) the prefects appear to have had general oversight of affairs of the temple and the appointing of high priests. After 44, these tasks rested with Herod of Chalcis and his successor, Agrippa II. Of the first governors only Pontius Pilate is documented to any extent. Josephus, Philo and the New Testament are unanimous in presenting Pilate as insensitive to Jewish customs and brutal in his suppression of dissent.

ROMAN GOVERNORS OF JUDAEA (AD 6–41 AND 44–66)

Coponius *c.* 6–9

Marcus Ambivulus *c.* 9–12

Annius Rufus *c.* 12–15

Valerius Gratus *c.* 15–26

Pontius Pilate *c.* 26–36

Marcellus *c.* 36–7

Marullus *c.* 37–41

Cuspius Fadus *c.* 44–46

Tiberius Julius Alexander *c.* 46–48

Ventidius Cumanus *c.* 48–52

Antonius Felix *c.* 52–60

Porcius Festus *c.*60–62

Albinus *c.* 62–64

Gessius Florus *c* 64–66

References: Josephus, *Antiquities* 20:1:1 to 20:11:1; *The Jewish War* 2:12:1 to 2:17:10; Matthew 27:1-26, 57-58 etc.; Acts 12:1-5, 23-24

A bronze coin of Pontius Pilate.

THE FIRST JEWISH REVOLT (AD 66–73)

The first Jewish revolt, which resulted in the destruction of the Jerusalem temple in AD 70, brought the history of ancient Israel to an effective end. It is true that hopes were entertained among Jews living in Judaea that the Romans would be defeated in the near future and that the temple would then be rebuilt – hopes that were fanned into the flames of the second Jewish revolt led by Bar Kokhba in AD 133–135; but if the war with Rome did not actually end until 135, the decisive battles had been fought 60 years earlier.

The first revolt brought to a head antagonisms towards Rome that had been smouldering for many years, and which had been nurtured especially by a nationalistic group known as the Zealots. The necessary causes of the revolt were the administration of Judaea by Roman governors who were often brutal and insensitive, and the resumption of that system after the brief rule of king Herod Agrippa (AD 41–44). The sufficient causes were two incidents in AD 66. In the first, the Jewish inhabitants of Caesarea were forced by the non-Jewish population to flee from the city; in the second,

the procurator Florus raided the temple treasury in Jerusalem, and then allowed Roman soldiers to rampage in the city. These actions were the green light for the Zealots, led by Eleazar, to revolt openly, seizing the fortress of Masada and occupying most of Jerusalem, in spite of attempts on the part of moderate Jews to prevent them. The Roman troops took refuge in the towers of Herod's upper palace, as important buildings were set on fire. Revolts broke out in other parts of the country.

Coin of the First Jewish Revolt. The reverse (left) has a lily and the words 'holy Jerusalem' and the obverse a chalice and 'shekel of Israel'.

With the failure of Florus and of the Roman governor of Syria to bring the situation under control, the emperor Nero despatched Vespasian to deal with the rebels. Arriving in Syria in the winter of AD 66–67 and assisted by his son Titus, Vespasian assembled three legions and various auxiliary troops. In the spring and summer of AD 67 he pacified

The Roman emperor Titus (AD 78–81), the son of Vespasian, conquered and destroyed Jerusalem in AD 70. His triumphal arch (below) erected in Rome was decorated with a frieze, a detail of which is shown here (opposite above). It portrays the bringing of the temple vessels to Rome, including the sacred trumpets, the table for the shewbread and the seven-branched menorah.

(Above) The discovery at Masada of 11 ostraca each with a different name may possibly be linked with the claim of Josephus (Jewish War 7:9:1) that ten men were chosen by lot to kill the survivors and then themselves rather than surrender to the Romans.

Galilee and quartered his legions in Caesarea and Scythopolis (Beth-shean) for the winter of AD 67–68. Meanwhile the Jews, both in Jerusalem and in unconquered parts of the country, were engaging in bitter struggles among themselves. A Zealot leader, John of Gishala, took control of Jerusalem, while Simon bar Giora rampaged through the countryside, marching on Jerusalem. He was admitted to the city in the spring of AD 69 by a populace tired of John of Gishala. John and the Zealots retired to the temple precincts.

Further Roman military action was postponed by events in Rome itself, and the emergence of Vespasian as emperor in the year of the four emperors (AD 69) following Nero's death. It was thus left to Titus to capture Jerusalem, which he did in the spring and summer of AD 70. The temple was set on fire, and Titus entered the Holy of Holies, while the Romans offered sacrifice to their ensigns. The city was destroyed, except for the three towers of Herod's upper palace. John of Gishala and Simon bar Giora were taken to Rome along with sacred vessels from the temple, to be displayed in the triumphal procession celebrating the Roman victory.

The conquest of Jerusalem did not signal the end of the revolt, however. The fortresses of Herodium, Machaerus and Masada remained in rebel hands. While the first two did not offer serious resistance, Masada held out until AD 73, when the defenders and their families took their own lives in a suicide pact rather than surrender.

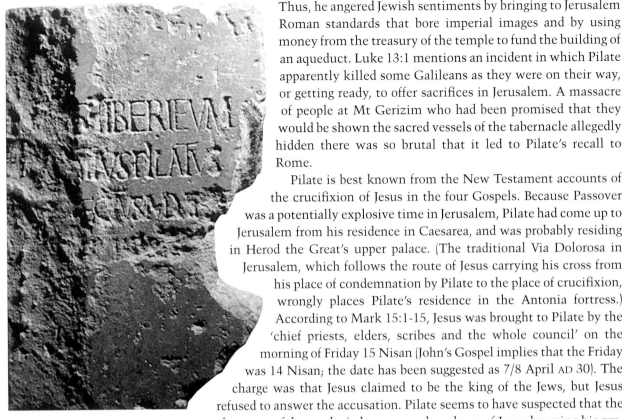

This inscription, discovered in Caesarea in 1961, reads 'TIBERIEM [PON]TIVS PILATVS [PRAEF]ECTVS IVDA[EA]E', indicating that Pilate held the title of prefect in Judaea during the reign of Tiberius (AD 14–37). This title is thought to indicate more a military than a merely administrative role for Pilate.

Thus, he angered Jewish sentiments by bringing to Jerusalem Roman standards that bore imperial images and by using money from the treasury of the temple to fund the building of an aqueduct. Luke 13:1 mentions an incident in which Pilate apparently killed some Galileans as they were on their way, or getting ready, to offer sacrifices in Jerusalem. A massacre of people at Mt Gerizim who had been promised that they would be shown the sacred vessels of the tabernacle allegedly hidden there was so brutal that it led to Pilate's recall to Rome.

Pilate is best known from the New Testament accounts of the crucifixion of Jesus in the four Gospels. Because Passover was a potentially explosive time in Jerusalem, Pilate had come up to Jerusalem from his residence in Caesarea, and was probably residing in Herod the Great's upper palace. (The traditional Via Dolorosa in Jerusalem, which follows the route of Jesus carrying his cross from his place of condemnation by Pilate to the place of crucifixion, wrongly places Pilate's residence in the Antonia fortress.) According to Mark 15:1-15, Jesus was brought to Pilate by the 'chief priests, elders, scribes and the whole council' on the morning of Friday 15 Nisan (John's Gospel implies that the Friday was 14 Nisan; the date has been suggested as 7/8 April AD 30). The charge was that Jesus claimed to be the king of the Jews, but Jesus refused to answer the accusation. Pilate seems to have suspected that the charge was false, and tried to secure the release of Jesus by using his prerogative to release a prisoner on the occasion of the festival. The crowd asked for the release of Barabbas (whose name, according to one tradition, was Jesus bar (son of) Abbas), a notorious criminal. Pilate, apparently more concerned with keeping order than doing justice, released Barabbas, and ordered the crucifixion of Jesus.

Between AD 41 and 44 the brief rule of Herod Agrippa interrupted the sequence of prefects. Then in the period AD 44–66 the prefects had to preside over a period of increasing unrest and chaos, both from organized groups of bandits and self-appointed prophets. A particular trouble spot was Caesarea, where the Jewish population, with no rights of citizenship, grew to outnumber the non-Jewish citizens, and demanded similar rights. Of these governors, Felix and Festus appear in Acts 23: 23–24:26 and 24:27–26: 32 respectively in connection with Paul's removal from custody in Jerusalem to Caesarea, where he was heard by both governors before being sent for trial to Rome.

The last two governors of Judaea, Albinus and Florus, are portrayed by Josephus as corrupt, unscrupulous, brutal and cunning, and prepared to let disorder rule so long as they could profit from whoever extracted money from others by force. Their rule only served to strengthen anti-Roman sentiments generally, and to hasten the tragic encounter with Rome that ended so disastrously for the province, Jerusalem and the temple.

SELECT BIBLIOGRAPHY

Aharoni, Y. et al., *The Macmillan Bible Atlas*. New York 1993.

Bahat, Dan, *The Illustrated Atlas of Jerusalem*. New York 1990.

Baines, John and Málek, Jaromír, *Atlas of Ancient Egypt*. Oxford 1980.

Barnett, R.D., *Illustrations of Old Testament History*. London 1977.

Ben-Tor, A. (ed.), *The Archaeology of Ancient Israel*. New Haven and London 1992.

Bimson, John J. (ed.), *Illustrated Encyclopedia of Bible Places*. Leicester 1995.

Biran, Avraham, *Biblical Dan*. Jerusalem 1994.

Bright, J., *A History of Israel*. Philadelphia and London 1981, 3rd ed.

Clayton, Peter A., *Chronicle of the Pharaohs. The Reign-By-Reign Record of the Rulers and Dynasties of Ancient Egypt*. London and New York 1994.

Comay, J., *Who's Who in the Old Testament*. London 1993.

Davies, G.I. (ed.), *Ancient Hebrew Inscriptions. Corpus and Concordance*. Cambridge 1991.

Davies, Philip R., *In Search of Ancient Israel*. Sheffield 1992.

Dietrich, Walter, *Die frühe Königszeit in Israel. 10. Jahrhundert v. Chr.* Stuttgart 1997.

Finkelstein, Israel, *The Archaeology of the Israelite Settlement*. Jerusalem 1988.

Freedman, David N. (ed.), *The Anchor Bible Dictionary*. 6 vols. New York 1992.

Fritz, Volkmar, *Die Entstehung Israels im 12. und 11. Jahrhundert v. Chr.* Stuttgart 1996.

Görg, Manfred, *Die Beziehungen zwischen dem Alten Testament und Ägypten von den Anfängen bis zum Exil*. Darmstadt 1997.

Grabbe, Lester L., *Judaism from Cyrus to Hadrian*. 2 vols. Minneapolis 1992.

Green, P., *From Alexander to Actium: the Hellenistic World*. London and San Francisco 1990.

Harris, Roberta L., *Exploring the World of the Bible Lands*. London and New York 1995.

Hepper, N., *Illustrated Encyclopedia of Bible Plants*. Leicester 1992.

Hopkins, David C., *The Highlands of Canaan. Agricultural Life in the Early Iron Age*. Sheffield 1985.

Isserlin, B.S.J., *The Israelites*. London and New York 1998.

Jamieson-Drake, David W., *Scribes and Schools in Monarchic Judah: A Socio-Archaeological Approach*. Sheffield 1991.

Jepsen, Alfred, and Schunk, Klaus-Dietrich (eds), *Von Sinuhe bis Nebukadnezar. Dokumente aus der Umwelt des Alten Testaments*. Berlin 1988 (4th rev. edition).

Josephus, Flavius, *De bello judaico* (Greek and German edition, ed. Otto Michel and Otto Bauernfeind) Darmstadt 1982 (3rd edition).

— *The Works*, translated by William Whiston. Edinburgh 1840.

Keel, Otmar and Uehlinger, Christoph, *Göttinnen, Götter und Gottessymbole. Neue Erkentnisse zur Religionsgeschichte Kanaans und Israels aufgrund bislang unerschlossener ikonographischer Quellen*. Freiburg-im-Breisgau 1992.

Key, Howard C. (ed.), *The Cambridge Companion to the Bible*. Cambridge 1997.

Kitchen, Kenneth A., *The Third Intermediate Period in Egypt (1100–650 BC)*. Warminster 1973.

Knight, D.F. and Tucker, G. (eds), *The Hebrew Bible and its Modern Interpreters*. Philadelphia 1985.

Kochav, Sarah, *Israel. Splendours of the Holy Land*. London 1995.

Lemche, Niels Peter, *Die Vorgeschichte Israels. Von den Anfängen bis zum Ausgang des 13. Jahrhunderts v. Chr.* Stuttgart 1996.

Lloyd, Seton, *The Art of the Ancient Near East*. London 1963.

May, H.G. (ed.), *Oxford Bible Atlas*. Oxford 1984.

Mazar, A., *Archaeology of the Land of the Bible, 10,000–586 BCE*. New York 1990.

Metford, J.C., *Dictionary of Christian Lore and Legend*. London and New York 1986.

Metzger, B.M. and Coogan, M.D. (eds), *The Oxford Companion to the Bible*. New York and London 1993.

Meyers, Eric M., *The Oxford Encyclopedia of Archaeology in the Near East*. 5 vols. New York 1997.

Mitchell, T.C., *The Bible in the British Museum: Interpreting the Evidence*. London 1988.

Oates, J., *Babylon*. London and New York, 1978.

Pritchard, James B., *Ancient Near Eastern Texts Relating to the Old Testament*. Princeton 1955 (2nd ed.).

— *The Ancient Near East. Supplementary Texts and Pictures Relating to the Old Testament*.

Princeton 1969.

— (ed.), *The Times Atlas of the Bible*. London 1987.

Renz, Johannes and Röllig, Wolfgang, *Handbuch der althebräischen Epigraphik vols. 1-2*. Darmstadt 1995.

Roaf, Michael, *Cultural Atlas of Mesopotamia and the Ancient Near East*. Oxford and New York 1990.

Rogerson, John, *Old Testament Criticism in the Nineteenth Century. England and Germany*. London 1984.

— *Atlas of the Bible*. Oxford and New York 1985.

Rogerson, John and Davies, Philip, *The Old Testament World*. Cambridge 1989.

Rogerson, John and Meyers, Eric M., 'The Old Testament' in Howard C. Key (ed.), *The Cambridge Companion to the Bible*. Cambridge 1997, pp. 32–287.

Sandars, N.K., *The Sea Peoples. Warriors of the Ancient Mediterranean*. London and New York 1985.

Scarre, Chris, *Chronicle of the Roman Emperors. The Reign-by-Reign Record of the Rulers of Imperial Rome*. London and New York 1995.

Schoors, Antoon, *Die Königreiche Israel und Juda im 8. Und 7. Jahrhundert v. Chr. Die Assyrische Krise*. Stuttgart 1998.

Schürer, Emil, *The History of the Jewish People in the Age of Jesus Christ (175 BC–AD 135)*. New English edition revised and edited by Geza Vermes and Fergus Millar. Edinburgh 1973.

Shanks, H. (ed.), *Ancient Israel: A Short History from Abraham to the Roman Destruction of the Temple* (Washington D.C. 1989).

Stern, E. (ed.), *The New Encyclopedia of Archaeological Excavations in the Holy Land*. Jerusalem 1993.

Thompson, Thomas L., *Early History of the Israelite People. From the Written & Archaeological Sources*. Leiden 1992.

Unterman, A., *Dictionary of Jewish Lore and Legend*. London and New York 1997.

Ussishkin, D., *The Conquest of Lachish by Sennacherib*. Tel Aviv 1982.

VanderKam, James C., *The Dead Sea Scrolls Today*. London 1994.

Vaux, R. de, *Archaeology and the Dead Sea Scrolls*. London 1973.

— *The Early History of Israel*, London 1978.

Vermes, Geza, *The Complete Dead Sea Scrolls in English*. London 1997.

Wiseman, D.J. (ed.), *Peoples of Old Testament Times*. Oxford 1973.

ILLUSTRATION AND TEXT CREDITS

Sources of illustrations

a=above, c=centre, b=bottom, l=left, r=right

The following abbreviations are used to identify sources and locate illustrations: AKG – Photo AKG, London; BL – By permission of The British Library; BM – © British Museum; BN – Bibliothèque Nationale de France, Paris; PW – Philip Winton (illustrator); ZR – Photo © Zev Radovan.

1 Israel Museum, Jerusalem. 2 BL. 5a–b Pinacoteca di Brera, Milan. Photo Alinari; Courtauld Institute of Art, London; Städelsches Kunstinstitut, Frankfurt am Main; BN. 6 Kunsthistorisches Museum, Vienna. AKG/Erich Lessing. 7 Ashmolean Museum, Oxford. 8 ZR. 10 PW/© Thames & Hudson Ltd, London. 11a PW/© Thames & Hudson Ltd, London. 11b ZR. 12 BL. 13 Reproduced by courtesy of the Director and University Librarian, the John Rylands Library of Manchester. 15l–r ZR; Rijksmuseum, Amsterdam; AKG; AKG. 16 National Museum, Damascus. 17a PW/© Thames & Hudson Ltd, London. 17b V&A Picture Library, London. 18 ZR. 19 ZR. 21 Münsterbauverein, Freiburg im Breisgau. 22 Musée des Beaux Arts, Tours. 23 Rijksmuseum, Amsterdam. 24 La Sainte Bible, Gustave Doré. 25 Österreichische Nationalbibliothek, Vienna. 26a AKG. 26b BL. 27 Gemäldegalerie, Alte Meister, Dresden. AKG/Erich Lessing. 28 Saint-Sulpice, Paris. Photo Bulloz. 29l PW/© Thames & Hudson Ltd, London. 29r Hans Holbein. 30–31 Fitzwilliam Museum, Cambridge. 31b AKG. 32a San Pietro in Vincoli, Rome. 32b BL. 33 Photo Scala. 35 Palacio de Liria, Madrid. 36a BL. 36b Photo Heidi Grassley/© Thames & Hudson Ltd, London. 37a BL. 37b Collection Israel Antiquities Authority, Jerusalem. 38a ZR. 38b PW/© Thames & Hudson Ltd, London. 38–39 John Rylands University Library, Manchester. 39b Sonia Halliday Photographs/Photo Jane Taylor. 40 BN. 41a Biblioteca Apostolica Vaticana. 41c&b Cairo Museum. 42a ZR. 42b BN. 43 ZR. 46 La Sainte Bible, Gustave Doré. 47a&b & 48 Herzog Anton Ulrich Museum, Brunswick. 49 La Sainte Bible, Lyon, 1553. 50a Courtesy of the Oriental Institute, Chicago University. 50b ZR. 52 ZR. 55 AKG. 56 Department of Antiquities, Amman. 57 ZR. 58 From Rudolf von Ems' World Chronicle. 59 Pierpont Morgan Library, New York. 60a Courtesy of the Oriental Institute, University of Chicago. 60b BM. 62 AKG. 63 Städelsches Kunstinstitut, Frankfurt am Main. 64a National Museum, Damascus. 64b From Sacred Art by A.G. Temple, 1898.

65a Oratory of Theodault, Germigny-des-Prés. Photo © Skira. 65b National Museum, Damascus. 67 Archiv für Kunst & Geschichte Berlin. AKG. 69l–r BN; AKG/Erich Lessing; BL; BL. 70 Städelsches Kunstinstitut, Frankfurt am Main. 71 BN. AKG/Erich Lessing. 72–73 Staatliches Museum, Schwerin. AKG. 73 Musée du Louvre, Paris. 74 Kunsthistorisches Museum, Vienna. 75 ZR. 76 Werner Neumeister. 77r Musée du Louvre, Paris. 78 ZR. 79 BN. 80 Museo Nazionale del Bargello, Florence. AKG/Erich Lessing. 81a&b ZR. 82 The City of David Archaeological Project, Prof. Y. Tsafrir, Hebrew University of Jerusalem. 83 PW/© Thames & Hudson Ltd, London. 84 BL. 85 AKG. 86a San Nazaro Maggiore, Milan. Photo Hirmer Fotoarchiv. 86b Musée de l'Homme, Paris. 87 ZR. 88a&b ZR. 89a&b ZR. 90a Jewish National University Library, Jerusalem. 90c&br George Taylor/© Thames & Hudson Ltd, London. 90bl ZR. 93l–r Musée de l'Ecole des Beaux-Arts, Paris. AKG; Österreichische Nationalbibliothek, Vienna. AKG; La Sainte Bible, Gustave Doré. 94 Musée de l'Ecole des Beaux-Arts, Paris. AKG. 95a&b Courtesy Oriental Institute, University of Chicago. 96 Musée de l'Ecole des Beaux-Arts, Paris. AKG. 97a&b ZR. 98 BM. 99 ZR. 101a Musée du Louvre, Paris. Photo © RMN. 101b ZR. 102 Musée du Louvre, Paris. 103a ZR. 103b ZR. 104a ZR. 104b Scarborough Borough Council. AKG. 105 By courtesy of Stephen Longstreet, Beverly Hills, CA. 106 all ZR. 107 Österreichische Nationalbibliothek, Vienna. AKG. 108 Österreichische Nationalbibliothek, Vienna. AKG. 110 La Sainte Bible, Gustave Doré. 111a Private collection. AKG. 111bl Musée du Louvre, Paris. Photo © RMN. 111br ZR. 112 BM. 114 Kunsthistorisches Museum, Vienna. AKG/Erich Lessing. 115 Musée du Louvre, Paris. 116 Israel Museum, Jerusalem. 117a ZR. 117b Corpus Christi College, Cambridge. Photo Courtauld Institute of Arts, London. 118 Bodleian Library, Oxford. AKG. 119 L. Cavro, Paris. 120 BN. 121a Musée du Louvre, Paris. 121c ZR. 121b Musée du Louvre, Paris. 123l–r AKG/Erich Lessing; Bodleian Library, Oxford; after Keel, 1992. 124 AKG/Erich Lessing. 125 Öffentliche Kunstsammlung, Basel. Photo M. Bühler. 126 Bodleian Library, Oxford. AKG. 127 ZR. 131 La Sainte Bible, Gustave Doré. 133 Henry E Huntington Library and Art Gallery, San Marino, CA. 134 Israel Museum, Jerusalem. 135al Israel Museum, Jerusalem. 135ar R. Sheridan. 135b Courtesy Y Aharoni Ramat Rahel Expedition of the Hebrew Univeristy of Jerusalem & University of Rome. 136 ZR. 137 BM. 138 Bodleian Library, Oxford. 139 La Sainte Bible, Gustave Doré. 140a Bodleian Library, Oxford. 140b BM. 140–141 PW/© Thames & Hudson Ltd, London. 141 BM. 142a BM. 142b Archaeological Museum, Istanbul. 143a ZR. 143b George Taylor/© Thames & Hudson Ltd, London. 144 after Keel, 1992. 145 BM. 146 La Sainte Bible, Lyon, 1553. 147 The University Museum, Philadelphia. 148 BM. 149 BL. 150 Courtesy Y Aharoni Ramat Rahel Expedition of the

Hebrew Univeristy of Jerusalem & University of Rome. 151 Corpus Christi College, Cambridge. 152 ZR. 153a Winchester Cathedral Library. 153b Courtesy of the Trustees of the late Sir Henry S Wellcome. 154 Staatliche Museen zu Berlin, © bpk. 154–155 Musée du Louvre, Paris. 155a Staatliche Museen zu Berlin, © bpk. 155b Sotheby's. 157l–r La Sainte Bible, Gustave Doré; Chora Monastery, Istanbul. AKG/Erich Lessing; AKG; ZR. 159a BM. 159b La Sainte Bible, Gustave Doré. 160a ZR. 160bl Museo Catedralicio, Toledo. AKG. 160br Sistine Chapel, Vatican. AKG. 161 La Sainte Bible, Gustave Doré. 162a Israel Museum, Jerusalem. 162b Biblioteca Medicea Laurenziana, Florence. 163l Tracy Wellman/© Thames & Hudson Ltd, London. 163r La Sainte Bible, Gustave Doré. 165 Brooklyn Museum of Art, Gift of Miss Theodora Wilbour from the Estate of her Father, Charles Edwin Wilbour 47.218.89. 166–167 Alinari. 166b Staatliche Museen zu Berlin, © bpk. 167a BM. 167b Drawn by Trevor Hodgson. 168a BM. 168b ZR. 169a ZR. 170 Winchester Cathedral Library. 171l &r BN. 172al&ar BN. 172b Israel Museum, Jerusalem. 173 University Library, Leyden. 174 BM. 176 Tracy Wellman/© Thames & Hudson Ltd, London. 177a&b ZR. 178 PW/© Thames & Hudson Ltd, London. 180a&b ZR. 181all ZR. 182 Reifenberg Collection, Israel. 183 Ny Carlsberg Glyptothek, Copenhagen. 184 Chora Monastery, Istanbul. AKG/Erich Lessing. 185 all ZR. 186a John G. Ross. 186b Chora Monastery, Istanbul. AKG/Erich Lessing. 186–187 ZR. 188 bl, br&a ZR. 189l Sonia Halliday. 189r ZR. 191 San Francesco, Assisi. AKG. 192a&b ZR. 192c PW/© Thames & Hudson Ltd, London. 193a&b ZR. 194 AKG. 195al&ar ZR. 195b The Metropolitan Museum of Art, New York. Rogers Fund, 1914. 196 Museo dell'Opera del Duomo, Siena. 197a&b ZR. 198a Alinari. 198bl&br ZR. 199ar ZR. 199c Anderson. 199b Georgina Masson. 200 ZR

Sources of quotations
The quotations in this book are taken from the following sources:

All quotes from the Bible are from the Revised Standard Version of the Bible, copyright 1952 [2nd edition, 1971] by the Division of Christian Education of the National Council of the Churches of Christ in the United States of America. Used by permission. All rights reserved.

Quotes from Josephus are taken from: Josephus, Flavius The Works, translated by William Whiston. Edinburgh 1840. Barnett, R.D., Illustrations of Old Testament History (London 1977), p. 52 [p. 121. Nimrud Prism].

Pritchard, James B., Ancient Near Eastern Texts Relating to the Old Testament. Princeton 1955 (2nd ed.), p. 284 [p. 120, 121, Tiglath-pileser III]; p. 288 [p. 141, Sennacherib]; p. 492 [p. 165, Elephantine papyrus].

INDEX

Page numbers in *italic* refer to the illustrations